T.S. Eliot's Theory of Poetry

By the same author.

Nature Imagery of the Major Romantic Poets
Essays in Criticism
Essays in Modern Criticism
Twentieth Century American Criticism

T.S. Eliot's Theory of Poetry

A Study of the Changing Critical Ideas in the Development of His Prose and Poetry

Rajnath

HUMANITIES PRESS
ATLANTIC HIGHLANDS, N.J.

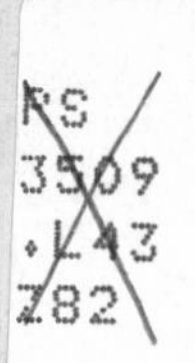

HUMANITIES PRESS INC.
ATLANTIC HIGHLANDS
NEW JERSEY 07719

First Published in India, 1980
by Arnold-Heinemann
Publishers (India) Pvt. Ltd.

First Published in the USA, 1980
ISBN O-391-01755-1

Printed in India

To
My Parents
with love and gratitude

Preface

The present work is meant to fill in a gap in the Eliot studies. There has been no comprehensive account of Eliot's critical concepts. Seán Lucy's *T.S. Eliot and the Idea of Tradition* deals with only one concept, while Fei-Pai Lu's *T.S. Eliot: The Dialectical Structure of His Theory of Poetry* studies mainly Eliot's critical method. The recent study by Mowbray Allan, *T.S. Eliot's Impersonal Theory of Poetry*, again, reckons with only one concept. So far there is no detailed discussion of Eliot's theory of the dissociation of sensibility. I have discussed in detail all the three major critical concepts of Eliot, namely tradition, impersonality, and the dissociation of sensibility, with the greater emphasis on the last.

The present work was originally submitted to the University of Leeds as a doctoral thesis and recommended by the examiners for publication. I have substantially revised it to make it more readable and added the concluding chapter which attempts an assessment of the critical achievement of T.S. Eliot. I must confess that in my approach to Eliot I have been influenced by two American critics, R.S. Crane and Edmund Wilson. The former has taught me that sense of discrimination which is the virtue of a literary critic, and in the absence of which he tends to make sweeping generalizations. This influence is particularly noticeable in the chapter on impersonal theory. From Edmund Wilson I have learnt how a critic should, as far as possible, present the reader with facts instead of influencing him with his opinions which can be postponed until after the discussions are over. This explains why I give my overall assessment of Eliot's literary criticism at the end of the book.

I take this opportunity to express my gratitude to all those who helped me at various stages of this work. My gratitude to Professor A. Norman Jeffares and the late Mr. K. Severs I can express only with a sense of inadequacy. A casual suggestion from Professor Jeffares several years ago proved invaluable. For this suggestion and for his tremendous interest in my research I feel highly indebted to him. Mr. Severs' suggestions, particularly on the stylistic side, have gone a long way to improve the work. For discussing Eliot with me I feel obliged to the late Dr. F.R. Leavis, and Professors G. Wilson Knight, Stephen Spender, Frank Kermode, Helen Gardner, M.C. Bradbrook, D.E.S. Maxwell, and D.W. Jefferson. I owe a debt of gratitude to Father Martin Jarrett-Kerr for many an interesting and fruitful discussion. To him and to Father Geoffrey Curtis, Rev. Michael Botting, and Mrs Ursula King I am grateful for helping me out of the mazes of Christianity and comparative religion. I am highly obliged to Mrs Valerie Eliot for helping me in various ways throughout my research, and for permitting me to quote several extracts from her husband's unpublished works the copyright of which is vested in her. Thanks are also due to her and Messrs Faber and Faber for quotations from Eliot's published works.

For their co-operation I wish to thank the librarian, Dr A.N.L. Munby, and the staff of the library of King's College, Cambridge, the librarians and staffs of the British Museum, London, the Bodleian library, Oxford, and the Brotherton library, Leeds.

In the end I will be failing in my duty if I do not thank the members of my family for their interest in my work, and my friend Dr. J.B. Beer for putting me in touch with several of his friends and colleagues during my stay in England.

University of Allahabad
India

RAJNATH

Contents

CHAPTER ONE

Eliot and his Critics

T.S. Eliot's literary criticism, like his poetry and plays, has been subjected to detailed analyses. As early as 1932, Ants Oras made a comprehensive examination of Eliot's criticism up to 1928. Oras was followed by Matthiessen who invoked Eliot's critical tenets to throw light on his practice. Among others who have worked on Eliot's criticism Sister Costello, Kristian Smidt, Victor Brombert, René Wellek, Seán Lucy, Vincent Buckley and Fei-Pai Lu deserve special mention. Sister Costello goes back to Aristotle in order to establish Eliot's *differentia* of poetry; Kristian Smidt relates Eliot's concept of poetic belief to his poetry; Victor Brombert examines the problems involved in Eliot's critical concepts; Vincent Buckley studies the relationship between poetry and morality in Eliot's criticism, Seán Lucy studies Eliot's idea of tradition and relates it to his poetry, and Fei-Pai Lu demonstrates the dialectical structure of Eliot's theory of poetry.

The above studies cover a wide area of Eliot's criticism and poetry. The system behind his criticism has been examined, the critical concepts, particularly those of poetic belief and tradition have been dealt with at length, and the relation between his criticism and poetry has been demonstrated. One may well wonder if there is still anything in Eliot left to examine. Despite all the studies mentioned above (except for Fei-Pai Lu's book which came out in 1966) Eliot said in 1961 in his convocation address at the University of Leeds :

> I find myself constantly irritated by having my words, perhaps written thirty or forty years ago, quoted as if I had uttered them yesterday. . . . rare is the writer who,

> quoting me, says "this is what Mr. Eliot thought (or felt) in 1933" (or whatever the date was).[1]

If we presume that Eliot had read all the criticism that had been written on him, and if there has been no work done since 1961 on the lines suggested by him, then there is obviously scope for a fresh study. There is no reason for questioning Eliot's acquaintance with his critics, since none of the critics referred to above have studied the development of his critical concepts. Eliot had not seen Lu's book but if he had, he would have called it another work of that "intelligent expositor of my work, who . . . discussed my critical writings some years ago as if I had, at the outset of my career as a literary critic, sketched out the design for a massive critical structure, and spent the rest of my life filling in the details."[2] As early as 1935 Matthiessen had hinted at the possibility of a work studying the development of Eliot's critical ideas in his remark that "*the evolution* both *of his critical tenets* and of his conception of the relation of the individual to society would make a good subject for another book."[3] (italics mine) The present work is a study in the evolution of Eliot's critical concepts.

The above remark of Eliot, quoted from "To Criticize the Critic," is not fortuitous since there are similar statements at other places, sometimes in more or less the same language. In his Introductions to the selections of Pound's and Valéry's essays, he seems to have his own essays at the back of his mind. In his Introduction to the selection of Pound's essays he says that he "has tried to establish as nearly as possible, the dates of all the pieces included" so that no 'malevolent' critic seeks "to quote and collate isolated sentences torn from their context and to quote what a writer said twenty or thirty years ago as if it was something he had said yesterday."[4] And in the Introduction to Paul Valéry's essays he writes :

> The writer whose critical essays have mostly been responses to particular situations is exposed, once the essays have been collected and published together, to a misunderstanding against which the prospective reader should be warned. In reading a volume of collected essays we are all, especially when approaching them for the first time, prone to expect a unity to which such work does not pretend.[5]

The danger and the difficulty that Eliot talks about in the context of Valéry's essays hold for Eliot as well. Eliot himself realized the danger to which he was exposed, and how often he was misunderstood by his readers, and misinterpreted by his critics. The works on Eliot's poetry have not been so unsatisfactory. The critics have analysed the development of his poetry, right or wrong, as is evident from several studies, particularly those by Frank Wilson and D.E.S. Maxwell[6] of which Eliot seems to be well aware. Distinguishing between the critics on his poetry and those on his criticism he stated in an unpublished address to The Authors' Club in 1955 :

> I am accustomed to critics tracing the rise and decline of my creative powers from poem to poem and play to play. But when it comes to my critical essays the criticism of *them* seems to assume that I wrote them all at once, and that it was designed to take its place in an orderly structure.[7]

In fact, much confusion has been created by the failure on the part of the critics of Eliot to attach due importance to the dates of his essays, and at times contradictions and inconsistencies have been pointed out between statements made at two different stages in the development of his criticism. That there was a shift in Eliot's criticism from aesthetics to religion or morality has not gone unnoticed. There might be differences regarding the date when the shift took place, but the critics have noted the shift and most of them have marked it around 1928, the year *For Lancelot Andrewes* was published. But there are also critics like Costello and Buckley who deny any marked change in Eliot's critical position. Costello quotes with approval R.A. Hodgson's observation that "there has been remarkably little change in his [Eliot's] position since 1917."[8] Buckley believes that Eliot's criticism has been fairly constant and that throughout his criticism he maintains faith in Hulme's distrust of personality.[9]

At the other extreme from Costello and Buckley are those who believe that Eliot's critical position underwent a radical change in the later phase. Delmore Schwartz, for instance, finds a sharp division between Eliot's early and later phase.

Taking 1922 as marking the beginning of the first phase and 1933 as marking the beginning of the second, he points out how Tennyson whom "Eliot scorned" in 1922 was "the object of serious and elevated commendation" in 1936. It is difficult to say why Schwartz takes 1922 as the beginning of the first phase when *The Sacred Wood* was published in 1920, and most of the essays in it were published in periodicals earlier still. Moreover, he has chosen a wrong example to illustrate his point. Eliot does appreciate and criticize Tennyson by turns but for different things. He criticizes Tennyson both in "The Metaphysical Poets" (1921) (I have no evidence of a critical piece published in 1922 in which Tennyson has been criticized) and "In Memoriam" (1936) for lack of thought in his poetry in the sense in which he finds it in Donne and other metaphysicals. Metaphysics dealing with permanent truths that the metaphysical poets use for poetic purposes, Eliot finds lacking in Tennyson in I921 as well as 1935. We are familiar with the well-known statement made in 1921 that "Tennyson and Browning are poets, and they think; but they do not feel their thought as immediately as the odour of a rose"[10] and that is because there is no thought in Tennyson and Browning such as we find in the metaphysical poets. This is the point that Eliot reiterates in 1936 in his essay on "In Memoriam".

> It [Tennyson's time] had, for the most part, no hold on permanent things, on permanent truths about man and God and life and death. The surface of Tennyson stirred about with his time; and he had nothing to which to hold fast, except his unique and unerring feeling for the sounds of words.[11]

Needless to say, what Eliot means by "permanent truths about man, and God and life and death" is the metaphysical thought, made use of by the metaphysical poets. Eliot does appreciate Tennyson but for a different quality. He sets great value on Tennyson's achievement in technical skill, particularly the manipulation of sounds.

> His [Tennyson's] variety of metrical accomplishment is astonishing.[12]
> He [Tennyson], has the finest ear of any English poet since Milton.[13]

Eliot's literary criticism does undergo a change, but in order to understand it aright one must avoid sweeping generalizations and pay due attention to the context.

Between Costello and Schwartz there are a host of critics who admit the change in Eliot's criticism but do not consider it as marking a sharp division between his two phases. Ants Oras confines his survey of Eliot's criticism to his output up to 1928, the year he takes as marking a "turning point in Mr Eliot's interests." Matthiessen believes that *For Lancelot Andrewes* marks a new stage in the growth of Eliot's criticism : "It was not until he returned to his own particular approach to art and society in *After Strange Gods* that he deepened the contours of his thought beyond *For Lancelot Andrewes*, 1928, as that volume of 'essays on Style and Order' had marked a different orientation from *Homage to John Dryden*, 1924."[14] Both Oras and Matthiessen believe that in his writing from *For Lancelot Andrewes* onwards, Eliot concerns himself increasingly with political, philosophical, and theological problems.

Like Oras and Matthiessen, Kristian Smidt believes that Eliot's criticism underwent a change, though the date he fixes is 1921, since when, he says, Eliot has been concerned with poetry as subordinated to metaphysical, political and cultural interests rather than as giving pure aesthetic pleasure. But this does not mean an absolute change in Eliot's critical position and "there still seems to be a residue of aestheticism unaffected by the conversion to Christian orthodoxy."[15]

The critics who admit the shift of emphasis in Eliot from the aesthetic to the ethical aspect of literature argue as if in the later essays his major preoccupation was the relationship between poetry and religion. From their discussions one gets the impression that in the later phase Eliot's earlier concepts yield place to ethical and theological considerations. To do justice to the later criticism critics often add a chapter on the religious and moral aspect of his criticism. Smidt, for instance, writes a section on "Poetry and Religion" in the chapter that deals with Eliot's criticism.[16] But in order to do full justice to Eliot's criticism on the whole, one should examine how he assimilates his earlier critical concepts to his growing concern with religion and morality, and what changes if any, this new concern brings about in the earlier concepts. Does Eliot, for instance, give up the theory of impersonality altogether in the later essays or assimilate it to theological values ? In most studies of Eliot's criticism theological values stand out of his earlier concepts and constitute an independent single unit.

The relationship between Eliot's criticism and poetry has been studied, among others, by Matthiessen. The great majority of Eliot's critics are of the view that Eliot's criticism and poetry go together. Eliot himself sets great store by the criticism of practitioners and talking about his own criticism affirms that "it is a by-product of my private poetry-workshop; or a prolongation of the thinking that went into the formation of my own verse."[17] From this it follows that Eliot's criticism, like that of other poet critics, is the formulation of his experience as a poet. The critics of Eliot have approached his critical pronouncements as an aid to the understanding of his poetry. Matthiessen, for instance, discusses Eliot's poetry in the light of his criticism. He writes a chapter on "Tradition and the Individual Talent" in which he first expounds Eliot's idea of tradition and then illustrates it from his poetry. But there is the possibility of another approach to Eliot's poetry and criticism, that is, to study his criticism in relation to his poetry. That there is such a possibility is confirmed by Eliot's own remark that "it is in relation to my own poetry that my criticism must be viewed."[18] If Eliot's criticism can be an aid to the understanding of his poetry, his poetry can also be an aid to the understanding of his criticism. There are many points in Eliot's criticism which become clear if explored in the light of his poetry. It is a commonplace of the Eliot criticism that in the later phase he lays emphasis on the religious and moral aspect of literature. The essay on "Religion and Literature" in comparison with "Tradition and the Individual Talent" is a clear pointer to it. But the reason for the shift of emphasis can be discovered best in Eliot's poetry. Even a random comparison of *The Sacred Wood* (1920) and *Homage to John Dryden* (1924) with *For Lancelot Andrewes* (1928) will bring out the shift of emphasis that has taken place in Eliot's criticism. Five of the eight essays in *For Lancelot Andrewes* deal with extra-literary interests such as religion, philosophy and politics as against *The Sacred Wood*, which is concerned primarily with aesthetic considerations.

One can explain away the shift in terms of Eliot's conversion to Anglo-Catholicism and naturalization as a British citizen. But this will be a rather facile explanation. All the three essays in *Homage to John Dryden* were written before the publication of *The Waste Land* (as evidenced by the dates mentioned against these essays in *Selected Essays*). That is to say, something happens in Eliot's poetical career after the publication of *The Waste Land* which is reflected in *For Lancelot Andrewes*. Only about a month after the publication of *The Waste Land* Eliot wrote to Richard Aldington : "As for *The Waste Land*, that is a thing of the past so far as I am concerned and I am now feeling towards a new form and style."[19] As the style is determined by the experience, a new style also means a new experience. The beginning of this new phase one finds in "The Hollow Men", the poem which followed *The Waste Land*. Though the poem has the vestiges of Eliot's early poetry, it also points to his later poetry both in theme and imagery. The change in Eliot's poetry is evidenced by such images in the poem as "the perpetual star" and "multifoliate rose." If "The Hollow Men" is the first important poem, "The Function of Criticism" is the first important critical piece Eliot published since the end of the first phase in 1922. One can easily see the change in Eliot's critical attitude in "The Function of Criticism." The main thing to notice in this essay is the attempt on Eliot's part to lend an extra-literary complexion to his earlier critical concepts, specially the idea of Tradition. Right at the outset of the essay, he reproduces the celebrated passage in the Tradition essay where he talks about the "existing monuments", and reaffirms his allegiance to the concept. But as he proceeds in his discussion, he expands the purely literary idea of Tradition into a general idea of order which literature possesses in common with religion and politics :

> If a man's interest is political, he must, I presume, profess an allegiance to principles, or to a form of government, or to a monarch; and if he is interested in religion, and has one, to a church; and if he happens to be interested in literature, he must acknowledge, it seems to me, just

> that sort of allegiance which I endeavoured to put forth in the preceding section [i.e., the allegiance to literary tradition].[20]

This statement of Eliot points to his laconic confession in the Preface to *For Lancelot Andrewes* (1928) where he admits that he is a "classicist in literature, royalist in politics, and anglo-catholic in religion." Eliot seems to forget that Pound could believe in literary tradition without espousing monarchy or Catholicism. But one thing is clear, that Eliot is trying to establish continuity between his early and later criticism. It is this attempt on the part of Eliot which has misled many critics. If we do not take Eliot at his word, we shall find that "The Function of Criticism" reflects an attitude which is substantially different from that of the early essays. Besides the change in his attitude towards tradition, there is in this essay a more sympathetic attitude towards extra-literary approaches to literature. In *The Sacred Wood* Eliot says that "the 'historical' and the 'philosophical' critics had better be called historians and philosophers quite simply."[21] And in "A Brief Treatise on the Criticism of Poetry" (1920) he writes : "The historical and the philosophical critic of poetry is criticizing poetry in order to create a history or philosophy."[22] But in "The Function of Criticism" he admits the usefulness of extra-literary data in literary criticism. "Scholarship, even in its humblest forms," writes Eliot "has its rights: we assume that we know how to use it, and how to neglect it."[23] Even the discovery of Shakepeare's laundry bills, he says, can be put to right use by a genius. As a matter of fact, Eliot has himself traced the development of his critical attitude in the Preface to 1928 edition of *The Sacred Wood.* Of this book and the essays in it, he writes :

> It is an artificial simplification, and to be taken only with caution, when I say that the problem appearing in these essays, which gives them what coherence they have, is the problem of the integrity of poetry, with the repeated assertion that when we are considering poetry we must consider it primarily as poetry and not another thing. At that time I was much stimulated and much helped by the critical writings of Remy de Gourmont. I acknowledge that influence, and am grateful for it; and I by no means

> disown it by having passed on to another problem not touched upon in this book : that of the relation of poetry to the spiritual and social life of its time and of other times.[24]

This is an unequivocal admission of the development from the aesthetic to the spiritual (moral/religious) and social aspect of literature. This should leave us in no doubt as to the development of Eliot's criticism. We may differ on the nature of development, but that there is a development cannot be denied.

Eliot had his later poetry, which is predominantly religious, at the back of his mind while writing his essay "Religion and Literature" published in 1935, the year which also saw the publication of "Burnt Norton" and *Murder in the Cathedral.* "Burnt Norton" and *Murder in the Cathedral* deal with the religious theme, and it is the religious point of view that is underlined in "Religion and Literature". Right at the outset of the essay Eliot writes :

> Literary criticism should be completed by criticism from a definite ethical and theological standpoint. . . . The 'greatness' of literature cannot be determined solely by literary standards; though we must remember that whether it is literature or not can be determined only by literary standards.[25]

He had already begun to look upon works of literature from a definite theological point of view. He considered *The Bhagawadgita* "the next greatest philosophical poem to The *Divine Comedy* within my experience,"[26] and the greatness of *The Divine Comedy* due to "the advantage of a coherent traditional system of dogma and morals like the Catholic."[27] Eliot who, in his early phase, was not at all prepared to admit extra-literary data into his critical fold confesses, in his later phase, that the greatness of literature can be judged only by theological and moral standards. Any failure to observe this development may be highly misleading. Eliot's criticism has been pressed into service by the exponents of his poetry. But a critic would be going amiss, if he judged Eliot's later poetry by the early critical formulas. C.K. Stead is one such critic who, by overlooking the development of Eliot's criticism, opines that in the *Four Quartets* Eliot failed to achieve the goal he set himself. Studying the evolution of Eliot's poetry Stead affirms that the early poetry becomes pure image, while the later poetry consisting of the *Four Quartets* attempts with failure to strike a compromise between discourse and image. The *Four Quartets,* he says, remains "imperfectly achieved with large portions of abstraction untransmuted into the living matter of poetry. The weakness of Stead's approach is the application of the early critical formula to both *The Waste Land* and the *Four Quartets.* If Eliot developed in his poetry, he developed in his criticism as well. If the early poetry can be understood in the light of the early essays, the later poetry is explained by the later essays, particularly "Dante" (1929) "Religion and Literature" (1935) and "The Music of Poetry" (1942). Eliot says in "Dante" that one learns from the *Purgatorio* how "straightforward Philosphical statement can be great poetry."[28] And in "The Music of Poetry" he writes that "in a poem of any length, there must be transitions between passages of greater and lesser intensity, to give a rhythm of fluctuating emotion essential to the musical structure of the whole."[29] The passages that Stead considers "*pure* discourse" and hence not poetry, Eliot would call passages of "lesser intensity" which are assimilated to those of greater intensity from which Stead quotes to demonstrate how Eliot occasionally achieves great poetry in the *Four Quartets.* By failing to pay due attention to Eliot's later essays Stead has completely misunderstood the pattern of the *Four Quartets.*

In discussing Eliot's criticism one needs to be careful in making generalizations, particularly when one is discussing Eliot on individual writers. The context in which Eliot talks is very important. An opinion on a particular aspect or quality of a writer must not be mistaken for an opinion on other qualities his work may possess, nor should an opinion on one poem or group of poems be taken as a judgement on the whole of the writer's work. Within his limitations Eliot tries his best to do justice to a writer by avoiding sweeping generalizations. It is seldom that Eliot aims at a wholesale condemnation or unqualified appreciation. He does not fail to notice good points, if there are any, in a writer whom he dislikes on the whole, or a weak point in a writer whom he likes on the whole. With his brilliant critical insight he can always single out good and bad points in a work, or a writer or a group of writers. Dante is the only writer for whom he has unqualified praise; that is to say, he appreciates all the aspects of all the poetry written by Dante. He has made reservations about the other two writers whom he rates very high and with whom he has striking similarities, namely Donne and Baudelaire. Compared with Dante, Donne has only "scraps of various philosophies"[30] and his poetry lacks the "organization" that one discerns in the poetry of Dante.[31] Of Baudelaire he says that "in Baudelaire, as well as in Goethe, is some of the out-moded non-sense of his time."[32] And compared with Dante, Baudelaire is nothing but a "bungler" in whom we do not find what we find in Dante, "the adjustment of the natural to the spiritual, of the bestial to the human and the human to the supernatural."[33] If, on the one hand, he can point out the limitations of Donne and Baudelaire for whom he has high admiration, on the other he can put his finger on the merits of Shelley whom he dislikes so much. The discussion of Shelley's criticism and poetry in *The Use of Poetry* went a long way to create the anti-Shelley attitude in the modern age, but in the same discussion Eliot singled out *The Triumph of Life* for special praise. He finds in it "a precision of image and an economy that is new to Shelley."[34] In "What Dante Means to Me?" (1950) Eliot says that "Shelley is the English poet, more than all others, upon whom the influence of Dante was remarkable."[35] He goes to the extent of quoting a passage from *The Triumph of Life* and admitting that "this is better than I could do."[36]

It stands out clear from the foregoing discussion that, in order to do justice to Eliot's criticism, one should avoid sweeping generalizations. One will be stating only partial truth if one says that Eliot likes Donne and Baudelaire and dislikes Shelley. What one should do is to point out what precisely he likes or dislikes in a particular writer or work.

The present work studies the evolution of Eliot's major critical concepts, and his poetry comes in only to illustrate his criticism. It is a study in which the primary emphasis falls upon Eliot's criticism, not upon his poetry. In my study of his criticism I confine myself to three major critical ideas, tradition, impersonality, and the dissociation of sensibility. All the three concepts undergo a shift of emphasis in course of the development of Eliot's poetry and criticism. In short, the three concepts which are originally purely litrary take on religious complexion in Eliot's later criticism. Tradition is used as a literary metaphor in the early essays, while in the later criticism it takes on a religious complexion as the Christian tradition. Similarly, impersonality which is a technical problem in the early criticism becomes a religious question in the later criticism. Impersonality in the later essays amounts to the acceptance of Christian orthodoxy. The theory of the dissociation of sensibility as formulated in the early critical pieces relates primarily to the "sensuous apprehension of thought",[37] whereas in the later criticism the metaphysical quality of feeling the thought, is said to be the product of metaphysics; the emphasis, thus, shifts from sensuousness to the metaphysical thought.

The development of Eliot's critical concepts should not be taken to mean that the later concepts supplant the early ones. In point of fact, the early concepts do not yield place to but only assimilate the later ones. Tradition, for instance, which is a literary metaphor combines in the later essays with the tradition which is a religious metaphor. Similarly with the other concepts. The religious dimension of Eliot's critical tenets that we find in his later essays is in comformity with the religious character of his later poetry. The present study demonstrates how Eliot's criticism follows the movements of his poetry and is the by-product or afterthought of his creative activity.

CHAPTER TWO

The Nature of Eliot's Development

Eliot, more than any other critic, has stressed the importance of a writer's development. Time and again, he points out how a writer shows a continuous development, and how his individual works constitute a unique organic whole. As early as 1917 he wrote anonymously :

> Any poet, if he is to survive as a writer beyond his twenty-fifth year, must alter; he must seek new literary influences; he will have different emotions to express.[1]

The development, Eliot concedes, may become disconcerting to the poet's readers who expect of the poet the same type of poetry. But the poet, in order to survive, must constantly grow, and if he does, one will find an organic relationship between his various works. In his essay on Dante (1929) Eliot underlines the pattern in Shakespeare's "carpet." "There is a relation," he writes "between the various plays of Shakespeare, taken in order, and it is a work of years to venture even one individual interpretation of the pattern in Shakespeare's carpet." He compares Shakespeare's pattern with Dante's and finds the former larger but the latter more distinct. Apparently, the pattern is the product of a writer's development. And if a writer has such a pattern, the critic, in order to do justice, must relate to each other his various works constituting the pattern. Each work sheds light on a writer's total corpus, and the whole corpus in turn illuminates the individual works. Eliot himself pays due attention to the pattern in a writer's "carpet" and writes in "What is Minor Poetry?" : "I could not say just why I think I understand *Comus* better for having read *Paradise Lost* or *Paradise Lost* better for having read *Samson Agonistes*, but I am sure that this is so."[2]

What Eliot says about the development of a creative writer holds for that of a critic as well. A critic develops just as much as a creative writer, and in order to do justice to him, one must take into account his total product while examining his individual pieces. As we noticed in the preceding chapter, Eliot himself regrets that the fact that his criticism has developed side by side with his poetry has gone unheeded by his critics. There are either those who wish to establish continuity in his criticism or those who find a complete break between his early and his later criticism.

The critics who find continuity in Eliot's criticism seek to trace his later critical ideas in his early criticism. Thus they tend to pay little attention to the shift in Eliot's criticism from the artistic to the theological aspect of literature. The two critics who deserve special mention here are Vincent Buckley and Fei-Pai Lu. Both maintain that Eliot's later emphasis on the ethical and theological element in literature is implied in his early essays. Vincent Buckley discusses at length the moral order behind Eliot's early critical principles such as tradition and impersonality and relates them to Eliot's acquiescence in Hulme's distrust of personality. He adduces Hulme's pronouncement that "the fundamental error is that of placing perfection in *humanity* thus giving rise to that bastard thing Personality, and all the bunkum that follows from it"[3], and says that Eliot pins his faith on this pronouncement throughout his criticism.[4] Buckley builds up his thesis on Hulme's pronouncement and points repeatedly to the moral order behind Eliot's early criticism. He says categorically that "we may see in his distrust of personality the roots of his later position : that the whole human order is more important than the individual insight, so far as that remains merely individual."[5] And of the shift of emphasis from art to morality he writes : "Eliot's moral interest and sense have not increased; it is only his explicit—and rather disproportionate—emphasis on them that has done so."[6]

Buckley seems to forget the simple fact that Hulme's *Speculations* was published only in 1924, and therefore it is open to question whether or not Hulme exercised any influence on the early Eliot. Moreover, Eliot himself admits that he came under Hulme's influence only in his later phase. The early influences on him were those of Irving Babbitt and Ezra Pound.[7] It is surprising that Buckley rests his entire thesis on Hulme-Eliot correspondence without taking into account the possibility of the former's influence on the latter. If we trust Eliot, and there is no reason to distrust him, then Buckley's thesis falls to pieces. In point of fact, Babbitt's influence on the early Eliot was much more decisive than is usually thought. This is evident from the striking parallels between Babbitt's critical pronouncements and Eliot's theories, particularly the ones on which Buckley centers his discussion, viz., tradition and impersonality. And if this is true, then the moral order behind the early Eliot is not Christian but humanistic. Both Buckley and Lu overlook the important distinction between ethics and theology, or, in other words, between morality and Christianity. While theology always includes in it ethics, ethics does not necessarily include theology : morality may be a revolt against what one finds in a particular religion. Both Babbitt and Lawrence, whom the later Eliot takes to task for being "after strange gods" and hence heretical, show a strong moral sense.

Even if we grant that the early Eliot was under Hulme's influence, we will still find Buckley's thesis untenable. The main charge against Buckley will be that he takes literally what is only metaphorically true. The relation between an individual and the church or state, and that between an individual writer and the literary tradition are only metaphorically identical. To take the latter as the same thing as the former is to miss the point. Buckley himself is aware of the danger in his approach, "the danger of taking for a declaration of fixed and central attitude what may be no more than an attempt, entered into at varying angles of interest, to re-assess the value which the literary past may have for the literary present."[8] One can only say that Buckley fails to avoid the danger, and it is only by using Eliot's later work that he has been able to find moral implications in Eliot's early criticism. If it is necessary to have a Christian attitude in order to formulate a theory of tradition, how could Pound set it forth, long before Eliot, while discarding

Christianity? Studying the development of Eliot's mind, John D. Margolis gives a persuasive account of the mind of Eliot at and around the time he wrote "Tradition and the Individual Talent." He quotes several pieces to demonstrate Eliot's sympathy with Christianity. I reproduce below a highly significant quotation he gives from Eliot's descriptive syllabus for the "Oxford University Extension lectures" (1916) :

> The beginning of the twentieth century has witnessed a return to the ideals of classicism. These may roughly be characterized as *form* and *restraint* in art, *discipline* and *authority* in religion, *centralization* in government .... The classicist point of view has been defined as essentially a belief in Original Sin—the necessity for austere discipline.
>
> It must be remembered that the French mind is highly theoretic—directed by theories—and that no theory ever remains merely a theory of art or a theory of religion or a theory of politics. Any theory which commences in one of these spheres inevitably extends to the others . . .
>
> The present-day movement is partly a return to the ideals of the seventeenth century. A classicist in art and literature will therefore be likely to adhere to a monarchical form of government, and to the Catholic Church. But there are many cross-currents. Our best procedure is to sketch briefly the relation of politics, literature and religion, and then consider the work of a few representatives of these three interests.[9]

Unfortunately, Buckley did not know this quotation, otherwise he could have done without drawing so heavily, and gratuitously, on Hulme's influence on Eliot. Margolis displays admirable caution in his discussion of the early Eliot. From the above quotation a critic like Buckley would have come to the conclusion that there was continuity in Eliot's criticism. But Margolis arrives at a most sensible conclusion which demolishes Buckley's thesis. "Eliot had," writes Margolis "lectured and written widely on extra-literary matters before the publication of *The Sacred Wood*; however, in that first volume of his essays, he scrupulously avoided such matters and insisted on their exclusion from literary criticism."[10] To prove his case he quotes from Eliot's "The Local Flavour" (1919) the following lines which again contradict Buckley :

> Most critics have some creative interest—it may be, instead of an interest in any art, an interest (like Mr Paul More's) in morals : *but interest in morals will not produce sound criticism of art*. Consequently, we may say that the only valuable criticism is that of the workman.[11] (italics mine).

There is all the difference between Buckley and Margolis, and it is Margolis who has got the point right.

Fei-Pai Lu commits more or less the same error as Buckley in seeking to establish continuity in Eliot's critical method which he designates as dialectical, i.e., built upon a dialectical opposition between art and morality. Lu sets himself in opposition to those who trace the development of Eliot from the aesthetic to the moral aspect of literature. "Historians," he writes "who found in Eliot's 'conversion' a development from aestheticism to moralism have committed historical inaccuracies."[12] He arrives at the conclusion that art or technique and morality, in a dialectical opposition, are simultaneously emphasized by Eliot : morality and art inform the early as well as the later criticism, and what is idealized is the resolution of their opposition. He forgets that in *After Strange Gods* Eliot talks of morality and orthodoxy to the exclusion of form. Where, one questions Lu, is the opposition and resolution of art and morality in *After Strange Gods*?

Even if one accepts Lu's argument that there is a co-presence of art and morality in Eliot's criticism, one cannot help raising a legitimate objection. The term "moral" or "morality" in Eliot's early essays does not carry the same connotation as it does in his later essays. The morality in the early criticism is humanistic, or, at the most Unitarian, whereas that in the later criticism is Christian. Morality for the later Eliot does not mean much unless it has behind it Christian sanctions. Lu ignores the distinction between the two types of morality presumably because it would undermine his argument. Both Buckley and Lu have misused the benefit of hindsight in tracing Eliot's preoccupation with Christian morality in his later essays to his early criticism. One does find traces of Eliot's early critical principles in his later essays but not the other way round. As Bergonzi and Coffman as well as Margolis point out, for all Eliot's later emphasis on the Christian experience, "Tradition and the Individual Talent" focuses on literary excellence.[13]

Eliot's literary criticism looked upon as a whole reveals a singular continuity in mutation. Christian values brought in by Eliot after the publication of *Homage to John Dryden* are absent from his early essays. The later Eliot does not denounce his early critical doctrines but combines them with Christian values. It is in this assimilation of the later Christian preoccupation to the early criticism that one finds continuity in his ideas. Tradition, impersonality, and the dissociation of sensibility, which are purely literary concepts in the early criticism, take on Christian meanings in the later criticism. This is what I mean by continuity in mutation.

When one comes to examine the criticism of Eliot's poetry, one finds that the critics of his poetry have used hindsight just as much as those of his criticism. The later Eliot is a Christian poet, while the early Eliot is not. By using hindsight the critics have traced his later Christian poetry to the poetry he wrote long before his conversion to Christianity. I am not denying the usefulness of hindsight but am protesting only against its abuse. In studying the development of a writer, a critic is apt to go wrong if he cannot resist the temptation of reading too much into the writer's early works. The critics are only too keen to establish continuity in a writer with the result that they often overlook the mutations which are at times more significant than continuity. Among the writers who find continuity in Eliot's poetry, R.P. Blackmur, Helen Gardner and Vincent Buckley deserve special consideration. These critics can be divided into two classes, the first comprising Blackmur, who finds no conversion in Eliot, and the other consisting of Gardner and Buckley, who accept continuity in Eliot with reservation, the reservation being that what is obvious in Eliot's later poetry constitutes only an undercurrent in his early poetry. Blackmur says categorically that "only those who never discerned a devout and savage Christian in *The Hippopotamus*, *Mr Eliot's Sunday Morning Service* and *The Waste Land*, have any cause to regret a change that never took place."[14] Thus to Blackmur, Eliot has been a Christian poet throughout, and his early poetry is no less Christian than his later poetry. Gardner and Buckley differ with Blackmur in so far as they maintain that Christianity, which is the theme of Eliot's later poetry, is no more than the underlying judgement in the early Eliot. Giving an account of the development of Eliot's poetry Helen Gardner writes:

> In the earlier poetry the apprehension is a kind of glass through which he views the world; it is a dark glass through which life is seen with a strange clarity, but drained of colour and variety. In the poetry that follows *The Waste Land* the apprehension itself becomes more and more the subject.[15]

Though Helen Gardner avoids using the term "Christian", what she actually means is the Christian apprehension. Her very remark that in the later poetry "the apprehension itself becomes more and more the subject" implies the Christian apprehension, as the later poetry is patently Christian. The early poetry uses Christian apprehension, believes Gardner, as a glass, i.e., as the criterion by which to judge the modern man.

Buckley is basically in accord with Helen Gardner. We have noticed above how he finds the traces of Eliot's later Christian preoccupation in his early criticism. And in examining Eliot's poetry he arrives at more or less an identical conclusion.

> The fact is that the preoccupations which we see as social or psychological are, in "The Waste Land," religious as well; and their religious character is seen not only in what we can extrapolate of the poem's 'themes' but also in what we respond to in the great, albeit confusing variety of its resonances.[16]

And, again,

> It [*The Waste Land*] is, in an extremely restricted sense, a religious poem, which binds its sections together by a theme of religious search, and seeks to affirm religious meaning by negation, by showing the dreariness associated with its absence. And it disguises the religious nature of the search by using anthropological and sociological terms to analyze the malaise of the civilization in which it was produced.[17]

I must point here to a difference between Gardner and Buckley. As is obvious from what I have said above, Gardner expresses her belief, though tacitly, that *The Waste Land* is a Christian poem. Buckley, on the other hand, believes that *The Waste Land* describes the "religious search" by negation, i.e., the poet has not yet arrived at a particular religion, though he is underlining its importance by demonstrating what life is like in its absence. One takes it that by negation Buckley implies not the negation of Christianity merely but of any religion. Buckley does not explain why the poem cannot be looked upon as having a Christian or a Hindu or a Buddhist bias. Moreover, how does one know that the poet is searching for a particular religion except by hindsight? Suppose Eliot had written nothing after *The Waste Land*, could we then say that in *The Waste Land* he was searching for a religion? As Eliot eventually did accept Christianity, it is easy to say that he was searching in *The Waste Land* for a religion which he found later.

Before I point out how the benefit of hindsight has been used by critics like Blackmur, Helen Gardner, and Buckley, I should like to quote Stephen Spender at some length.

> Most recent critics seem to read Eliot's conversion of 1927 into *The Waste Land* which was published in 1922. They do not seem to reflect that if Joyce had, like Graham Greene, written novels of wry Catholic orthodoxy, instead of *Finnegans Wake*, they would have been reading his reversion into Ulysses . . . .
>
> With all its virtues, the danger of critical analysis is that in tracing the graph of a writer's development it arrives at a pattern which looks like a rigid plan. Eliot lends himself particularly to this kind of treatment on account of declarations like the famous one about his being royalist and Catholic, and the still more famous one about the "progress of an artist" being a continual self-sacrifice, a continual extinction of personality." . . . In deciding, for example, whether *The Waste Land* adumbrates a Christian orthodoxy which became clarified in the *Four Quartets* I.A. Richards' view (put forward in 1926) that it was a poetry "severed from all beliefs" should be taken into account just as much as the view of someone today using hindsight sees *The Waste Land* almost as a Christian poem. A different evolution of Eliot's ideas was possible, and if it had happened, would have made Richards right.[18]

Spender suggests, and rightly, how a critic should approach the work of a writer who has completed his literary career. When the total work of a writer is available, the critic will be tempted to establish continuity in the writer and may in the process go amiss. I do not mean, and Spender does not seem to mean either, that it is futile to look for continuity in a writer. But the continuity must be discovered with due caution and not be traced in any direction or all directions. Joyce did not undergo the kind of conversion that Eliot did, but both manifest some sort of continuity in their total corpus. And we must not forget that continuity does not imply sameness and that continuity is not thematic only. Continuity implies that there is some link between different stages of a writer's development. And the development is not restricted to theme only but includes in it technical development as well.

Spender has rightly pointed out that in his poetry Eliot develops from anthropology to Christianity.[19] And in a brilliant discussion of the "transposition of the fertility myths", Maxwell argues that

> the basic symbol of the death that must be experienced before new spiritual life can be won, is taken over from the early poems, and transposed from the background of the fertility myths to that of Christianity and the Bible. Instead of in the symbolism of the Hanged Man, the reminiscences of the Corn God's burial, and the Fisher King, "Journey of the Magi" and "A Song for Symeon" concentrate the notion of rebirth in variations on the theme of Christ's birth.[20]

Spender and Maxwell are basically in accord, as they both hold that Eliot's early poetry draws on anthropology, while the later poetry concentrates on Christian tradition. The question which has been left unanswered by the two critics is whether or not anthropology lends itself to the same treatment as Christianity. Christianity is the theme of Eliot's later poetry, but is anthropology the theme of his early poetry? Eliot's own well-known pronouncement on the mythical method used in Joyce's *Ulysses* is worth considering.

> In using the myth, in manipulating a continuous parallel between contemporaneity and antiquity, Mr Joyce is pursuing a method which others must pursue after him . . . It is simply a way of controlling, of ordering, of giving a shape and significance to the immense panorama of futility and anarchy which is contemporary history . . . . It is a method for which the horoscope is auspicious. Psychology . . . . ethnology and the Golden Bough have concurred to make possible what was impossible even a few years ago. Instead of narrative method we may now use the mythical method.[21]

Eliot had already used the mythical method in *The Waste Land* when he said this. A significant point that emerges from the above passage is that the anthropological structure of *The Waste Land* plays the same role as the Homeric scaffolding in *Ulysses.* This is the point that Bernard Bergonzi makes when he writes, after refuting G.S. Fraser's view that "the ritual regeneration of the barren land is 'the underlying theme' of the poem," that "important though it is, I would prefer to describe it as a guide that Eliot used in composing the poem just as Joyce employed the *Odyssey* as a scaffolding in writing Ulysses."[22] Joyce used Homer's *Odyssey* to describe what he observed in his own age, and in his own country ; in other words, the Homeric myths are used as a technique or the mythical method. Just as Joyce is not writing about *Odyssey* but drawing on it for technical purposes, so is Eliot not writing about anthropology but only using it as a method to lend form to what was in and around him.[23] I find convincing Bergonzi's argument that the theme of *The Waste Land* is to be found not in the anthropological structure as such but in what the structure is used for.

If the above interpretation is accepted, then the question of the poet's belief in the anthropological structure of *The Waste Land* does not arise. The myths used in the poem have the same role to play as symbols, metaphors and similes ; in other words, they are poetical devices. M.H. Abrams defines mythology as "any religion in which we no longer believe."[24] And he goes on to say : "Poets, however, long after having ceased to believe in them, have persisted in using the myths of Jupiter, Venus, Prometheus, Wotan, Adam and Eve, and Jonah for their plots, episodes or allusion."[25] Discussing the use of mythology in modern literature Abrams, like Bergonzi, groups Joyce's *Ulysses* (and *Finnegans Wake*) with Eliot's *The Waste Land*. Abrams does not mention any Christian myths possibly under the impression that Christianity is a religion in which we still believe. But if we accept the anthropological findings which repudiate any difference between one religion and another, we cannot mark off Christianity from other religions. For anthropologists, all religions have their common roots and Christianity is not different from Paganism.

I suspect that the overriding factor behind Eliot's tremendous interest in anthropology was his Unitarian background. After all, one cannot go very far in one's interest in anthropology without sharing in the attitude of the anthropologists which is very similar to the Unitarian attitude. They are far from regarding Christianity as a new covenant or Christ as superior to the gods in other religions. It is a well-known fact that Eliot drew heavily on Miss Jessie L. Weston's *From Ritual to Romance* which he recommended to the readers of his *The Waste Land*. And here is Miss Weston's remark :

> That Christianity might have borrowed from previously existing cults certain outward signs and symbols, might have accommodated itself to already existing Fasts and Feasts, may be, perforce has had to be, more or less grudgingly admitted ; that such a *rapproachment* should have gone further, that it should even have been inherent in the very natureof the Faith, that, to some of the deepest thinkers of old, Christianity should have been held for no new thing but a fulfilment of the promise enshrined in the Mysteries from the beginning of the world, will to many be a strange and startling thought. Yet so it was, and I firmly believe that it is only in the recognition of this one-time claim of essential kinship between Christianity and the Pagan Mysteries that we shall find the key to the secret of the Grail.[26]

This observation may have startled the later Eliot, an orthodox Christian as he was. What Miss Weston is driving at is not the similarity between Christianity and Paganism in sheer formalism but that in faith. That is to say, Christianity and the Pagan Mysteries are essentially the same, which is well borne out by the very title of her book. The Grail which was originally associated with Pagan rituals took on the Christian complexion in the medieval romance. The sub-title of the book reads : "An account of the Holy Grail from ancient ritual to Christian symbol." The Holy Grail associated with the Christian Eucharist has been traced by Miss Weston to Pagan ritual. The striking parallel between Paganism and Christianity established so emphatically by her strikes at the very root of Christianity, which looks upon the Nativity of Christ as marking the end of the old dispensation and the beginning of the new.

Miss Weston confesses her indebtedness to Sir J.G. Frazer's *The Golden Bough*, the two volumes of which, *Adonis, Attis and Osiris,* have been drawn on by Eliot in *The Waste Land.* One has only to skim through Frazer's chapter on "Oriental Religions in the West" to realize how perplexing his conclusions would have been to a Christian. In point of fact, Frazer makes no secret of his attitude towards religion, Pagan as well as Christian. He points out how in the beginning Pagans and Christians took issue with each other, "the Pagans contending that the resurrection of Christ was a spurious imitation of the resurrection of Attis, and the Christians asserting with equal warmth that the resurrection of Attis was a diabolical counterfeit of the resurrection of Christ."[27] But for an anthropologist, there is no question of which god is superior to which, since to him they point to the same working of the human mind. For an anthropologist, Christianity is the continuation of Paganism, though Frazer goes even beyond this parallel and collates Christ and the Buddha. Of Christianity and Buddhism he writes :

> Both systems were in their origin essentially ethical reforms born of the generous ardour, the lofty aspirations, the tender compassion of their noble founders, two of those beautiful spirits who appear at rare intervals on earth like beings come from a better world to support and guide our weak and erring nature.[28]

The collocation of Christ and the Buddha has far-reaching implications. The Buddha was not a god, though he was, no doubt, a great religious reformer and the founder of the religion called after his name. And if Christ is compared to the Buddha, then Christ ceases to be the God of Christianity and comes down to the level of a reformer. Here we find a typical anthropological attitude to religion in general and Christianity in particular. In fact, Frazer goes to the extent of criticizing the excessive value set on spirituality in Christianity and Buddhism at the early stages. He says categorically that "by their glorification of poverty and celibacy both these religions struck straight at the root not merely of civil society but of human existence."[29] Of the impact of the oriental religions in the west Frazer writes :

> Men refused to defend their country and even to continue their kind. In their anxiety to serve their own souls and the souls of others, they were content to leave the material world, which they identified with the principle of evil, to perish around them. This obsession lasted for a thousand years. The revival of Roman Law, of the Aristotelian philosophy, of ancient art and literature at the close of the Middle Ages, marked the return of Europe to native ideals of life and conduct, to saner, manlier views of the world. The long halt in the march of civilization was over.[30]

With the close of the Middle Ages, believes Frazer, "the long halt in the march of civilization was over." Needless to say, the later Eliot, a neo-scholastic, would not have been in a position to sympathize with Frazer's attitude. For him, as for Hulme, another neo-scholastic, "the halt in the march of civilization" started with the close of the Middle Ages.

I have discussed at some length the anthropological attitude to religion in order to emphasize that this attitude is at odds with the Christian attitude of the later Eliot but in accord with the Unitarian attitude of the early Eliot. That there is a striking similarity between the anthropological and the Unitarian attitudes is borne out by the following observation by R.N. Cross, a Unitarian :

> The Christian Trinity has had quite another derivation, due partly to that process of deification of heroes or profoundly great men in religion which has parallels everywhere, and in a feebler form is to be seen in the canonizing

> of saints in certain sections of the Christian Church. Christ, like Buddha, in spite of himself, came to be worshipped as a God.[31]

The juxtaposition of Christ and the Buddha reminds us of a similar juxtaposition by Frazer above. Like Frazer, Cross looks upon Christ as a great man in religion, i.e., a religious reformer turned into God by his followers. The Unitarian attitude with its striking resemblance with the anthropological attitude is also very similar to the humanistic attitude of men like Babbitt and Foerster with whom Eliot took issue. We must bear in mind that it was the later Eliot, and not the Eliot of *The Waste Land* and the poems which preceded it, who expressed his differences from the humanists. The early Eliot was deeply saturated in Babbitt's thinking, though a detailed account of Babbitt-Eliot relationship has yet to come. There was a long controversy over the new humanism in the pages of *The Criterion* and articles for and against the humanistic position were written.[32] There is no point in going into the details of the controversy, as Eliot's position is fairly clear. After his conversion to Christianity he cannot accept humanism, though he can still recognize its value as far as it goes. The early Eliot with whom we are concerned here was a Unitarian, and as such in sympathy with humanism. Indeed, the borderline between Unitarianism and humanism is so thin that it is difficult to draw a line between them. If Unitarianism can at all be deemed a religion, Babbitt is quite prepared to sympathize with the religious attitude. He goes at one place to the extent of saying that "though religion can get along without humanism, humanism cannot get along without religion."[33] Babbitt discarded the idea of the outer authority of church and pleaded for the inner check. The following statement by a Unitarian can well sum up Babbitt's position :

> Our modern view insists on the *universality* of revelation—that the light of God is given direct to every man—not first of all handed by God to certain privileged intermediaries and then passed on to the rest of us. *It is God himself—nothing less—who comes to us in Nature, in Conscience, in human intercourse, in Jesus.*[34] (italics mine)

The only difference between Unitarians and Babbitt one can envisage is that the former place Jesus above other saviours,[35] while the latter places Confucius and the Buddha above Jesus.[36] But this is a rather superficial difference and at bottom they remain the same.

The above discussion leads us to the conclusion that the attitude of the early Eliot can be designated as anthropological, Unitarian or humanistic but not Christian. One can here raise a question as to the references to Christ in Eliot's early poetry. And it is here that one can see the use of hindsight at its worst. The later Eliot is a Christian and so the critics using hindsight take the references to Christ in the early Eliot, particularly "Gerontion" and *The Waste Land*, in the Christian and not anthropological spirit. What anthropology does is to transform Christianity or, any other religion, for that matter, into mythology with the result that the religious dogmas become myths. The mistake that the Eliot critics have made is to take the Christian myths in Eliot's early poetry as Christian dogmas. So they think that every reference to Christ points in the direction of the later Eliot, without realizing that it does not suggest any more than a reference to Paganism, Hinduism or Buddhism. Surprisingly enough, when there is an allusion to Pagan ritual, it is taken as a myth, but when there is a reference to Christ it is taken as a dogma by the critics trying to prove that the early Eliot is a Christian, just as the allusions to Hinduism and Buddhism are taken as dogmas by the critics interpreting the early Eliot as a Hindu or a Buddhist poet. But if we view the early Eliot through the anthropological glass, we will find that there is no difference for him between one religion and another, and that there are no religious dogmas but only religious myths in his early poetry.

The critics who find continuity in Eliot's poetry embedded in Christianity forget, in the first place, that the early Eliot had launched a severe attack on church and Christian formalism in poems like "A Fable for Feasters," "Hippopotamus" and "Mr Eliot's Sunday Morning Service," and, secondly, that Christianity in Eliot's early poetry is Christian mythology and not Christianity as a religious institution. Anyone looking upon "Gerontion" in the Christian spirit will make one mistake, i.e., he will be quick to point out that Gerontion is lamenting the loss of Christian beliefs in the following lines :[37]

> Signs are taken for wonders, "We would see a sign"
> The word within a word, unable to speak a word,
> Swaddled with darkness. In the juvescence of the year
> Came Christ the tiger.

The tiger springs in the new year. Us he devours. But if we examine the these utterances of Gerontion in the anthropological spirit, we will arrive at an altogether different conclusion : we will find that Gerontion's attitude towards what Christ stands for is ironical rather than appreciative. In his discussion of Eliot in the Christian perspective, Neville Braybrooke makes a significant observation :

> The difference between seeing Gerontion as a symbol, and Gerontion himself using people as symbols is a subtle, but vital, one, if the poem is not to be falsely interpreted as a piece of Christian propaganda. . . . At one remove, readers who happen to be Christian may find in the poem an illustration of spiritual drought—though all that Gerontion himself finds is his dislike of Christianity further increased by musing on the religious superstitions that have been practiced by so many believers whom he has known. Nor does his criticism stop short at Christianity : it applies to all forms of faith.[38]

And it is true that the critics have ignored the simple fact that Gerontion is "a character in a dramatic situation"[39] and as such is not a spokesman of the poet. He has an ironical attitude not only towards spiritual regeneration suggested by the references to Christ but all higher values like virtue and heroism as is evident from the following lines :

> Unnatural voices
> Are fathered by our heroism. Virtues
> Are forced upon us by our impudent crimes.

The Waste Land has been looked upon as a Christian, a Buddhist, and a Hindu poem. Critics like Helen Gardner and Vincent Buckley, as we have observed, look upon *The Waste Land* as covertly Christian. Cleanth Brooks supports them when he intimates that "the Christian material is at the centre, but the poet never deals with it directly."[40] And the critics interpreting *The Waste Land* as a Hindu or a Buddhist poem are equally emphatic. Raymond Tschumi writes : "More than a disguise of Eliot's convictions as a Christian, the allusions to Indian rituals are the whole foundation of the poem."[41] And after examining the Hindu allusions in *The Waste Land*, John Holloway affirms that "Eliot, when he wrote this poem [*The Waste Land*], was not an English poet and was not drawing on anything that English culture had given him."[42] Though Holloway does not say it in so many words, what he actually implies is that *The Waste Land* is not a Christian but a Hindu poem. The critics maintaining that *The Waste Land* is a Buddhist poem are not very clear on the difference between Hinduism and Buddhism. Harold Mc-Carthy is aware of but does not enlarge upon the difference between them, while Craige Raine simply ignores it. At any rate, the difference between the two religious systems is irrelevant to our present discussion. Both McCarthy and Raine attach great importance to the Buddhist element in Eliot's poetry, though the former concentrates on *The Waste Land*, while the latter on the *Four Quartets*. Of his approach to Eliot, McCarthy writes : "I agree with most critics that much of Eliot's work remains obscure unless seen within the context of the Christian tradition. But I am also convinced that an approach from the point of view of Buddhism can be peculiarly illuminating."[43] McCarthy's conclusion comes down to the belief that the Buddhist element in Eliot's poetry is as pervasive as the Christian. In his poetry, he believes, Eliot brings together the eastern and western religious traditions. Raine sums up his conclusion in the remark that "it [*The Waste Land*] is a poem about ennui because it is a Buddhist poem about reincarnation."[44]

Without advancing a detailed refutation of the views above, I can say that *The Waste Land* is not a Hindu or a Buddhist poem for the same reason for which it is not a Christian poem, i.e., as there are no religious dogmas but only myths from various religions employed for evocative purposes. *The Waste Land* is not a religious poem at all, unless we consider Unitarianism or humanism a religion.

Eliot's Christian poetry begins after *The Waste Land*. His development as poet and critic is not from the covertly Christian to the overtly Christian but from Unitarianism or humanism to Christianity.[45] Eliot's own admission in his thesis on Bradley that "I am as good a materialist as any-body"[46] suggests that in his early phase he could go to the other extreme from chirstianity. "The Hollow Men" is a transitional poem which looks backward to the early poetry which is not Christian and anticipates the later poetry which is markedly Christian. Where I differ with critics like Northop Frye and Helen Gardner, who also deem the poem transitional,[47] is in denying that it brings to surface what was implicit in the early poetry. "The Hollow Men" brings a new element in conjunction with what characterizes the early poetry. And this new element points to the Christian experience embodied in such poems as "Ash Wednesday" and the *Four Quartets*, It is difficult to accept Frank Wilson's view that " 'The Hollow Men' marks, not a development but a new beginning."[48] In point of fact, "The Hollow Men" can be looked upon as a bridge across Eliot's early and later poetry : it is a poem in which his early phase passes into his later phase. I shall touch here only on one element in the poem which links up Eliot's two phases. The point that I have in mind has been suggested, though somewhat vaguely, by Raymond Tschumi in his remark that " 'The Hollow Men' awakens in the reader a spiritual longing."[49] Tschumi believes that the emptiness in "The Hollow Men" is essentially the same as that in *The Waste Land*, and hence his admission that "the theme of *The Waste Land* is similar to that of "The Hollow Men!"[50] In fact, the emptiness in "The Hollow Men" combines the emptiness in *The Waste Land* with that in the *Four Quartets*. In *The Waste Land* men and women are spiritually empty despite the whole material world, because they lack spirituality, while in the *Four Quartets* the emptiness is caused by the deprivation of worldly associations which is a pre-requisite for the communion with the Divine.

I must point here to a significant difference between Eliot's early and later poetry. The early poetry uses religious myths, while the later poetry deals with religious dogmas. This difference has gone completely unnoticed by Eliot's critics. If religions are treated as constituting religious mythologies, myths from different religions can go side by side, as there is no question of believing in myths. But if they are taken as religious systems, they provide not myths but dogmas, and the dogmas from different religions cannot be brought together without thinning those religions to a point where they cease to be religions. Dogmas, unlike myths, are believed in and one cannot be an orthodox believer in two religions at the same time. It is for this reason that I believe that the Hindu and the Buddhist elements in Eliot's later works are out of place. I shall consider here only two attempts on the part of the later Eliot to combine the Indian religious tradition with Christianity, one in the *Four Quartets* and the other in *The Cocktail Party*.

The most dominant element in the *Four Quartets* is Christian mysticism such as one finds in St John of the Cross.[51] Even a cursory glance at the works of St John of the Cross will be sufficient to persuade one that his emphasis falls upon contemplation which demands, to use Eliot's words, "desiccation of the world of sense." The introduction of the *Bhagwadgita* in "The Dry Salvages" is out of place as the general tenor of Krishna's argument is not contemplation but action. There are two ways to God according to Lord Krishna, the way of knowledge or wisdom and the way of action.[52] It is the former that can be compared to St John of the Cross's mysticism, but it is the latter on which Krishna's emphasis falls. All Krishna's argument is directed at exhorting Arjuna to act. And, therefore, S. Radhakrishnan is right when he says,

> It [the *Bhagwadgita*] raises the question whether action or renunciation of action is better and concludes that action is better. . . . He [Krishna] recommends the full active life of man in the world with the inner life anchored in the Eternal Spirit. The *Gita* is therefore a mandate for action.[53]

With its emphasis on action the *Bhawadgita* does not fit into a poem which is so influenced by St John of the Cross.

If the *Gita* is out of place in the *Four Quartets*, Buddhism is out of place in *The Cocktail Party* which is patently Christian.

Celia's eventual crucifixion should leave us in no doubt as to the Christian bias of the play. Eliot tries very tactfully to bring together Christianity and Buddhism in the psychiatrist Reilly's exhortation to Celia as well as to Edward and Lavinia. He says to them : "Work out your salvation with diligence." This is the last speech of the Buddha to his disciples.[54] Eliot avoids quoting from the New Testatment where St Paul says : "Work out your own salvation with fear and trembling."[55] The Buddhist utterance in a Christian play points to Eliot's attempt to unite Buddhism with Christianity. He does not seem to realize that this is an attempt which is not expected of an orthodox Christian like himself. The word "diligence" in the Buddha's utterance and the words "fear and trembling" in St Paul's letter hint at the basic difference between Buddhism and Christianity. In Buddhism, with its emphasis upon meditation, salvation is achieved by one's own effort, while in Christianity it cannot be attained without the grace of Jesus. The difference between Christianity and Buddhism has been clearly expressed by Henry Clark Warren whose *Buddhism in Translations* has been mentioned by Eliot in his notes to *The Waste Land*.

> Protestant Christianity teaches salvation by faith, while Buddhism places its greatest reliance in meditation. And it is not strange that the methods of the two religions should be so different, when we consider the very different meanings attached by Buddhists and Christians to the word "salvation,"—the latter wishing to be saved from sin and hell, the former from Karma and rebirth.[56]

It is enough to point out that there is no rebirth in Christianity in the Buddhist sense. Eliot adopts in the *Four Quartets* and *The Cocktail Party* a syncretic attitude without realizing that, being an orthodox Christian, he cannot do so. Christianity reconciled with Hinduism or Buddhism is Christianity reinterpreted, and this reinterpretation will not be acceptable to an orthodox Christian. We are reminded here of Eliot's own *After Strange Gods* where writers are attacked for reinterpreting Christianity. What I am suggesting is not that syncretism itself is an impossibility, but that it cannot be achieved while retaining Christian orthodoxy. Visser 't Hooft rightly points out that "a Christianity which should think of itself as one of many diverse contributions to the religious life of mankind is a Christianity that has lost its foundation in the New Testament."[57] Eliot wants to retain Christian orthodoxy and at the same time syncretize it with other religions. But the two do not go together. One is bound to deviate from the New Testament in direct proportion to one's movement towards syncretism. In a rather neglected Preface Eliot rejects precisely what syncretism will result in :

> I am aware. . . . that there are readers who persuade themselves that there is an "essence" in all religions which is the same, and that this essence can be conveniently distilled and preserved, while every particular religion is rejected. Such readers may perhaps be reminded that no man has ever climbed to the higher stages of the spiritual life, who has not been a believer in a particular religion or at least a particular philosophy.[58]

Syncretism is the distilling of the essence in various religions that Eliot disapproves of. Eliot wants to have his cake and eat it too : he wants to retain Christian orthodoxy and at the same time syncretize it with other religions. In order to bring together various religions Eliot needs to revert to his Unitarianism.

CHAPTER THREE

Tradition

The term "tradition" as used by Eliot is a metaphor that can be applied to any number of subjects. Eliot himself applies it to several disciplines such as literature, culture, education, philology, sociology, and politics. But if we leave aside for a while his critical works published after *Homage to John Dryden*, which marked the end of the early phase of his criticism, the metaphorical nature of the term becomes less significant, since his early criticism deals only with literary tradion. As we shall see later, tradition, which is only a metaphor in Eliot's early phase, takes on the extra-literary complexion in his later phase.

The metaphorical nature of tradition has not gone unnoticed by the critics of Eliot. Among those who have noticed it F.R. Leavis and Vincent Buckley deserve special mention.[1] Leavis, who doesn't approve of the impersonal theory formulated in "Tradition and the Individual Talent", himself applies the metaphor of tradition to English studies. Pressing the metaphor into service, Leavis pleads for the teaching of modern literature. He argues that "it is only from the present, out of the present, in the present that you can approach the literature of the past. To put it in another way, it is only in the present that the past lives."[2] Like Leavis, Buckley treats tradition as a metaphor that takes on the extra-literary implications in Eliot's later criticism, as is evident from his assertion that "the centre of attention is not now [in the later essays] an objectively existing literary order ('tradition'), but an equally objective cultural order on which literature depends."[3] Here I must add that neither Leavis nor Buckley brings out all the complexity of the term "tradition" as a metaphor. The metaphorical implication that comes out of Leavis's discussion is nominal: it is extending the argument of Eliot to English studies rather than explaining the metaphorical nature of tradition. And, in fact, Eliot himself advanced the same argument as Leavis in "On Teaching the Appreciation of Poetry."

> The pupils who have some aptitude for enjoyment and understanding of what is good in literature . . . will find that their knowledge of the great poetry which has had the approval of successive generations will sharpen their discrimination and refine their enjoyment of the poetry written in their own time; and their enjoyment of the poetry written in their own time will help them towards the enjoyment of the classics of literature. For our own poetry of today and of our forefathers, the foundations upon which we build and without which our poetry would not be what it is, will eventually be seen as forming one harmonious whole.[4]

Buckley has restricted the application of tradition to certain disciplines such as literature, culture, and religion instead of recognizing the infinite flexibility of the term. The term, a metaphor as it is, can be stretched in any direction. In the following extract, for instance, we can notice how Eliot draws on the metaphor of tradition in his discussion of education :

> More than ever, we should look to education today to preserve us from the error of pure contemporaneity. We look to institutions of education to maintain a knowledge and understanding of the past. And the past has to be reinterpreted for each generation, for each generation brings its own prejudices and fresh misunderstandings.[5]

Compare this extract with the following comment of Eliot regarding the critic reinterpreting the literary tradition :

> From time to time, every hundred years or so, it is desirable that some critic shall appear to review the past of our literature, and set the poets and the poems in a new order. . . . each generation, like each individual, brings to the contemplation of art its own categories of appreciation, makes its own demands upon art, and has its own uses for art.[6]

It is the same interaction between the past and the present that Eliot has emphasized in education as well as in literary criticism. He extends the metaphor of tradition to philology in his comment that "we need to understand the way in which our words have been used in the past, how they have developed and altered their meanings, in order to understand how we are using them ourselves."[7] And tradition becomes a cultural metaphor in his remark that "the baffling problem of 'culture' underlies the problems of the relation of every part of the world to every other."[8]

The metaphor of tradition has no restriction of application whatsoever : it can be applied to education as well as to literature. The relationship between the past and the present, or, in other words, between tradition and contemporaneity is the relation between the whole and the parts. And the relation between the whole and the parts that Eliot idealizes is the organic relationship. Before entering on a discussion of the organic nature of Eliot's tradition it is worthwhile to reflect for a while on the meaning and characteristics of organic unity. There is no point in tracing the origin and development of the idea of organic unity, though in England, Coleridge can be said to be the popularizer of it. The relation between the whole and the parts is basic to the concept of organic unity. In the organic unity the parts and the whole are inextricably related to each other. In a machine it is the parts which come first and the whole emerges out of their assemblage but, conversely, in a tree it is the whole that comes first and the parts grow out of it. Coleridge himself remarks : "Depend on it, whatever is grand, whatever is truly organic and living, the whole is prior to the parts."[9] Eliot's idea of tradition is closely related to the emphasis on the whole in Coleridge's concept of organic unity. As M.H. Abrams points out, since the origin of a plant lies in the seed, Coleridge thinks that "the elementaristic principle is to be stood on its head; that the whole is primary and the parts secondary and derived."[10] Similarly, in Eliot's theory of tradition it is the whole, the literary tradition, that comes first and the individual talent emerges out of it. The terms "secondary" and "derived" should not be taken in a derogatory sense, but only as implying that they come after the whole. In point of fact, the parts are as important for the whole as the whole is for the parts, for the simple reason that the whole is after all formed by the parts.[11] Coleridge rightly says that in a living organization there is "the connection of parts to a whole, so that each part is at once end and means."[12] The parts and the whole act and interact upon each other : a part contributes as much to the whole as the whole to the part. If a part of a living organism is chopped off, it is not only the part that is affected but also the whole. This is what Eliot implies when he says that the whole tradition is stirred with the introduction of a new work of art. Eliot's idea of tradition and the individual talent is summarily expressed in the following extract :

> The existing monuments form an ideal order among themselves, which is modified by the introduction of the new (the really new) work of art among them. The existing order is complete before the new work arrives, for the order to persist after the supervention of novelty, the *whole* existing order must be, if ever so slightly, altered; and so the relations, proportions, values of each work of art toward the whole are readjusted, and this is conformity between the old and the new.[13]

The whole is the organic whole in which each part is doubly related, related to the whole and related to the other parts in the whole. As an inevitable corollary of the introduction of a new part to the whole, not only is the whole altered but also the relationship among various parts in the whole. Eliot becomes increasingly conscious of organic unity which is employed frequently in the discussions of extra-literary subjects in his later criticism.

II

The source of Eliot's theory of tradition has been traced to various writers and critics. I should like to confine myself to four major figures behind Eliot's concept of tradition, namely, Arnold, Babbitt, Hulme and Pound.[14] Arnold's is a peculiar case for the Eliot critics. Eliot, they argue, has drawn heavily on Arnold and hence his attack on the latter is best seen as stemming from his general anti-Victorian attitude. Vincent

Buckley, for example, remarks that "what set him [Eliot] against Arnold is what set him against the Romantics' century—the nineteenth. His total position is one of reaction against that century, and an affirmation of a scheme of values alternative to it."[15] One can say that Eliot is being dishonest in not expressing what he genuinely feels about Arnold. But to say this is to miss the point. As has been said, the context is very important in Eliot's criticism, and one should bear in mind that Eliot does not criticize Arnold for what the critics have found him indebted to Arnold for. As a matter of fact, he has acknowledged the importance of Arnold's work as a bridge across the English Channel.[16]

Eliot himself has touched upon the sources he tapped in evolving his theory of tradition. In his appraisal of his own criticism in "To Criticize the Critic" he confesses that in writing his "Tradition and the Individual Talent", he drew on Irving Babbitt and Ezra Pound. This influence, he says, later combined with that of T.E. Hulme and Charles Maurras.[17] Though one should think twice before taking a writer at his word, yet I find no reason to distrust Eliot. The two common points between Arnold and Eliot that Lucy shows—the idea of European tradition and of external authority—are there in Eliot, but he could as well have got them from Babbitt and Pound. The idea of external authority expressed in Arnold's "The Literary Influence of Academies" and "On Translating Homer" is different from Eliot's tradition. There are two major differences between Arnold's academical authority and Eliot's literary tradition. First, the relation between Arnold's authority and individual is one-sided ; that is to say, it is the authority that affects the individual and not the other way round. Conversely, Eliot's theory of tradition centers on an interaction between tradition and the individual talent. Secondly, Arnold lays his emphasis on the repudiation of provinciality through the influence of academy. "The less a literature has felt," writes Arnold, "the influence of a supposed centre of correct information, correct judgement, correct taste, the more we shall find in it this note of provinciality."[18] But with Eliot, on the other hand, provinciality is not discarded but only transfused into universality. In an essay published in 1922 under the title "The Three Provincialities", Eliot talks about the Irish, the English, and the American literatures and points out that in order to attain not merely local but European significance these literatures must seek literary excellence not in nationality but in language. Joyce, Eliot believes, has raised what is national and racial to the level of what is international and thus produced literature for Irish as well as for European public. In his postscript to the essay written in 1950 Eliot says :

> True literature has in it something which can be apprecia-ted by intelligent foreigners who have a reading knowledge of the language, and also something which can only be understood by the particular people living in the same place as the author.[19]

I do not contend that there is nothing in common between Arnold and Eliot. I find striking similarities between Arnold's view of modernity expressed in an essay called "On the Modern Element in Literature" and Eliot's concept of tradition. Like Eliot's tradition, Arnold's modernity is a matter of what is relevant to the present. It is in relation to the present that he finds the Greek literature of the 5th century B.C. modern. Like Eliot he underlines the need for placing one literature in relation to other literatures in order adequately to evaluate it : "no single event," says he "no single literature is adequately comprehended except in its relation to other events, to other literatures."[20] And compare with this Eliot's remark that "no poet, no artist of any art, has his complete meaning alone. . . .You cannot value him alone ; you must set him, for contrast and comparison, among the dead."[21] Moreover, Eliot's distinction between two types of tradition[22] can be traced to Arnold's distinction between "a significant spectacle" and a point of view from which the spectacle is surveyed. "He who has found that point of view, he who adequately comprehends this spectacle, has risen to the comprehension of his age."[23] But nevertheless, there are basic differences between Arnold's and Eliot's attitudes. First, there is no such emphasis in Arnold on the individual writer or work as we find in Eliot. And, secondly, the idea of organic unity that is basic to Eliot's theory of tradition is missing from Arnold.

Both as teacher and writer Babbitt exercised a decisive influence on Eliot's entire anti-romantic attitude. Babbitt had attacked the traditional humanism, Baconian (i.e., materialistic) as well as Rousseauistic (i.e., emotional), and pleaded for his own critical humanism with its emphasis on the inner check. The main point in Babbitt's humanism that Eliot has absorbed is the balance, the golden mean, between the extremes of romanticism and neo-classicism, the former stressing the repudiation of all standards and the latter simply setting out to imitate certain models. In the critical language of Eliot one can say that the romantics were anti-tradition, whereas the neo-classicists were anti-individual. Babbitt makes it sufficiently clear that romanticism that sprang from the Rousseauistic philosophy believed in emotional imperialism and was averse to any restraint whatsoever. Of the romantic genius he writes : "Everything that limits temperamental expansion is dismissed as either artificial or mechanical ; everything on the contrary that makes for the emancipation of temperament, and so for variety and difference, he welcomes as vital, dynamic, creative".[24] The neo-classicists, whom Babbitt calls pseudo-classicists, on the other hand, looked upon classical writers as representing ideals and sought to imitate them in their works : thus they aimed at not true imitation in the Aristotelian sense but "the imitation of models."[25]

Like Arnold, Babbitt emphasised the importance of the literature of the past in relation to the present. Both Arnold and Babbitt set great value on Greek literature of which the latter writes :

> Nothing was more remarkable about Greek literature than the balance it maintained between the forces of tradition and the claims of originality so that Greek literature at its best is a kind of creative imitation.[26]

It is the "creative imitation" which Babbitt finds lacking in the English neo-classicists. He anticipates Eliot and reminds one of Arnold in his belief that the works of a writer should be estimated "as links in that unbroken chain of literary and intellectual tradition which extends from the ancient to the modern world."[27] Eliot must have noticed Babbitt's remark that,

> What we are seeking is a critic who rests his discipline and selection upon the past without being a mere traditionalist; whose holding of Tradition involves a constant process of hard and clear thinking, a constant adjustment, in other words, of the experience of the past to the changing needs of the present.[28]

Moreover, Eliot echoes Babbitt in his view of originality. Babbitt said that "Genuine originality . . . usually gains more than it loses by striking deep roots into the literature of the past."[29] And Eliot writes that "not only the best, but the most individual parts of his [poet's] work may be those in which the dead poets, his ancestors, assert their immortality most vigorously."[30]

The above discussion brings out how Babbitt influenced Eliot in evolving his theory of tradition. But it would be wrong to make a wholesale identification of Babbitt's critical humanism and Eliot's tradition. For all that Babbitt says about humanism he remains basically individualistic in his belief in the inner check exercised by higher will. He admits that he is with the naturalists to the extent of rejecting "outer authority in favour of the immediate and experimental."[31] It is the inner control and not the imitation of models that he finds emphasised by Aristotle. It is in his emphasis on the inner check that Babbitt differs from Eliot. For Eliot tradition constitutes an external authority to which an individual writer submits in such a way that not merely is he affected by the tradition but the tradition, too, is in turn affected by him. But Babbitt's tradition either becomes a blemish when looked upon as a model, or helps an individual with the exercise of his talent while itself remaining unaffected.

Pound's impact on Eliot was no less decisive than Babbit's. The two critics are at one as regards the importance of tradition and the way it acts and interacts upon the individual talent. Both postulate that it is tradition in the true sense and not originality that a writer should aim at. " 'Originality'," in the words of Pound "when it is most actual, is often sheer lineage, is often a closeness of grain."[32] Pound not only set forth his idea of tradition in his early writings including *The Spirit of Romance* (1910) but used it in the first collection of his poems, *A Lume Spento* (1908). In *The Spirit of Romance* he evolves a tradition for himself. His exaltation of Dante and denunciation of Milton, and also his comparison of Dante with Shakespeare, anticipate Eliot. In his Preface to *Poetical Works of Lionel Johnson* (1913) he expresses the view that "one should weigh Theocritus and one's neighbour in one balance."[33] And compare it with Eliot's remark that "we need a digestion which can assimilate both Homer and Flaubert."[34] It is in Pound for the first time that we discern that interaction between "Tradition and the Individual Talent" which is basic to Eliot's concept of tradition as an organic whole. In his "Date Line" Pound enumerates different types of criticism, and the most intense form according to him is "criticism in new composition." He illustrates this type of criticism from Eliot's "Fragment of an Agon" which to him is a better piece of criticism of Seneca than Eliot's essay on Seneca.[35] One can instance *The Waste Land* in which the whole tradition undergoes a metamorphosis at the hands of Eliot. There is a close interaction between Eliot and each of the writers used in the poem. When Dante is quoted in "The Burial of the Dead", it is not only that Dante contributes to the total meaning of the poem but also the total meaning of the poem sheds light on Dante. It is this interaction that Pound means by "criticism in new composition."[36]

For all the parallels between Pound and Eliot it is difficult to side with Hugh Witemeyer in the complete identification of the two critics on tradition.[37] For a start, the writers constituting tradition for Eliot are not the same as those composing tradition for Pound. Virgil and Donne, to whom Eliot attaches so much importance, are not so important for Pound, while writers like Homer and Swinburne who are significant links in Pound's tradition are certainly not Eliot's favourites. But, in fact, the question of links in tradition is a minor one compared with the organic relationship of links. A more important difference between Eliot and Pound is that the former is more systematic in building up his tradition than the latter. The unity of Eliot's tradition is much more clear than that of Pound's : the moment we look at Eliot's tradition, the entire history of literature udergoes a marked change. Pound's tradition is fragmentary compared with Eliot's. The writers in Eliot's tradition have a twofold relationship; they are related at once to Eliot and to each other. That is why we find that the writers constituting Eliot's tradition have certain points in common with each other. One can at a glance see similarities between Dante, Donne and Baudelaire, to mention three of the several writers in Eliot's tradition : they are all poets who give us sensuous embodiment of thought. But what, one asks, are the common points uniting the writers in Pound's tradition such as Homer, the troubadours, Dante, Cavalcanti, Chaucer, Rossetti, Swinburne, and Henry James? Though Pound is aware of the interaction between the past and the present, yet the organic relationship in his tradition is only onefold, while the true organic relationship is twofold. Pound, unlike Eliot, seems more fascinated by the technical accomplishment of a writer than the total excellence of his work.[38] Eliot himself confesses that he is "seldom interested in what he [Pound] is saying but only in the way he says it."[39]

Seán Lucy and Vincent Buckley talk of the influence of Hulme on the whole of Eliot, but, as we shall see later, Eliot is right in saying that he came under Hulme's influence only in his later phase, since the influence is visible only in his later criticism with its emphasis on the Christian tradition.

III

Eliot formulated his theory of tradition in the first section of "Tradition and the Individual Talent" where, surprisingly enough, he refrained from instancing any writer embodying it in his works. At any rate, in the other essays in *The Sacred Wood*, and also elsewhere, Eliot does apply his theory of tradition to various writers. Discussing Ben Jonson he points out the failure of Gregory Smith to look upon Jonson as our contemporary, i.e., as part of our tradition. "Of all the dramatists of his time," says Eliot "Jonson is probably the one whom the present age would find the most sympathetic, if it knew him."[40] The difference between Smith's and Eliot's approaches to Jonson is virtually the difference between historical criticism and the historical sense as defined by Eliot.[41] Smith examines Jonson in the context of Jonson's own age, while Eliot estimates him in the modern context. And to assess Jonson in the modern context one needs the histroical sense that will put Jonson in our age rather than putting us into the seventeenth century. Eliot advances an identical comment on Professor Gilbert Murray's translation of Euripides; that is, that Murray "leaves Euripides quite dead", since his Euripides belongs to the past with nothing of use to us. Eliot, on the other hand, desiderates a translation that amounts to re-creation, that shows whether or not Euripides can be made use of by those writing today. Professor Murray's failure, for the most part, is due to the fact that he is a creative writer of little significance. But even the translations by H.D. and other creative writers in "Poets Translation Series", says Eliot, "have so far done no more than pick up some of the more romantic crumbs of Greek literature."[42] What Eliot implies is that the poet translators have moved to the other extreme from Professor Murray by not paying sufficient attention to the pastness of Greek literature. "We need an eye," he writes "which can see the past in its place with its definite differences from the present, and yet so lively that it shall be as present to us as the present."[43] This is the type of eye that Pound is gifted with. Eliot's comment on Pound's translations of Chinese poems in *Cathay* is significant. He predicts "that in three hundred years Pound's *Cathay* will be a 'Windsor translation' as Chapman and North are now 'Tudor translations' : it will be called (and justly) a magnificent specimen of XXth century poetry, rather than a 'translation'. Each generation must translate for itself."[44] The type of translation that Eliot approves of is a blend of the pastness and the presentness of a work.

The interaction between the past and the present forms the very foundation of Eliot's theory of tradition. The idea of the present being directed by the past is not new, since we discern it in earlier writers including the English neo-classicists. What is new in Eliot's doctrine of tradition is the idea of the past also being altered by the present. And in order to attain the interaction between the past and the present, one needs the historical sense which is defined as follows :

> The historical sense involves a perception, not only of the pastness of the past, but of its presence; the historical sense compels a man to write not merely with his own generation in his bones, but with a feeling that the whole of the literature of Europe from Homer and within it the whole of the literature of his own country has a simultaneous existence and composes a simultaneous order. This historical sense, which is a sense of the timeless as well as of the temporal and of the timeless and of the temporal together, is what makes a writer traditional.[45]

Eliot forestalls the objection that it is humanly impossible for a writer to acquaint himself with all that has been written in the past. In the first place, knowledge is not a matter of sheer acquisition of information but absorption. Shakespeare, for instance, "acquired more essential history from Plutarch than most men could from the whole British Museum."[46] And, secondly, the acquaintance with the past is a matter of procuring the consciousness of the past, and once one has procured it, one can go on developing it throughout the rest of one's career.

In his *The New Criticism* Ransom has called attention to the employment in Eliot's criticism of the tools of comparison and analysis and the way they are related to his idea of tradition. Ransom quotes from Eliot's essay on Swinburne where Eliot places Swinburne in relation to writers like Campion, Shelley, Shakespeare, Wordsworth and the provençal. Indeed, such comparative estimates one comes across in almost every critical piece of Eliot. The following is an example from his essay on "Ben Jonson" :

> We have no difficulty in seeing what brought him [Jonson] to the pass; how in contrast, not with Shakespeare but with Marlowe, Webster, Donne, Beaumont and Fletcher, he has been paid out with reputation instead of enjoyment. He is no less a poet than these men, but his poetry is of the surface. Poetry of the surface cannot be understood without study, for to deal with the surface of life, as Jonson dealt with it, is to deal so deliberately that we too must be deliberate, in order to understand. Shakespeare, and smaller men also, are in the end more difficult, but they offer something at the start to encourage the student or to satisfy those who want nothing more; they are suggestive, evocative, a phrase, a voice; they offer poetry in detail as well as in design. So does Dante offer something, a phrase

> everywhere (*tu se' ombra ed ombra vedi*) even to readers who have no Italian; and Dante and Shakespeare have poetry of design as well as of detail.[47]

Eliot sets Jonson, for comparison and contrast, among other writers like Shakespeare, Marlowe, Webster, Donne, Beaumont, Fletcher and Dante and thus practises in his criticism what he advocates in his theory. From this it follows that not only writers but also critics need to acquire the historical sense. And the historical sense is very different from what Ransom calls historical criticism. It is surprising that Ransom calls Eliot a historical critic despite Eliot's own denunciation of historical criticism. A historical critic concerns himself with background data of a writer. But Eliot, on the contrary, is not bothered about the background of a writer. He lifts a writer, as it were, out of his historical setting and focuses his attention on his works. And this is in conformity with Eliot's tradition where time does not matter. A historical critic takes the reader to the period to which the writer under examination belongs, while Eliot brings a writer of the past to the present age.

Pound exemplifies Eliot's concept of tradition and the individual talent. As early as 1918 he wrote : "Pound's erudition, his interest in the past, and his interest in the present are one."[48] Eliot distinguishes between false and true originality, the former being "in the bad sense 'subjective' with no relation to the world to which it appeals" and the latter only the development of what has already been done by others. Pound's originality is true originality : "his versification is a *logical* development of the verse of his English predecessors."[49] Moreover, Pound has gone back to the literary tradition of Europe from the ancient age to the recent past and made it a part of his individual talent. Eliot traces the influence on Pound of various poets from the troubadours, Cavalcanti and Dante down to Browning and Yeats. Pound, says Eliot, looks upon the Provencal and Italian poets as his contemporaries; "that is to say, he grasped certain things in Provence and Italy which are permanent in human nature.'[50] In such a use of tradition the influence operates both ways : Pound is as much acted upon by the tradition as he himself acts upon it.

> It is probable that the Chinese, as well as the Provençals and the Italians and the Saxons, influenced Pound, for no one can work intelligently with a foreign matter without being affected by it; on the other hand, it is certain that Pound has influenced the Chinese and the Provençals and the Italians and the Saxons—not the matter *an sich*, which is unknowable but the matter as we know it.[51]

It is this subtle interaction between tradition and the individual talent that Eliot has advocated throughout his criticism. Virgil's *Aeneid*, which is the only universal classic by Eliot's standards, strikes a balance between tradition and the individual talent. Eliot holds that Virgil had a critical sense of the past with the result that he could suitably use the Greek and Latin traditions existing before him. The English neo-cassical literature Eliot reckons "minor classical literature." As has been said, Babbitt considers English neo-classical poetry "pseudo-classical" as it aims at imitating models rather than doing something original in the manner of great classical writers. Babbitt is not opposed to the use of ancient classicists in the manner of, say, Eliot and himself admires Pope's *Epistle to Augustus* which to him is a "genuine creation." In *Epistle to Augustus* Pope has imitated Horace to express a contemporary situation and such an imitation comes very close, is almost akin, to Eliot's use of tradition.[52] What Babbitt says of *Epistle to Augustus* one can say of many other poems of Pope which are not imitations in a pejorative sense but genuine creations. *The Rape of the Lock* and *Moral Essays*, besides *Epistle to Augustus*, are Pope's original creations, though we do feel behind them the presence of classical writers. Even imitations of Horace are all creations, though it is difficult to draw a line between the use of Horace for individual experiences and the use of certain experiences that can be fitted into the Horatian models. At any rate, Eliot is right in saying that Pope and other neo-classical poets lacked amplitude and catholicity. "In the eighteenth century," remarks Eliot "we are oppressed by the limited range of sensibility, and especially in the scale of religious feeling."[53] Religious feeling may not be so important for us as for Eliot, but there is no denying that the eighteenth-century sensibility was highly restricted. Moreover, an important difference between the neo-classicists' use of mythology and Eliot's use of tradition is that in the former the classical mythology itself remains unaffected, while in the latter tradition not only modifies the individual talent but is also in turn influenced by it.

The way a mature writer makes use of other writers is different from the way an immature writer imitates others. In his essay on Massinger, Eliot divides writers into various categories, according as they use other writers, particularly their predecessors.

> One of the surest of tests is the way in which a poet borrows. Immature poets imitate; mature poets steal; bad poets deface what they take, and good poets make it into something better, or at least something different. The good poet welds his theft into a whole of feeling which is unique, utterly different from that from which it was torn; the bad poet throws it into something which has no cohesion.[54]

Eliot demonstrates through various examples that Massinger fails to make with his borrowings from Shakespeare what is expected of a good poet. Virgil, on the other hand, improves upon any phrase or device that he borrows from his predecessors and, thus, in a way, re-writes Latin poetry.

IV

Besides examining other writers in the light of his theory of tradition, Eliot evolves a tradition for himself and uses it in his poetry. Eliot's tradition as it emerges from his early essays can be described as the metaphysical tradition. Eliot pronounces time and again that a change for the worse took place in English poetry after the poets and dramatists of the early seventeenth century. He sets much importance on dramatists like Marlowe, Webster, Tourneur and Shakespeare, and poets like Donne and Marvell. These writers, he says, "had a quality of sensuous thought, or of thinking through the senses, or of the senses thinking."[55] In his essay on Andrew Marvell, Eliot traces a long tradition of metaphysical wit which he holds in high estimation. The tradition covers a large number of writers like Horace, Catullus, Lucretius,

Dante, Propertius, Ovid, and the English writers of the Elizabethan and Jacobean periods like Shakespeare, Ben Jonson, Donne, Marvell, and the French writers of the nineteenth century such as Gautier, Baudelaire, and Laforgue. Massinger in drama and Cowley in poetry are the transitional writers through whom the metaphysical wit starts disappearing. It is this tradition of metaphysical wit that constitutes Eliot's tradition.

In his poetry Eliot draws heavily on the metaphysical tradition. He is in accord with the metaphysical poets in resolving disparate experiences. He cannot be identified with any of the poets in his tradition, whether Dante, or Donne, or Baudelaire but at the same time these poets have gone into the making of his individual talent. It is a commonplace of modern criticism that the whole vogue of metaphysical poetry began with Eliot, which is to say that the metaphysical poets were affected by the introduction of Eliot's works. In point of fact, it was not only metaphysical poetry of the early seventeenth century but the entire tradition of English poetry that was affected by the emergence of Eliot and "the relations, proportions, values of each work of art toward the whole [were] readjusted."[56] It was due to Eliot that the metaphysicals came into the limelight and the romantics and Victorians lost much of their significance.

Besides the whole body of Eliot's work constituting a unit and acting upon the tradition of English poetry, the fragments from individual writers pass into his works undergoing a metamorphosis. He does with his borrowings from other writers what a good poet is expected to do, i.e., make them better or at least different. A good poet lifts a fragment from one context and puts it in an altogether different one, with the result that the two contexts act upon each other producing a congeries of fresh meanings. Eliot's epigraphs are mostly lifted from writers remote in time and placed in a new context. Of the major poems "Prufrock" carries the epigraph from Dante's *The Divine Comedy*; "Gerontion's" epigraph is from Shakespeare's *Measure for Measure*; *The Waste Land's* epigraph from Conrad's *Heart of Darkness* was changed to the Sybil epigraph from the Roman writer, Petronius; "The Hollow Men's" epigraph is from Conrad; "Ash Wednesday" has no epigraph; and "Burnt Norton" 's epigraph is from Heraclitus. "A good poet," says Eliot "will usually borrow from authors remote in time, or alien in language, or diverse in interest."[57] Dante, and Petronius, and Heraclitus are both remote in time and alien in language, Shakespeare is remote in time and diverse in interest, and Conard is diverse in interest. All these epigraphs throw tremendous light on the poems to which they have been appended. An interesting point to note about Eliot's epigraphs is that they have been borrowed mostly from writers whom Eliot values highly. The epigraphs operating in two different contexts at once illustrate Eliot's "Tradition and the Individual Talent."

Besides epigraphs, Eliot has used extracts from other writers in his poems so much so indeed that at the early stage he had to face the charge of plagiarism. The fragments borrowed from other writers have been transformed into fresh meanings in the new contexts. The way Eliot handles the fragments from other writers points to his historical sense. In the context of his poems the fragments are reproduced not by the poet but by the personages created by him. The way the memory of Prufrock or Gerontion or Tiresias, to mention three major personages in the early poetry, operates is precisely the way the mind of the poet functions within the framework of tradition. In short, past and present coalesce in the memories of Eliot's personages in the same way as they do in his own mind. *The Waste Land*, supposedly Eliot's masterpiece, at least of the early phase, abounds in fragments from other writers. The fragments have been used either to demonstrate the parallel or to underline the contrast. In "The Burial of the Dead" Eliot uses a fragment from Dante's *Inferno* ("I had not thought death had undone so many") to describe city clerks going across London Bridge.

Eliot would not say that what he made with the fragment was something better than what Dante did with it, but he was definitely doing something different. In the *Inferno*, Dante describes the spirits of the people who are being punished for their deeds on earth. Thus it is the real hell that Dante describes, whereas Eliot describes the hell on earth formed by its inhabitants living a life of purposelessness and indecision. Eliot communicates the horror of the modern Waste Land effectively through a parallel between Dante and himself. This is one way of using fragments from other writers : the other way is to emphasise the contrast rather than the parallel. Eliot uses a fragment from Goldsmith's *The Vicar of Wakefield* ("When lovely woman stoops to folly") to express the reaction of the typist girl to her copulation with the carbuncular young man. In Goldsmith's novel Olivia repents over her seduction, and says in her song that the only way left for a woman in her position is to die. The typist girl in her complete indifference to seduction offers a sharp contrast to Olivia. The fragments from other writers used as epigraphs or parts of the poem point to the literary tradition used by Eliot. But it would be wrong to make a complete identification of these fragments with Eliot's concept of tradition. We should bear in mind that there are two types of tradition; first, the literary tradition comprehending the entire literary history and, second, the tradition evolved by an individual writer. The twofold division of tradition is evident from the following comment :

> The poet must be very conscious of the main current, which does not at all flow invariably through the most distinguished reputations. He must be quite aware of the obvious fact that art never improves, but that the material of art is never quite the same. He must be aware that the mind of Europe—the mind of his own country—a mind which he learns in time to be much more important than his own private mind—is a mind which changes, and that this change is a development which abandons nothing *en route*, which does not superannuate either Shakespeare, or Homer, or the rock drawing of the Magdalenian draughtsmen.[58]

The main current of which Eliot wants the poet to be conscious will vary from poet to poet for the simple reason that each poet will discover a current for himself. But the mind of Europe, the development of which leaves nothing *en route*, includes the entire literary history of Europe. The two traditions— the main current and the mind of Europe— are not completely separate, since the former is culled out of the latter. When I say that the literary tradition as the mind of Europe comprises the entire literary history, I do not equate the literary tradition with the literary history. A vital difference between the two is that in history writers hold a fixed position according to the period to which they belongs, but in the literary tradition time does not matter and writers belonging to different periods—Homer and Flaubert, for instance—come into contact with and act upon each other. For all Eliot's emphasis on impersonality tradition does have a subjective side, since it is useful only for the writer who evolves it : another writer needs to evolve another tradition. (In his thesis on Bradley, Eliot himself denies a water-tight division between the "subjective" and "objective".)[59] The fragments from other writers used by Eliot are only a part, though a significant one, of his total view of tradition :[60] they only suggest that time does not matter in literary tradition, since fragments from writers of different times and places go side by side in a new context. The fragments from Dante and Baudelaire in the first section of *The Waste Land* are an instance in point. But among the fragments, there are also those that come from writers who do not belong to Eliot's tradition, Goldsmith for instance.

B. Ifor Evans points to a discrepancy in Eliot's concept of tradition. He argues that "T.S. Eliot, who in his prose has advocated tradition, has in his poetry been more responsible than any other writer for the break with the past."[61] And the main point in Eliot's poetry, for Evans, that marks a break with the tradition is its allusiveness. There have been poets in the past, he says, abounding in allusions, Milton for instance. But their allusiveness is of a different nature. When Milton picks up a Virgilian phrase, he lends it an additional richness in his context but without distorting the meaning of the original. But Eliot employs his borrowings, says Evans, in such a way that "the magnificence of the original passage is torn down and trampled."[62] True, and this is precisely what Eliot aims at. Eliot does not mean by tradition mere conformity to the literature of the past but the use of it for the formation and restraint of the individual talent. The employment of fragments from other writers affecting the original as well as bringing forth fresh meanings is basic to Eliot's theory of tradition. What Evans calls the "tearing down" and "trampling" of the original only points to the tradition being stirred by the individual talent.

V

Eliot's literary tradition formulated in his early essays, particularly "Tradition and the Individual Talent," and used in his early poetry, principally *The Waste Land*, does not yield place to but assimilates the Christian tradition of the later criticism and poetry. That is to say, in his later works Eliot does not give up his theory of literary tradition but includes in it the Christian tradition. If "Tradition and the Individual Talent" formulates Eliot's literary tradition, *After Strange Gods* sets forth his Christian tradition.

I have already said that Hulme's influence impinged on Eliot only in his later phase. In his long essay, "Humanism and the Religious Attitude," Hulme demonstrates the inadequacy of humanism and pleads for the religious attitude centering on the Christian dogma of Original Sin. Humanism with its belief in the fundamental goodness of man attaches extreme importance to personality in literature. Conversely, the religious attitude postulates the imperfection of man in the light of the absolute values of religion and ethics.

> In the light of these absolute values, man himself is judged to be essentially limited and imperfect. He is endowed with Original Sin. While he can occasionally accomplish acts which partake of perfection he can never himself *be* perfect. Certain secondary results in regard to ordinary human action in society follow from this. A man is essentially bad, he can only accomplish anything of value by discipline—ethical and political. Order is thus not merely negative, but creative and liberating. Institutions are necessary.[63]

Eliot himself quotes this extract from Hulme in his essay on Baudelaire with the remark that Baudelarie would have approved of it. That is to say, Eliot himself approves of Hulme's belief in the Original Sin, the imperfection of man, and the importance of institutions, since he is in agreement with what he discovers in Baudelaire. The institution that is most important for man to achieve anything valuable is the Church.

It is the religious attitude that is all-important in Hulme's discussion, and the classical literature is only the by-product of it. He divides literature, and also philosophy, according to the humanistic and religious attitudes. It is the humanistic attitude that brings forth romanticism in art, while classicism is the product of the religious attitude. The Greek and Renaissance arts are based upon the humanistic attitude, and it is against this attitude, says Hulme, that the moderns have started reacting. The Byzantine, Egyptian and Indian arts, which Hulme calls geometrical, embody the religious attitude. In this attempt to revive the geometrical art the moderns were being at once traditional and untraditional, traditional in that they were reviving the Byzantine tradition, but untraditional, since they were breaking away from the Renaissance tradition.

In Hulme the religious and literary traditions go together and it is the religious attitude advocated by him that influenced Eliot. As regards the literary tradition, Eliot differs from Hulme on several points. For a start, Eliot does not believe in the revival of a particular tradition. His tradition is more subjective than Hulme's in that a writer has to evolve a tradition for himself, and it is not restricted to a particular period in history but is constituted by individual writers. Moreover, the whole idea of organic unity that forms the very backbone of Eliot's tradition is repugnant to Hulme. He contrasts the "vital" or "organic" with the "mechanical" and attacks "the vital art of Greece and the Renaissance." Of the new art which he advocates he writes : "As far as one can see the new 'tendency towards abstraction' will culminate, not so much in the simple geometrical forms found in archaic art, but in the more complicated ones associated in our minds with the idea of machinery."[61] The most striking point in his concept of religious tradition that Eliot has in common with Hulme is the belief in the dogma of Original Sin.

Here, it is worth our while to clarify the distinction between literary tradition and its religious counterpart. And in order to point out the difference, I shall draw on a rather commonplace distinction, the distinction between form and content The literary tradition is a matter of form, while the Christian tradition is a matter of content. Literary tradition helps a writer with formal problems, while the Christian tradition helps him evolve a view of life. At two places in *After Strange Gods* does Eliot mention the term "Original Sin", and doubts whether what he says will convey much sense to one who does not believe in the dogma.

In both literary and religious contexts Eliot takes exception to originality. In "Tradition and the Individual Talent" he criticises the tendency of dwelling "with satisfaction upon the poet's difference from his predecessors"[65], and in his Introduction to Pound's poems he avers that "the poem which is absolutely original is absolutely bad."[66] Originality in the literary context means that the writer has no point of contact with the writers of the past, whereas in the religious context it points to the attempt on the part of a writer to evolve his own philosophy and thus try to act like a Messiah.

Right at the outset of *After Strange Gods* Eliot writes, referring to "Tradition and the Individual Talent," that

> I do not repudiate what I wrote in that essay any more fully than I should expect to do after such a lapse of time. The problem, naturally, does not seem to me so simple as it seemed then, nor could I treat it now as a purely literary one.[67]

Eliot is right and the extra-literary complexion that the problem takes on in *After Strange Gods* is religious. In this book Eliot talks of the inadequacy of the terms "romanticism" and "classicism" and instead uses "orthodoxy" and "heterodoxy" (which he replaces by "heresy"). He also points out the difference between tradition and orthodoxy, saying that the former is unconscious while the latter is conscious. Distinguishing between tradition and orthodoxy he writes :

> I hold . . . that a *tradition* is rather a way of feeling and acting which characterises a group throughout generations; and that it must largely be, or that many of the elements in it must be, unconscious whereas the maintenance of *orthodoxy* is a matter which calls for the exercise of all our conscious intelligence.[68]

Since the way of feeling and acting of a society goes on changing, tradition is subject to change. Moreover, since tradition manifests itself in the behaviour of the people, it cannot exist independently of the social group. Orthodoxy, on the other hand, exists whether people believe in it or not.

Eliot draws on the Christian tradition for his literary evaluations. He takes to task all those writers who take on the role of a Messiah and seek to convey their own message to the world. Such writers, he believes, are "after strange gods" rather than the God in Christian theology. In his essay on Blake, Eliot deprecates Blake for creating a philosophy of his own, while his genius required "a framework of accepted and traditional ideas." On the other hand, he admires Dante for using the philophy of St Thomas Aquinas for poetic purposes. But the tool that Eliot applies to Blake and Dante in these essays is not specifically Christian. A poet should borrow his philosophy from philosophers, he says, but the philosophy he draws on may not of necessity be Christian. But in *After Strange Gods* Eliot's critical criterion is out and out Christian and his concern is not whether a particular philosophy used by a writer is borrowed or fabricated but whether or not it is Christian. In this book Eliot has criticized writers like Hardy, Lawrence, Yeats and Pound for not conforming to Christian orthodxy, and appreciated Baudelaire, Conrad and James Joyce for their Christian beliefs. He takes up for a comparative study three stories, one each by Katherine Mansfield, D.H. Lawrence, and James Joyce. In the first two there is no moral struggle, while in the story of James Joyce there is a strong moral sense. All three stories centre on the same theme of disillusionment; in Mansfield's story the moral struggle is negligible within the setting. In Lawrence's story, on the other hand, the moral struggle cannot be neglected, but what we find, in fact, is "the absence of any moral or social sense." And this absence Eliot finds not only in the story under eximination but in the whole of Lawrence. "The point is," says Eliot, "that Lawrence started life wholly free from any restriction of tradition or institution, that he had no guidance except the Inner Light, the most untrustworthy and deceitful guidance that ever offered itself to wandering humanity."[69] If Lawrence had not been guided by the deceptive

Inner Light and looked to the Church, an outer authority, for Christian values, he would have realised that what he considered spiritual was Evil. The type of intellectual independence that Lawrence had results in original thinking which can be highly misleading.

The absence of tradition and orthodoxy Eliot discerns even in a writer like Pound whom he always admired for literary tradition. Eliot's movement from literary to Christian tradition is best exemplified by his commentaries on Pound. Out of Eliot's discussions Pound emerges as at once traditional and untraditional, traditional, since his individual talent operates within the framework of a literary tradition, but untraditional, since he seeks to create his own philosophy independently of Christian orthodoxy. The description of Hell in *The Cantos* uses a literary tradition to be sure, if only because it draws on the tradition of a literary device, the device of undertaking a journey to the underworld, first employed by Homer and used, among others, by Virgil, Dante and Joyce. But Eliot finds Pound's Hell unorthodox, since it does not rest on Christian dogmas. As there is no objective standard to judge the nature of Evil—the standard can be provided only by the Christian Tradition—Pound can place anybody he dislikes in Hell. "Mr Pound's Hell," writes Eliot "for all its horrors, is a perfectly comfortable one for the modern mind to contemplate, and disturbing to no one's complacency : It is a Hell for the *other People*, the people we read about in the newspapers, not for oneself and one's friends."[70] The limitations of Pound's Hell will stand out clear, if we compare it with Dante's *inferno* in which there is an objective standard provided by Christian orthodoxy as interpreted by St Thomas Aquinas.

Pound, according to Eliot, "is an individualist, and still more a libertarian." Pound finds Guido Cavalcanti much more sympathetic than Dante, and Guido is for Eliot a heretic. It is in his discussion of Pound that Eliot attempts the following generalization which applies not only to Pound but all the heretics :

> With the disappearance of the idea of Original Sin, with the disappearance of the idea of intense moral struggle,

> the human beings presented to us both in poetry and in prose fiction to-day, and more patently among the serious writers than in the underworld of letters, tend to become less and less real. It is in fact in moments of moral and spiritual struggle depending upon moral sanctions, rather than in those "bewildering minutes" in which we are all very much alike, that men and women come nearest to being real.[71]

It is the disappearance of the idea of Original Sin that Eliot finds in the heretics from George Eliot to Ezra Pound. Tradition in the religious sense such as we find in *After Strange Gods*, is not a matter of the writers one draws on, but the type of human beings one presents in the work. If, for example, the characters in a work submit themselves to their emotional excitements with the full approval of the writer, without any resistance engendering moral struggle, then the writer of the work is not traditional in the Christian sense howsoever traditional he may be in the literary sense.

As is suggested by the sub-title of the book, in *After Strange Gods* Eliot concerns himself principally with the heretics, and the orthodox writers come in only for contrast. Nevertheless, the orthodox writers, though briefly touched on, point significantly to Eliot's idea of the Christian tradition. Writers like Dante, Baudelaire and James Joyce, among others, orthodox though they are, are not concerned to disseminate a Christian message but rather their writings are penetrated by the Christian point of view. The main point that Eliot makes in his two essays on Baudelaire is that in his description of Paris as the modern *inferno*, Baudelaire emerges as a great Christian poet. In the writings of James Joyce including "The Dead", which is discussed as a contrast to Lawrence's "The shadow in the Rose Garden", there is a strong moral struggle. Dante invariably is a great poet for Eliot by any standards, let alone Christian.

In *After Strange Gods* Eliot's concept of tradition is religious rather than literary. This should not lead one into thinking that he has given up altogether his concept of literary tradition, since it has been invoked at several places in his later criticism. One can, for instance, refer to "What is a Classic ?" where the criterion of literary tradition has been applied to Virgil. What deserves particular attention is the way Eliot assimilates the Christian tradition to his literary tradition. In the early essays one discerns only the literary tradition, while in the later essays one comes across not the Christian tradition alone but a co-presence of the literary and Christian traditions. What Eliot arrives at in the later essays comes down to this : that a writer is truely traditional only if he discovers a literary tradition for himself as well as draws on Christian orthodoxy.

VI

Eliot's development from literary to Christian tradition is in conformity with the progress of his poetical career. That is to say, the early poetry embodies the literary tradition without being Christian, while the later poetry is at once Christian and traditional in the literary sense.

That Eliot's poetry up to and including *The Waste Land* is not Christian has been demonstrated at length in the preceding chapter. Here I shall touch on only one point relating to *The Waste Land*. *The Waste Land* has been compared to Dante's *Inferno*. The analogy between the two is easy to establish, since Eliot has reproduced lines from Dante's *Inferno* to describe the inhabitants of the Waste Land. In the third Canto of the *Inferno* Dante, guided by Virgil, enters the Vestibule which is inhabited by the Futile, i.e., those who made no choice of Good or Evil. The spirits of the Futile share the abode with the angels, who made no choice at the time of Satan's rebellion. Explaining who the Futile are Virgil says to Dante :

> The dismal company
> Of wretched spirits thus find their guerdon due
> Whose lives knew neither praise nor infamy ;
> They're mingled with the caitiff angel-crew
> Who against God rebelled not, nor to Him
> Were faithful, but to self alone were true ; [72]

After the explanation Dante says : "It never would have entered in my head/There were so many men whom death had slain." Eliot quotes Dante's remark in *The Waste Land* as "I had not thought death had undone so many." In the fourth canto of the *Inferno,* Dante enters the Limbo where dwell the Unbaptized and the Virtuous Pagans. Describing the inhabitants of the Limbo Dante writes :

> We heard no loud complaint, no crying there,
> No sound of grief except the sound of sighing
> Quivering for ever through the external air ;

Eliot continues his quotation from Dante with an extract from the above lines as "sighs, short and infrequent, were exhaled." With the help of the quotations from Dante, Eliot describes city clerks as follows :

> Unreal city,
> Under the brown fog of a winter dawn,
> A crowd flowed over London bridge, so many,
> I had not thought death had undone so many.
> Sighs, short and infrequent, were exhaled,
> And each man fixed his eyes before his feet

The city, critics have pointed out, is not only London but also Dante's Limbo and Baudelaire's Paris with all their associations. Cleanth Brooks's comment on the Dante passage in the above lines is significant.

> The references to Dante are most important. The line, 'I had not thought death had undone so many', is taken from the Third Canto of the *Inferno* ; the line, 'Sighs, short and infrequent, were exhaled', from the Fourth Canto. Mr Matthiessen has already pointed out that the Third Canto deals with Dante's Limbo which is occupied by those who on earth had "lived without praise or blame." [73]

And, again,

> These various allusions drawn from widely differing sources enrich the comment on the modern city so that it becomes "unreal" on a number of levels, as seen through "the brown fog of a winter dawn"; as the medieval waste land and Dante's Limbo and Baudelaire's Paris are unreal. [74]

Cleanth Brooks is right in paraphrasing Matthiessen's view but wrong in giving assent to it. Matthiessen is wrong in saying that Dante's Limbo is "the region of those dead who while on earth had "lived without praise or blame."[75] It is the Vestibule which lies outside the actual *inferno*, and not the Limbo, where Dante comes across those who made no choice. Limbo is the first circle in the *Inferno* which is occupied by the Unbaptized and the Virtuous Pagans. The two quotations from Dante in the passage in question come from two different cantos of the *Inferno*, one dealing with the Vestibule and the other with the Limbo. It is surprising that both Matthiessen and Brooks overlook the distinction between the Vestibule and the Limbo. I am deliberately emphasising this distinction, as this is basic to our understanding of *The Waste Land*.

An examination of *The Waste Land* will bring home to us that it is the quotation from the Vestibule, and not the one from the Limbo, that is at the centre of *The Waste Land*. The point that Eliot underlines throughout *The Waste Land* is that its inhabitants do not exist, because they have chosen neither Good nor Evil. This, in fact, is the point in quoting Dante. When Eliot says, "I had not thought death had undone so many" he refers not to those actually dead, but people in the modern waste land, living a mechanical life, as they do, are dead, not physically but spiritually because of their purposelessness and lack of direction. The carbuncular young man and the typist girl are not different from city clerks, since they, like the latter, chose neither Good nor Evil, in their copulation. Since they do not make a choice, their copulation is akin to that of animals. This is a point well borne out by Eliot's own comment in his essay on Baudelaire :

> So far as we are human, what we do must be either good or evil ; so far as we do evil or good, we are human ; and it is better, in a paradoxical way, to do evil than to do nothing ; at least, we exist. [76]

And, again,

> Baudelaire has perceived that what distinguishes the relation of man and woman from the copulation of beasts is the knowledge of Good and Evil.[77]

Buadelaire's world is the world of Evil, because in it people have made the choice of Evil. The view of *The Waste Land* as a Christian poem will collapse at once, if the Vestibule described by Dante has no Christian sanctions. Dorothy L. Sayers, who can be trusted as regards Dante and Christian theology that went into the formation of *The Divine Comedy*, makes the following comment on the Vestibule :

> *The Vestibule* was presumably suggested to Dante by the description in *Aeneid* VI where, however, it is tenanted by rather a different set of people. It does not, I think, occur in any previous Christian eschatology. [78]

And John D. Sinclair, another translator of *The Divine Comedy* writes :

> The first class of the lost, the Neutrals, angels and humans, is an original and most characteristic invention of Dante's, outside of all the traditional systems. [79]

That is to say, the idea of a neutral position is Dante's own invention, not derived from Christian theology. In Christianity there is choice of either Good or Evil. According to the New Testament, one who is not with Jesus is against him, that is to say, a person in the neutral position is doing Evil. Jesus says : "He who is not with me is against me, and he who does not gather with me scatters."[80] In fact, in one place in the New Testament the possibility of a neutral position has been conceded, but the judgement is against it.

> I know your work : you are neither cold nor hot : would that you were cold or hot, so because you are lukewarm, and neither cold nor hot, I will spew you out of my mouth.[81]

Though there is a possibility, as Dorothy L. Sayers points out, of imagining a third category of those who make no choice, there is no Christian evidence for it, and a poet who draws so heavily on this new category is obviously not Christian. Thus the criterion that Eliot applies to the inhabitants of the Waste Land is not Christian, whatever else it may be.

Maxwell points out, and I think rightly, that the motif of Eliot's early poetry is aridity which suggests emptiness of the modern man. In poem after poem Eliot has underlined this emptiness which recurs conspicuously in the transitional poem, "The Hollow Men." What Eliot describes in detail in "The Hollow Men" has been touched on, implicitly, throughout his early phase. As the title itself indicates, the Hollow Men are empty men with nothing inside except straw. Hence they say,

> Our dried voices, when
> We whisper together
> Are quiet and meaningless
> As wind in dry grass
> Or rat's feet over broken glass
> In our dry cellar.

"As wind in dry grass" reminds one of Gerontion's confession that he is "an old man in a draughty house/Under a windy knob." The house that Gerontion inhabits is symbolic of Gerontion himself. His thoughts, which are "thoughts of a dry brain in a dry season," are "tenants" of this house. It is this emptiness and hollowness that we find about the protagonist of "Portrait of a Lady" who says, "I must borrow every changing shape/To find expression," which points to the following lines uttered by one of the Hollow Men :

> Let me also wear
> Such deliberate disguises
> Rat's coat, crowskin, crossed staves
> In a field
> Behaving as the wind behaves

It is hollowness which is the predominant theme of the early poems, leading up to and including *The Waste Land.* Compare the lines adduced from "Portrait of a Lady", "Gerontion", and "The Hollow Men" with the following from *The Waste Land*:

> What is that noise ?
> The wind under the door.
> What is that noise now ? What is the wind doing ?
> Nothing again nothing.

Like city clerks in *The Waste Land,* the protagonist of

"Portrait of a Lady", Gerontion, and the Hollow Men do not exist, since they have chosen neither Good nor Evil.

It should be obvious from the above quotations and comments that the major preoccupation of Eliot on the negative side is not Evil but the absence of both Evil and Good leading to the non-existence of the modern man. But, there is no evidence in Christian theology for such a predicament. The fact that Eliot is critical of the modern man without any sense of value should not lead one into thinking that he is necessarily Christian. There are many other writers who have criticized the modern world but have no faith in Christianity. Pound is an emphatic instance in point. Eliot does have a moral criterion behind all that he describes in the early poetry, but it has no Christian sanctions. And the moral criterion does not necessarily have to be religious, let alone Christian : it may as well be humanistic.

Eliot's Christian poetry begins with "The Hollow Men", which has also traces of the early poetry, and culminates in "Ash Wednesday" and the *Four Quartets*. This development of Eliot's poetry is consonant with the development of his criticism. The first phase of Eliot's criticism ends with *Homage to John Dryden* (1921, 1924) and of poetry with *The Waste Land* (1922). "The Hollow Men" and "Journey of the Magi" are Christian poems, but the most Christian of Eliot's poetry is "Ash Wednesday" which abounds in liturgical references. As the title indicates, "Ash Wednesday" deals with the Christian dogmas of Original Sin and Incarnation. Ash Wednesday is the first day of Lent, a period of forty days, during which Christians repent for their past sins and turn to God. Leonard Unger has rightly pointed out that St John of the Cross's *The Dark Night of the Soul* stands in the same relation to "Ash Wednesday" as Miss Weston's *From Ritual to Romance* to *The Waste Land*. Unlike the personages in *The Waste Land*, the protagonist of "Ash Wednesday" has made a choice and is described at the transitional stage between the glory of the material world and that of God. The Christian idea of penitence which is related to the dogma of Original Sin has been emphasised in the poem.

Pray for us sinners now and at the hour of our death
Pray for us now and at the hour of our death

The theme of the *Four Quartets* with which Eliot rounds off his poetical career is the Christian dogma of Incarnation. That the Incarnation is at the very centre of Christian revelation is evident from Eliot's observation that "Christian revelation is the only full revelation; and that the fullness of Christian revelation resides in the essential fact of the Incarnation; in relation to which all Christian revelation is to be understood."[82] The Incarnation of Christ was the moment of intersection of time and Eternity. God, who was above the flux of time before the Incarnation, appeared in time in the form of Christ, and the daily ceremony in the Church is the repetition of the unique moment of the union of time and Eternity. It is in this sense that,

While the light fails
On a winter afternoon, in a secluded chapel
History is now and England.

Just as in Eliot's later criticism, so in his later poetry, the literary and Christian traditions go together, though the predominant element is the latter rather than the former. The opening lines of "Ash Wednesday" which deal with the Dark Night of the Soul remind the reader at once of Guido Cavalcanti's ballata and Lancelot Andrew's sermon. And a few lines later when the poet says, "Desiring this man's gift and that man's scope" the reader is reminded of Shakespeare's sonnet. We can see how the poet is pressing into the service of his Christian experience the writers in the literary tradition. In the *Four Quartets*, again, Eliot occasionally draws on the literary tradition in order to give form to his Christian experience. In the description of the air-raid in the second movement of "Little Gidding" Eliot draws at once on the Bible in which the Holy Spirit is symbolised by the dove, and Dante's *Inferno* in which Dante meets his old teacher, Brunetto Latini. Thus the Christian and literary traditions go hand in hand.

CHAPTER FOUR

Impersonality

Much controversy has centered round the question whether Eliot is a romanticist or a classicist. Since the impersonal theory is bound up with the question regarding romanticism/classicism, I should like to consider it at the very outset of this chapter.

Eliot has been called both a romanticist and a classicist, and the reason why critics turned their attention to the problem of categorization is not far to seek. In his early criticism Eliot repeatedly expressed his predilection for classical standards. Reviewing George Wyndham's *Essays in Romantic Literature*, Eliot said categorically that "there may be a good deal to be said for Romanticism in life, there is no place for it in literature."[1] Eliot was still more dogmatic in his denunciation of romanticism in his essay on "The Function of Criticism" (1923), in which he took issue with Middleton Murry. Expressing his disagreement with Murry he wrote; "With Mr. Murry's formulation of Classicism and Romanticism I cannot agree; the difference seems to me rather the difference between the complete and the fragmentary, the adult and the immature, the orderly and the chaotic;"[2] that is to say, romanticism is fragmentary, immature and chaotic. And, again, in his review of James Joyce's *Ulysses* he conceded that "Mr Aldington and I are more or less agreed as to what we want in principle, and agreed to call it classicism."[3] Eliot makes it sufficiently clear that romanticism and classicism are two different attitudes and that classicism is not just an alternative to romanticism but embodies the ideal. In 1928 came Eliot's laconic statement on his stance in literature, politics and religion in the Preface to *For Lancelot Andrewes*. Speaking of his general point of view he said that it "may be described as classicist in literature, royalist in politics, and anglo-catholic in religion."

It was but natural for critics to take the cue from Eliot's admissions and investigate the nature of his classicism. The critics examining this aspect of Eliot can be grouped into two different categories. There were those who took Eliot at his word and sought to demonstrate the elements of his poetry and criticism that made him a classicist. And then there were those who questioned Eliot's admission, and on an exploration of his works, arrived at the conclusion that for all his anti-romantic and pro-classical pronouncements, Eliot remained at bottom a romanticist. Critics like D.E.S. Maxwell, Philip Wheelwright, René Taupin, and Allardyce Nicoll believe that Eliot is a classicist, while Herbert Read, C.K. Stead, Frank Kermode, John Bayley and Donald E. Stanford place Eliot in the romantic tradition.[4]

The critics above have expressed diametrically opposed views, but the truth lies somewhere in between. I have already stated that the critics erred in taking an extreme position either with or against Eliot. It was not long before Eliot himself realized the unsuitability of the terms "classicism" and "romanticism" and admonished critics to eschew them in order to arrive at the truth.

Even before making the straightforward statement, at the instance of Irving Babbitt, in the Preface to *For Lancelot Andrews,* Eliot was not very sure whether the term "classicism" as used conventionally could formulate his position effectively. The early enthusiasm for classical position had faded as early as 1926, when he said in *The Criterion* :

> I believe that the modern tendency is toward something which, for want of a better name, we may call classicism. I use the term with hesitation, for it is hardly more than analogical ; we must scrupulously guard ourselves against measuring living art and mind by dead laws of order.[5]

Eliot is well aware that the term "classicism" will send critics back to the writers of antiquity, who are supposed to embody the ideal to be followed by a classicist. This is precisely what Eliot intends to avoid. But the critics did set out to look for the parallels between Eliot and the neo-classicists despite his disapproval of the term "neo-classicism" only the following year.[6] The year 1928 is an important date in Eliot's career, when he professed at once to be a romanticist and a classicist. In the well-known statement in the Preface to *For Lancelot Andrewes*, he defines his position in literature as classicist, while in his Introduction to Pound's *Selected Poems* he alleges that his taste is possibly too romantic to appreciate Pound's epigrams. When Eliot was termed a "self-confessed romantic" by the *TLS* reviewer, he resented it and sought clarification. And when the reviewer offered clarification by referring to Eliot's comment on Pound's epigrams, he drew attention to his classical position confessed the same year in *For Lancelot Andrewes*. All this goes to show that Eliot never had in mind a water-tight division between romanticism and classicism. His clear-cut classical position in the early essays is probably meant to draw attention away from the decadent romanticism rather than to define his actual position. Eliot knows the difficulties of stating his position in terms of classicism/romanticism. This is the reason why in the later essays he emphasises time and again the inappropriateness of these terms. Writing on "Experiment in Criticism" in 1929 he expressed dissatisfaction with the moralistic critic who is prone to pigeonhole literature under categories. "When he upholds 'classicism' and denounces 'romanticism' he is likely to give the impression that we should write like Sophocles or Racine".[7] Discussing the modern mind in 1933 Eliot underlined the inaptness of the terms romanticism and classicism. "In the interest of clarity and simplicity," he said "I wish myself to avoid employing the terms Romanticism and Classicism, terms which inflame political passions, and tend to prejudice our conclusions."[8] In 1934, in his contribution to the *Companion to Shakespeare Studies*, he pointed to the critical admonition expressed in Dr. Johnson's remark on the players dividing Shakespeare's work into comedies, histories and tragedies : "To those who would divide periods and segregate men, neatly into classical and romantic groups, I commend the study of this sentence [the sentence in which Johnson disapproves of the categorization of Shakespeare's works]."[9] In "What is a classic ?" (1945)

Eliot found the antithesis between "classic" and "romantic" a hinderance rather than help. Eliot's last statement on romanticism/classicism came in "To Criticize the Critic" (1961) where he said: "as for Classicism and Romanticism, I find that the terms have no longer the importance to me they once had."[10]

It should be clear from Eliot's own utterances that gradually he came to realize that the two terms are in the nature of party-politics rather than literary criticism. A literary critic should feel free to point to merits and defects irrespective of the fact whether a particular work is traditionally romantic or classical.

Eliot is neither a romanticist nor a classicist but a unique mixture of the two. When Eliot refers to the party spirit evoked by the two terms, he seems to have at the back of his mind his own earlier statements made in that spirit. The critics of Eliot, who have designated him a romanticist or a classicist have singled out only those aspects of his criticism which serve their purpose and left out the others. In fact, Eliot's criticism has all those elements that his critics have pointed out in calling him a romanticist, but then it has something more, something that flies in the face of their contention. Let us take, for instance, Read and Stead. Read is right in saying that Eliot "writes verse with a minimum consciousness of rules,"[11] and Stead is right, too, in calling attention to Eliot's emphasis on the "dark embryo"[12] which puts him in line with the romantics. But both Stead and Read are only partly right. An important fact that Eliot has stressed is that the poet cannot have the premonition of the final results of the poetic process, mysterious as it is.[13] But there is a great amount of preparation expected of a poet before he sets out to write, and a great deal of labour to be expended on the first results of the creative process. A typical romanticist will place excessive weight on inspiration. Eliot is a critic who defies being categorized as a romanticist or a classicist. If, on the one hand, he recognizes the role of inspiration, on the other he puts due emphasis on preparation and organization. In an unpublished address called "The Idea of a European Society" (1949), he discusses inspiration vis-a-vis organization.

> In writing a poem of any length—a poem which requires *labour*—I find in retrospect that I cannot wholly distinguish, in the result, what was calculated from what was spontaneous, what was conscious from what was unconscious, what was growth from what was construction. I know that the unexpected arrives, and I know that I have given many hours of conscious toil.[14]

He repeated this view in *The Use of Poetry* in his remark that "organization is necessary as well as inspiration."[15]

Stead has called attention to the creative process as described by Eliot to prove that Eliot is a romanticist, but it is here that one can see Eliot's combination of romanticism and classicism at its best. I am reproducing below Stead's argument expressed in the tabular form and then quoting Eliot to demonstrate how a critic can go awry by making sweeping generalizations. Stead's table runs as follows :[16]

"impersonal"		"personal"
"unconscious"	(conscious)	"mind"
"feelings"		"emotions"
"images, phrases"		"structure"
"detail"		"design"

And here is an extract from Eliot's Introduction to Pound's poems :

> The development of *experience is largely unconscious*, subterranean so that, we cannot gauge its progress except once in every five or ten years; . . . . a poet's work may proceed along two lines on an imaginary graph; one of the lines being his *conscious and continuous effort in* technical excellence . . . .[17] (italics mine)

Stead argues that for Eliot emotion (i.e., cxperience) is conscious, while "images and phrases" (i.e., technique) are unconscious, but Eliot himself says that experience is unconscious, while technique is conscious. We must not forget that all this holds for Eliot before the actual creation. The actual creation is for Eliot a "mysterious" process which is difficult to define. The experience and technique dive together, as it were, in the mind of the poet at the rare moment of creation, and emerge combined into one, i.e., poem, which is different from either experience or technique existing separately before the creation.

Just as critics have gone wrong in calling Eliot a romanticist, so they have gone amiss in calling him a classicist. Alardyce Nicoll, for instance, commits many an error by grouping Eliot with the English neo-classicists. Without explaining what precisely he means by imitation, Nicoll writes : "Conscious imitation becomes one of the poet's duties, for by imitation he serves to call into the minds of his readers (as by symbols) some at least of this intellectual inheritance."[18] The term "imitation" was used in an honorific sense in the neo-classical, period but with Eliot it takes on a pejorative implication. Distinguishing between influence and imitation Eliot writes : "the difference between influence and imitation is that influence can fecundate whereas imitation—especially unconscious imitation—can only sterilize."[19] Nicoll, again, goes wrong when he says that "in his critical work Mr Eliot never tires of emphasizing . . . tradition, just as classicists in a previous age had emphasized the glory that was Greece and Rome."[20] Nicoll fails to notice that Eliot's attitude to tradition is different from that of the neo-classicists' towards Greece and Rome. In short, Eliot's attitude towards tradition is highly critical, while the neo-classicists had unqualified praise for "the glory that was Greece and Rome."

II

Just as in the classification of romanticism and classicism, so in that of personality and impersonality, the critics of Eliot are sharply divided. And just as critics have pointed out that despite his avowed classicism Eliot is at bottom a romanticist, so they have demonstrated that he is an upholder of the theory of personal expression for all his insistence on impersonality.

The critics of Eliot discussing his impersonal theory can be divided into two categories, namely those who emphasise the invalidity of the theory and those who find the theory basically a personal one. F.R. Leavis is a critic of the first category who does not tire of repeating the untenability of the impersonal theory.[21] John Casey expresses an identical view to Leavis' in his belief that "Eliot's remarks about the impersonality of art form perhaps the most confusing part of his critical theory."[22] There are other critics who are concerned with the simple fact that Eliot's theory of impersonality is basically a theory of personal expression. In his essay on "T.S. Eliot in his Criticism" Stephen Spender, for instance, points out how Eliot's theory of impersonality formulated in the Tradition enay is rooted in the personality of the writer. Allen Austin is not different from Spender in maintaining that Eliot believes in "the indirect expression of personality."[23] Discussing the dialectical structure of Eliot's theory of poetry, Fei-Pai Lu opines that Eliot's criticism displays two opposite types of personality and impersonality and emphasizes the balance of personality with impersonality.

The foregoing discussion is an evidence of how divergent are the views expressed about Eliot's theory of impersonality. The main source of confusion regarding the theory is the sweeping generalizations made by the critics. The critics have failed to descriminate sufficiently between the different types of personality and impersonality in Eliot's criticism. Let us take, for instance, the case of F.R. Leavis who denounces vehemently Eliot's theory of impersonality and in opposition to it sets forth his own theory of personal expression. But he fails to notice that Eliot himself has set considerable value on personality, specially in *The Sacred Wood* where he evolves his theory of impersonality. And Lu, who doesn't fail to notice Eliot's use of personality in the honorific sense, overlooks the personality that Eliot has criticized in the later essays. He distinguishes between two types of personality and two types of impersonality when, in fact, Eliot's essays display three types of personality and three types of impersonality.

Before entering upon a detail discussion of the different types of personality and impersonality in Eliot's essays, I give a summary account of them in the tabular form.

Personality	(1)	Criticized in the early essays
Personality	(2)	Criticized in the later essays
Personality	(3)	Appreciated throughout

Impersonality (1) Appreciated in the early essays
Impersonality (2) Appreciated in the later essays
Impersonality (3) Criticized throughout.

I shall begin with personality (3) and impersonality (3), one appreciated throughout Eliot's criticism and the other depreciated throughout. The personality which Eliot has exalted throughout his criticism is the personality that emerges out of the design of experiences in the work, and can be identified with "point of view." Writing anonymously about Pound's metric and poetry in 1977, he brings out the writer's "point of view" which is an indication of his maturity. In the reviews contributed to *Athenaeum* for the year 1919, Eliot stresses time and again the significance of the "point of view" in a work which reveals the writer's personality. In his review of *The Years Between* by Rudyard Kipling, Eliot writes, contrasting Swinburne and Kipling with other writers such as Shakespeare and Dante :

> Some poets, like Shakespeare or Dante or Villon, and some novelists like Mr Conrad, have, in contrast to ideas or concepts *points of views*, or "worlds"—what are incorrectly called "philosophies." . . . Mr Conrad has no ideas but he has a point of view, a "world", it can hardly be defined, but it pervades his work and is unmistakable.[24] (italics mine)

The point of view for Eliot will be discernible only in the work of a writer with personality. The personality does not imply holding on to certain ideas and forcing them on the audience (as is done by Swinburne and Kipling), but revealing one's attitude through the organization of experiences in the work. Contrasting the humanist's personality with the scientist's or artist's, Eliot avers that "in the man of scientific or artistic temper the personality is distilled into the work, it loses its incidents, it becomes, as with Montaigne, a permanent point of view, a phase in the history of mind."[25] It is obvious that the personality of a writer is distilled into a point of view ; that is to say, the point of view is not personality in the sense of biography with all its personal incidents but personality shorn of incidental elements and transformed into an impersonal (or what Eliot calls permanent) point of view. When we read a work with such a point of view, we feel the presence in it, not of the writer talking to us but only his individuality, not expressed in individual utterances but diffused throughout the work.

Eliot frequently applies the criterion of personality in his evaluations. The most emphatic instance of the application of this criterion occurs in his demonstration of the inferiority of Massinger to writers like Marlowe, Jonson and Shakespeare.

> The inferiority of Massinger to Jonson is an inferiority, not of one type of art to another, but within Jonson's type. It is a simple deficiency. Marlowe's and Jonson's comedies were a view of life; they were, as great literature is, the transformation of a personality into a personal work of art, their lifetime's work, long or short. Massinger is not simply a smaller personality: his personality hardly exists. He did not, out of his own personality, build a world of art, as Shakespeare and Marlowe and Jonson built.[26]

Thus Massinger is inferior to Marlowe, Jonson, and Shakespeare because he, as against the latter, has no personality to express. Needless to say, the personality can be transformed into a work of art only when a writer has a personality to express. The transformed personality which is a work of art is personal in that it reflects an individual point of view in the sense explained above.

The personality that I have been discussing Eliot has exalted not only in his early essays but throughout his criticism. In his essay on Ford (1932) he emphasizes the revelation of Shakespeare's personality uniting all his works into a whole, and then advances the following generalization:

> A man might, hypothetically, compose any number of fine passages or even of whole poems which would each give satisfaction, and yet not be a great poet, unless we felt them to be united by one significant, consistent and developing personality.[27]

The revealed personality becomes increasingly important in Eliot's criticism, and the Elizabethan playwrights are repeatedly estimated on this criterion as is evident from his essays on Thomas Middleton (1927), Cyril Tourneur (1930), Thomas Heywood (1931), John Ford (1932) and John Marston (1934). Whereas Middleton, Heywood and Ford are disparaged for lack of personality, Tourneur and Marston are applauded for the personality expressed in their works. Of Middleton, for example, Eliot says that "it is difficult to imagine his personality." As regards Tourneur, "in no play by any minor Elizabethan is a more positive personality revealed than in *The Revenger's Tragedy*." The criterion in these essays is the same as the one in the earlier essays on the Elizabethan playwrights such as "Ben Jonson" (1919) and "Philip Massinger" (1920).

Writing on Yeats in 1940 Eliot reiterated the importance of personality. What he says in his essay on Yeats is in line with what he had been saying from the very beginning. Hence it is difficult to explain, except in terms of the lapse of memory, why he thinks that "in giving as a reason for the superiority of Yeats' later work the greater expression of personality in it, I am contradicting myself."[28] The essay on Yeats furnishes me with the starting point to discuss the impersonality disapproved of by Eliot throughout his critical programme. Feeling that in extolling Yeats' later work he is contradicting his earlier stance on impersonality, he distinguishes between two types of impersonality—one that he depreciates and the other that he acclaims. And the impersonality that he acclaims is the same as the personality discussed above.

> There are two forms of impersonality: that which is natural to the mere skillful craftsman, and that which is more and more achieved by the maturing artist. The first is that of what I have called the "anthology piece"' of a lyric by Lovelace or Suckling, or of Campion, a finer poet than either. The second impersonality is that of the poet who, out of intense and personal experience, is able to express a general truth; retaining all the particularity of his experience, to make of it a general symbol.[29]

The impersonality of the first type that Eliot attributes to a mere anthology piece is impersonality without personality.

Since there is no personality to express, there is no question of personality being transmuted into impersonality. Eliot has defined what he means by an "anthology piece" in "What is Minor Poetry?" In an anthology we find both minor and major poets represented, and a minor poet is one who does not arouse any curiosity in the reader to read beyond the piece (or pieces) in the anthology. The curiosity to go beyond the anthology piece will be aroused only by a poet with personality which is the first characteristic of a major poet. Eliot's comment on Campion who is impersonal without personality is significant. "I should say," writes Eliot "that within his limits there was no more accomplished craftsman in the whole of English poetry than Campion" but still "we do not feel, after reading Campion, that we know the man Campion, as we do feel after reading Herrick."[30] It is this extraordinary craftsmanship without personality that makes Campion impersonal in the sense that does not make one a major poet.

The impersonality that Eliot disapproves of in the essay on Yeats he had been crying down all along. In "Seneca in Elizabethan Translation" (1927) he compares Greek plays with those of Seneca and the differences that he discerns between them are the same as those between the later Yeats and Campion.

> Behind the dialogue of Greek drama we are always conscious of a concrete visual actuality, and behind that of a specific emotional actuality. Behind the drama of words is the drama of action, the timbre of voice and voice, the uplifted hand or tense muscle, and the particular emotion. The spoken play, the words which we read, are symbols, a shorthand, and often, as in the best of Shakespeare, a very abbreviated shorthand, indeed, for the acted and felt play, which is always the real thing. . . . In the plays of Seneca, the drama is all in the word, and the word has no further reality behind it. His characters all seem to speak with the same voice, and at the top of it, they recite in turn.[31]

The difference between Greek plays and those of Seneca is virtually the difference between the plays reflecting a personality and those not reflecting one. Both the types of plays are impersonal but whereas in the former the impersonality is the transmutation of personality, in the latter the impersonality is of mere craftsmanship. This is the reason why Eliot says later that "in the tragedies of Seneca the centre of value is shifted from what the personage says to the way in which he says it."[32]

When a writer is impersonal in a pejorative sense, the way of expression tends to take precedence over what is expressed. What for Eliot is true of Seneca holds also for writers like Philip Massinger and Swinburne. In a passage already adduced Eliot says that Massinger's personality simply does not exist. And this absence of personality is a concomitant of "Massinger's feeling for language . . . . [outstripping] his feeling for things."[33] Swinburne is the extreme instance of an impersonal writer who delights exclusively in words and their sounds. Eliot says unequivocally that the world of Swinburne is impersonal, but it has the impersonality of a mere craftsman. Swinburne's absence of personality goes side by side with his intemperate interest in expression. "It is, in fact, the word," writes Eliot "that gives him the thrill, not the object."[34]

There remain two other types of personality and impersonality to be discussed. Personality (2) condemned in the later essays and impersonality (2) appreciated in the later essays I shall discuss later. At the moment I concern myself with personality (1) which is decried and impersonality (1) which is exalted in the early essays.

I have already dwelt at some length upon the impersonality emerging out of the transformation of personality. Eliot's impersonality in the honorific sense cannot be attained without personality. In his "Tradition and the Individual Talent" he says emphatically that "only those who have personality and emotions know what it means to want to escape from these things." And he reiterates this view in his Introduction to Paul Valréy's *Le Serpent* where he writes :

> It [*Le Serpent*] is "impersonal" in the sense that personal emotion, personal experience, is extended and completed in something impersonal—not in the sense of something divorced from personal experience and passion."[35]

Personality and emotion are the necessary prerequisites of impersonality. What a great artist does is to escape, through a process of transmutation, into a work of art which combines particularity with generality or, to use Eliot's familiar terms, personality with impersonality. (It is this combination of opposites which, among other things, marks off Eliot from the neo-classicists on the one hand and the romantics on the other.) Let us examine now the way personality is transformed into impersonality, or in other words, particularity is generalized. And here comes in Eliot's celebrated critical formula called the objective correlative.

As has been pointed out, there are two types of personality, one that stands outside the work and can be identified with the writer's biography, and the other that emerges from inside the work. It is the objective correlative that plays the most vital role in the transformation of the former into the latter. Since the creative process is mysterious, it is difficult to say what precisely happens in the process of transmutation.

Before the actual transmutation takes place, there are present in the mind of the artist two things—first, the experience that has accumulated unconsciously and, secondly, the objective correlative devised consciously. The relation between the two forms the basis of the well-known definition of the objective correlative set forth by Eliot in his essay on *Hamlet*.

> The only way of expressing emotion in the form of art is by finding an "objective correlative" ; in other words, a set of objects, a situation, a chain of events which shall be the formula of that *particular* emotion ; such that when the external facts, which must terminate in sensory experience, are given, the emotion is immediately evoked.[36]

Before entering on a discussion of the objective correlative it is worthwhile to examine the term "emotion". C.K. Stead equates "structural emotion" with the objective correlative. The main weakness of Stead is his sweeping generalization. Consequently he fails to distinguish between different types of emotion that Eliot describes. In the table already reproduced Stead has grouped "emotion" with "structure" and in a footnote he identifies Eliot's distinction between "structural emotion" and "floating feelings" with Ransom's between "structure" and "texture." The very fact that Stead equates both "emotion" and "structural emotion" with "structure" in Ransom's sense shows that he does not distinguish between these two types of emotion. If we examine closely the emotional terms employed by Eliot, we shall find that they are of four different types. And unless we bear in mind the distinction between the four types, we are likely to commit the same error as Stead. There is, without doubt, a type of emotion which can be identified with Ransom's structure, but then this is only one of the several types. The following are the extracts from Eloit's essays containing emotional terms of different types.

> It is not in his *personal emotions*, the emotions provoked by particular events in his life, that the poet is in any way remarkable or interesting.[37] (italics mine).
>
> This [the balance of the contrasted emotions of beauty and ugliness in an extract adduced] is, so to speak, the *structural emotion*, provided by the drama. But the whole effect, the dominant tone, is due to the fact that a number of floating feelings, having an affinity to this emotion by no means superficially evident, have combined with it to give us a new *art emotion*.[38] (italics mine).

The personal emotion is, Eliot makes it sufficiently clear, the emotion evoked by events in the life of the poet, the structural emotion is the emotion that we find *in* the poem, and the artistic emotion is the emotion that stems from the work as a whole out of the combination of emotion and feeling. There is a fourth emotion also which is not qualified by any adjective but is used as a synonym for any of the three emotions. When Eliot uses the word "emotion" in the passage where he defines the objective correlative, he uses it as a synonym for the personal emotion. But when the term comes in conjunction with feeling, it is used in the sense of "structural emotion." And whenever Eliot talks of "the effect of a work of art" he has at the back of his mind "the artistic emotion", since the effect is after all the emotional effect.

It should be clear now that only the structural emotion can be identified with Ransom's structure. And Ransom's structure can in turn be equated with the objective correlative. But I must hasten to add that the objective correlative as it exists before the actual creative process begins cannot arouse the original emotion : it can become an effective formula for the arousal of emotion only after combining with feeling.

If we have the above creative process in mind, many of Eliot's statements which sound enigmatic stand out clear. In view of the foregoing analysis, it should not be difficult to understand Eliot's well-known utterance in "Tradition and the Individual Talent" that "the poet has, not a 'personality' to express, but a particular medium, which is only a medium and not a personality, in which impressions and experiences combine in peculiar and unexpected ways."[39] Before commenting on this pronouncement I must call attention to the fact that Eliot has taken here an extreme stance which he modifies later in "Four Elizabethan Dramatists," where he writes :

> No artist produces great art by a deliberate attempt to express his personality. He expresses his personality indirectly through concentrating upon a task which is a task in the same sense as the making of an efficient engine or the turning of a jug or a table leg.[40]

At first sight one may find a discrepancy between the two utterances of Eliot : in one he says that the poet does not have a personality to express, while in the other he admits that the poet expresses his personality, though indirectly. But the truth of the matter is that there is no discrepancy between the two statements. (The extreme view in the first statement was, I believe, necessary for combating the emphasis that had been laid on personality for over a century.) There is a difference between direct and indirect expression of personality : in the indirect expression of personality what the poet expresses is not personality but an equivalent of it, or, to use Eliot's term, the objective correlative. Eliot speaks of the task of artistic production and compares its product to objects like engine, jug and table leg. Eliot is right from his own point of view. An artist, he maintains, produces a work of art not by expressing his personality but by designing an objective correlative which, combined with formal elements, brings into being a work of art. The designing of an objective correlative is a task in the same sense as the making of any other object, an efficient engine, for instance.

The medium which is the mind of the poet has an important role to play in Eliot's theory of impersonality. Eliot has drawn a chemical analogy to describe how the medium operates. He says that when oxygen and sulphur dioxide come into contact with platinum, they form sulphurous acid, though the platinum itself remains unaffected and the new gas contains no traces of platinum. This is precisely what takes place in the artistic creation. The objective correlative and the formal elements are transformed into a work of art by the operation of the poet's mind. However, one can see a serious lacuna of the chemical analogy. As applied to poetry, it means that the poem has no traces of the poet's mind. But, according to Eliot's own arguments, the work of a significant artist bears the imprint of his personality, and how can this personality be completely abstracted from the poet's mind which is the medium ?

III

Eliot's theory of impersonality is bound up with his own practice. Eliot's two theories—Tradition and Impersonality—were formulated in the same essay. In the preceding chapter I dealt with the use of tradition in Eliot's poety, and here I must point out how tradition is related to impersonality before passing on to demonstrate their co-presence in Eliot's poetry.

"Tradition and the Individual Talent" was originally published in *The Egoist* in two instalments—the first dealing with the theory of tradition and the second with the impersonal theory. Pointing to the link between the two parts of the essay Eliot writes :

> I tried to point out the importance of the relation of the poem to other poems by other authors, and suggested the conception of poetry as a living whole of all the poetry that has ever been written. The other aspect of this Impersonal theory of poetry is the relation of the poem to its author.[41]

It is clear from this passage that a poem stands in a twofold relation—related to the literary tradition and related to the author. What is not clear is the way the two aspects of the poem are related to each other. We can, however, see some link between the two aspects. As we have observed, what a poet seeks to convey is not emotion as such but its objective correlative which, combined with feelings (which are primarily images), arouses the original emotion. The role of tradition in artistic creation is primarily with images. I do not equate tradition with feelings, since images are also drawn from sources other than literary tradition. Nevertheless, literary images go a long way to evoke the original emotion that the artist set out to communicate.

In his poetry Eliot is concerned to evolve the objective correlatives for his emotions. Eliot's poetry is dramatic, and in order to comprehend the nature of the objective correlatives in his poetry it is necessary to bear in mind the relation in which the characters in a drama stand to the dramatist. This is to avoid the mistake into which critics fall by identifying Eliot's pesonages with Eliot himself. Just as in a drama, so in the dramatic monologues of Eliot, there may be certain resemblances between the writer and the personages, but this does not warrant any wholesale identification of the two.

When I am making this point and separating Eliot from his personages, one may refer to Eliot's own comments on dramatic monologue in "The Three Voices of Poetry", where he identifies the speaker in a dramatic monologue with the writer himself. But, in fact, Eliot's analysis of dramatic monologue, and its distinction from drama, is rather unsatisfactory. Nevertheless, it needs to be taken into account in order to see what light it can shed on Eliot's own early poetry. Distinguishing between drama and dramatic monologue Eliot writes :

> The fact that a number of characters in a play have claims upon the author, for their allotment of poetic speech, compels him to try to extract the poetry from the character, rather than impose his poetry upon it. Now, in the dramatic monologue we have no such check. The author is just as likely to identify the character with himself, as himself with the character : for the check is missing that will

> prevent him from doing so—and that check is the necessity for identifying himself with some other character replaying to the first.[42]

Eliot's point is that it is the dialogue form that prevents a playwright from identifying himself with his personages. After all, a writer can identify himself with one character only, and since there are at least two characters involved in a dialogue, the identification is not possible. In a dramatic monologue, on the other hand, there is only one character speaking and so the writer tends to identify himself with the speaker. What Eliot fails to notice is that there is more than one type of dramatic monologue and that it is not always possible to identify the speaker with the writer. We should be on guard against one pitfall in any discussion of dramatic monologue : we should not try to read a writer's biography into his poetry.

George T. Wright has distinguished between the romantic lyric and the dramatic monologue of Browning, saying that in the former the poet talks to the reader from a high pedestal, while in the latter the poet and the reader join in watching the personage. And, again distinguishing between Browning's dramatic monologues and those of Yeats, Pound and Eliot he writes : "Browning meets his reader at a point where they can survey the poet's material; Eliot, Yeats, and Pound meet their readers at a point where they can survey the poet's treatment of his material—his song."[43] Wright's point is that in a modern dramatic monologue it is the total poem, and not just the personage, that is viewed by the reader along with the poet.

Eliot has grouped Browning and Pound together, while Wright has noted at least one point of difference between them. But the lacuna of both Wright's and Eliot's approaches is the same the lack of sufficient distinction. All Browning's dramatic monologues are not of the same type, and whereas in one monologues the speaker may talk to the reader precisely as in a romantic lyric, in another he may talk to another personage who may not be actually present but whose presence may be felt. Let us compare Browning's "Porphyrio's Lover" with his "Andrea del Sarto." The speaker of the former talks to us, while that of the latter talks to his wife. When the monologue is of the latter type, it comes very close to the actual drama. "Porphyrio's Lover" describes a past experience, while "Andrea del Sarto" is the actual enactment of experience such as we find in a drama.

When we come to Eliot's early poetry, we find that his dramatic monologues are nearer to "Andrea del Sarto" than to "Porphyrio's Lover." His dramatic monologues are "interior dialogues", since inside their heads the protagonists are in conversation with other personages. As against Browning's monologues, the dialogues of Eliot have listeners not merely whose presence is felt but who also speak. This is true of such poems as "Prufrock", "Portrait of a Lady" and "Rhapsody on a Windy Night." In "Prufrock" both the listener and the women speak in the mind of the protagonist. The listener's question we know only from the answer given by the protagonist.

> Oh, do not ask, "What is it?"
> Let us go and make our visit.

while the speeches of the women are reproduced !

> (They will say : 'How his hair is growing thin !)
>
> (They will say : 'But how his arms and legs are thin !)
>
> If one, settling a pillow by her head
> Should say : "That is not what I meant at all.
> That is not it, at all."

In "Portrait of a Lady" the dialogue form is much more marked, though the dialogue remains interior, since it takes place in the mind of the protagonist.

> The voice returns like the insistent out-of tune
> Of a broken violin on an August afternoon :
> "I am always sure that you understand
> My feelings, always sure that you feel,
> Sure that across the gulf you reach your hand.
>
> You are invulnerable, you have no Achilles' heel.
> You will go on, and when you have prevailed
> You can say : at this point many a one has failed.
> But what have I, but what have I, my friend,
> To give you, what can you receive from me,
> Only the friendship and the sympathy
> Of one about to reach her journey's end."

The first two lines clearly indicate that the lady is conversing with the protagonist in his mind. And the long speech of the lady with the protagonist places the two characters in a dramatic situation so much so indeed that the reader watches them precisely as he does characters in a dramatic dialogue.

In "Rhapsody on a Windy Night" the protagonist is spoken to by the street lamp. The speeches in this poem, as in the others, constitute interior dialogue. But there is a major difference between the poems discussed above and a poem like "Gerontion" in which there is only Gerontion's speech. In what sense, one may ask, is Gerontion in a dramatic situation? On the face of it, this poem reads like Browning's dramatic monologue of the first type mentioned above. But there is a difference between "Porphyrio's Lover" and "Gerontion." The difference can be seen most clearly in Gerontion's self-critical irony. Eliot has confessed to having started writing poems under the impact of Laforgue, and nowhere is Laforgue's influence more marked than in self-critical irony. The self-critical irony touches deeper than appears. In a drama one personage is criticized by another, while in the self-critical irony the personage gives a deprecatory account of himself. So when Gerontion talks to us we get the impression as if he were being examined by someone else. It is this self-critical irony and the conflicting views that constitute the dramatic situation in "Gerontion."

What we find in the poems discussed above is not the poet talking to us in his own person, but only presenting before us certain characters in certain situations arousing certain emotions through certain images. It is probable that the emotions aroused are the personal emotions of the poet himself, but we do not know anything about them except through the emotions stemming from the objective correlatives.

Eliseo Vivas seeks to demolish Eliot's theory of the objective correlative on the ground that the emotion which the objective correlative actually expresses is not that which the poet felt before the poem was written : the original emotion suffers a sea-change in the course of composition.[44] Allen Austin, on the other hand, charges Vivas with taking the character's emotion in Eliot's theory of the objective correlative for what is the poet's emotion. And one can in turn blame Austin for his confusion between a work of art and a particular character in it.[45] The truth of the matter is that Eliot concerns himself with all the three emotions—the emotion of the poet, of the character, and that which emanates from the work as a whole—with the main emphasis on the work as a whole. The objective correlative as a finished product, i.e., not as originally planned by the writer but as actually expressed through images can be identified with the work as a total construction. And since the character is only one among several components of a work, it is merely contributory to the emotional effect of the total work. That is to say, the characters in a drama cannot be estimated in isolation from the total structure of which they form parts. When Eliot discusses Hamlet's emotion, he is concerned with Hamlet as he exists in the total design of the play. And it must needs be stressed that Hamlet, after all, is the protagonist of the play and therefore his emotion will be in direct relation to the overall emotional effect of the play. So when Eliot says that the motif of the earlier play was revenge, while Shakespeare was trying to impose on its material the effect of the mother's guilt upon the son, he is referring both to the character's emotion and the play's. The reason why Hamlet is an artistic failure is the lack of correspondence between Hamlet's emotion and the facts constituting the objective correlative for him. And the absence of a proper objective correlative for Hamlet means also the absence of one for Shakespeare. The reason why Hamlet does not find a suitable objective correlative for his emotion is that Shakespeare himself fails to find one for his own emotion.

The problem of the objective correlative presented itself in its greatest complexity in *The Waste Land*, where Eliot was trying to express a most complex emotion. I hasten to add that the complexity of emotion one learns from the poem itself, and not from what was in the poet's mind. The predominant emotion, or what Eliot calls art emotion, of *The Waste Land* has been interpreted variously. The interpreters can be roughly divided into three categories represented by F.R. Leavis, Helen Gardner and John Peter. In his pioneer work on modern English poetry Leavis says that the poem purports to describe the present state of civilization which is best brought out by "the seeming disjointedness" of the form.[46] Writing fifteen years after Leavis, Helen Gardner argued that the early critics of *The Waste Land* went wrong by overlooking the religious implication of *The Waste Land* and discovering in it the disillusionment of a generation.[47] Gardner's argument is partly confirmed by Eliot's own comment on *The Waste Land* in "Thoughts After Lambeth," where he disapproves of those critics who find in the poem "the disillusionment of a generation.[48] I say partly because Eliot only tells us what was not his intention, and maintains diplomatic silence, as it were, over what it was.[49] John Peter unearths the poet's intention and arrives at the conclusion that *The Waste Land*, like *In Memoriam* of Tennyson, describes the personal grief of the poet occasioned by the loss of his friend.[50]

I skip over Helen Gardner's exegesis of *The Waste Land*, since I have already refuted it. As regards the other two interpretations, one has only to look at Eliot's own comments to find out that they are not necessarily antithetical. In "Shakespeare and the Stoicism of Seneca" Eliot says that "the great poet, in writing himself, writes his time." And in his essay on *In Memoriam* he advances a more elaborate explanation : "It happens now and then that a poet by some strange accident expresses the mood of his generation, at the same time that he is expressing a mood of his own which is quite remote from that of his generation."[51] The two moods seem to have coincided in *The Waste Land*, and since it is a coincidence of, and not an antithesis between, the two, the predominant emotion remains the same.

As the title itself indicates, the emotional effect of *The Waste Land* is of sterility, and whether the sterility was personal or of the age that Eliot was expressing in the poem is an insignificant question. The idea of sterility has been effectively communicated to us through the objective correlative. The sterility in the poem operates on two levels, namely sexual and spiritual, and the two levels combine in the Grail myth described in Miss Weston's *From Ritual to Romance* which is the chief source of *The Waste Land's* objective correlative. How important is the idea of the Waste Land in *From Ritual to*

Romance is evidenced by the following remark of Miss Weston's :

> As a matter of fact I believe that the "Waste Land" is really the very heart of our problem ; a rightful appreciation of its position and significance will place us in possession of the clue which will lead us safely through the most bewildering mazes of the fully developed tale [i.e., the Grail story].[52]

The objective correlative derived from *From Ritual to Romance* is filled in with the imagistic details so much so indeed that one cannot think of it in isolation. The idea of sterility derived from Miss Weston's book has been given textural details by the images that come from different literary sources such as Dante's *The Divine Comedy*, Chaucer's *Prologue to Canterbury Tales*, Shakespeare's *The Tempest* and Goldsmith's *The Vicar of Wakefield*. The poet is nowhere present in the poem, the different components of which are united by Tiresias. When we read the poem, we stand face to face not with the poet but only a set of images presenting characters in different situations. The nature of the objective correlative of *The Waste Land* stands out clear if we compare it with, say, Matthew Arnold's *The Scholar Gipsy* which also deals with the malaise of the age. Arnold comes out openly to state the "strange disease of modern life" and contrasts it with the life of the scholar gipsy who embodies the ideal. On the contrary, the poet of *The Waste Land* never appears in the poem and the disease of the modern life is communicated only through the projection of the objective correlative.

IV

The impersonality in the early essays is different from the one that Eliot postulates in the later essays. Going back to my earlier distinction of personality and impersonality, it is personality (2) and impersonality (2) that are Eliot's main concern in his later essays. When I make this comment, I certainly do not mean that the other concepts of personality and impersonality, that we have already dealt with, disappear altogether from the later essays. They are very much there, but they combine with the new concepts.

The new concepts of personality and impersonality one can see at their best in *After Strange Gods* where the criterion of assessment is Christian orthodoxy. As I have said in the preceding chapter, the literary tradition in the early essays combines with the Christian tradition later. Similarly, the impersonality which is the outcome of the literary tradition in the early essays is supplemented by the impersonality which is the product of Christian orthodoxy. The personality that has been condemned in the early phase exists independently of the literary tradition, while the one that has been attacked in the later essays is personal in the sense that it is not sanctioned by Christian orthodoxy. The writers who are most personal by the later criterion are those who have deviated most from Christian dogmas. For Eliot, Christian orthodoxy constitutes an impersonal background against which a writer operates in literary creations.

In his later writings Eliot has stressed the importance of religious standards in literary assessments. In *Notes Towards the Definition of Culture* he writes that "the artistic sensibility is impoverished by its divorce from the religious sensibility, the religious by its separation from the artistic . . . ."[53] In "Religion and Literature" Eliot goes to the extent of wishing for "the existence of two literatures, one for Christian consumption and the other for the Pagan world."[54] He calls upon Christians to maintain consciously "certain standards and criteria of criticism over and above those applied by the rest of the world."[55] Apparently, the criteria which are specifically Christian will relate to the beliefs expressed in a work rather than the literary form. As René Wellek points out, Eliot is pleading for "a double standard", one Christian and the other literary, one by which the greatness is to be judged and the other whereby the "artness" (René Wellek's coinage) is to be decided.[56]

The Christian beliefs and personality in the sense of point of view discussed earlier should not be confused. I have already demonstrated how personality as point of view has been exalted by Eliot throughout his criticism. A writer may have a point of view without being Christian, Shakespeare, for instance. Similarly, a writer who is Christian may also have an individual attitude, Dante, for example. This will refute the notion that since a Christian writer shares in a common set of beliefs he does not have his individuality. His individuality lies in the way he feels his material and gives it a form. Thus both Christian and non-Christian writers can have individuality. The difference lies in the fact that the attitude of the former will have behind it Christian sanctions, while that of the latter will not. In his early essays Eliot appreciates a personal point of view emerging from within the work whether it is orthodox or heretical, whereas in his later essays he idealizes the point of view which is both individual and orthodox.

Eliot has made a threefold division of literature in relation to religion ; first, religious literature such as the authorized translation of the Bible, or the works of Jeremy Taylor ; secondly, religious or devotional poetry which, for the great majority of people, means the poetry that deals with religious dogmas, and, thirdly, the literature that aims at forwarding the religious cause. Of the three categories of literature, Eliot approves of the second with some modification, the modification being that a religious poet is not necessarily a poet restricted to a narrow area of subject matter. A great religious writer such as Dante, or Corneille, or Racine is concerned with the religious spirit informing the whole range of subject matter that he covers rather than the religious subject only. Eliot compares these writers with Vaughan, Southwell, and George Herbert who are religious poets in a restricted sense.

Eliot is careful to distinguish the writer who accepts Christian orthodoxy from the one who reinterprets it. The former gives, says Eliot, "poetic form to 'theological thought'",[57] while the latter distorts Christianity to his own idiosyncracy. Eliot's comments on Blake and the metaphysical poets in the same address bring out significantly the distinction between the two types of poets. According to Eliot, Blake "is a great poet, and a religious poet if there ever was one ; but whose Christianity is so individual and eccentric that it is extremely difficult to define.' "[58], And of metaphysical poetry of the seventeenth century he writes that it "is impressively impersonal, it is the work of men who were Christians in a Christian society."[59] The personality of Blake and the impersonality of the metaphysicals that Eliot speaks of are different from the personality and impersonality of his early essays. The personality is an attitude emerging out of a system of beliefs which have no Christian sanctions, while the impersonality is enshrined in Christian orthodoxy. The difference between a metaphysical poet and Blake is that the former accepts orthodoxy, while the latter reinterprets it to the point of heresy.

It is the heretical point of view which is the main target of Eliot's criticism in the later phase, particularly *After Strange Gods*. He desiderates an objective moral standard, which for him could be provided only by Christian orthodoxy, and regrets the fabrication of individual morality.

> When morals cease to be a matter of tradition and orthodoxy—that is, of the habits of the community formulated, corrected, and elevated by the continuous thought and direction of the Church— and when each man is to elaborate his own, then *personality* becomes a thing of alarming importance.[60]

This is the reason why he takes exception to the bishops' reliance on "the individual conscience" in the Lambeth report, and the emphasis placed by Babbitt and other humanists on the inner check to be exercised by individuals on themselves. In "Religion and Literature" he criticizes "censorship" "because it acts only from custom and habit, not from decided theological and moral principles."[61] In *After Strange Gods* Eliot categorizes writers according to the beliefs expressed in their works. The list of writers who are heretical includes, among others, Yeats, Pound and D.H. Lawrence. Eliot contrasts them with the orthodox writers such as Baudelaire and Joyce.

The heretical writer seeks to evolve his own set of beliefs independently of Christian orthodoxy. That Eliot's concern with impersonality in the later essays relates not to the technique employed by the writer but the experience and beliefs expressed in his work is amply borne out by the fact that Pound is here considered heretical. If Pound has discarded Christianity, Yeats and Lawrence have striven to fabricate a religion of their own, which is heretical to the extent that it deviates from orthodox Christianity. Eliot quotes Yeats' own confession that he "had made a new religion, almost an infallible church of poetic tradition." Yeats not only believes, like Arnold, that poetry can substitute for religion but constructs "an *individual* religion." D.H. Lawrence is an extreme form of Yeats. If in Yeats's religion there are components which are derived from religions other than Christianity and others which are purely personal interpretations of the Christian beliefs, Lawrence's religion is, as Graham Hough affirms, an inverted form of Christianity.[62] That Lawrence was vehemently opposed to Christian orthodoxy is obvious from several comments in his novels on Christ and the Christian beliefs. The following comes from Lady Chatterley who is, for the most part, Lawrence's spokesman in *Lady Chatterley's Lover* :

> The human body is only just coming to real life. With the Greeks it gave a lovely flicker, then Plato and Aristotle killed it and Jesus finished it off. But now the body is coming really to life, it is really rising from the tomb.

But, on the other hand, Lawrence draws heavily on the Christian terminology to describe sexual union. In point of fact, he places flesh on a par with spirit in Christianity. And once one accepts, like Eliot, the sanctity of Christian orthodoxy and applies it in literary assessments, Lawrence turns out to be the advocate of Satanism.

Eliot contrasts the heretics discussed above with orthodox writers like Baudelaire, Conrad, and James Joyce. The comparison between Lawrence and Baudelaire becomes significant in view of the fact that both focus their attention on Satanism. But whereas Baudelaire examines it critically, Lawrence approves of it. So, for Eliot, Lawrence is a heretic, while Baudelaire is a Christian religious poet. He takes issue with Arthur Symons on the nature of Baudelaire's poetry. Symon's image of Baudelaire is more or less identical with Eliot's view of Lawrence. Symons believes that Baudelaire is "an ascetic of passion, a hermit of the Brothel" who glorifies Evil. Eliot, on the contrary, argues that Baudelaire is essentially a Christian poet who, concerned with the problems of Good and Evil as he is, describes the power of Evil which by implication points to "the need for prayer."

Eliot traces the development of English fiction in terms of Christian orthodoxy and discovers the first traces of heresy in George Eliot. Novelists before George Eliot such as Jane Austen, Dickens and Thackeray were "orthodox enough according to the light of their day." The heresy beginning with George Eliot and passing through Thomas Hardy culminates in D.H. Lawrence. Among the modern writers Lawrence and James Joyce represent for Eliot the opposite poles—Lawrence the heretical and Joyce the orthodox. The concept of morality with its distinction between Good and Evil is the criterion that Eliot applies to judge whether a writer is heretical or orthodox. If the concept is without any basis in Christian orthodoxy, it will make the writer a heretic. Thus the fact that Lawrence may be considered a moralist by a sympathetic critic will not refute Eliot's charge, since he himself looks upon George Eliot as a serious moralist but deplores her "individualistic morals." Joyce's work, says Eliot is "penetrated with Christian feeling"; that is to say, the moral point of view that emerges out of Joyce's work has behind it orthodox Christian sanctions. Eliot himself has examined Joyce's "The Dead" to demonstrate the "orthodoxy of his sensibility." One can refer to the other works of Joyce as well to explain what Eliot suggests. As against Lawrence's, Joyce's characters appeal to both the sides of human personality, which Eliot would call Good and Evil in the Christian sense. An interesting instance of how the two sides combine in the same character one finds in *A Portrait of the Artist as a Young Man*, where Stephen looks at the voluptuous girl with her bare legs and thighs, soft bosom and long hair and, in emotional excitement.

> —Heavenly God ! cried Stephen's soul, in an outburst of profane joy.
>
> *   *   *
>
> A wild angel had appeared to him, the angel of mortal youth and beauty, an envoy from the fair courts of life, to throw open before him in an instant of ecstasy the gates of all the ways of error and glory.

"Profane joy", "wild angel" and "error and glory" bring out the two sides of human personality. The conflict between flesh and spirit that Stephen Dedalus feels is a pointer to the conflict between Good and Evil. Joyce's characters feel the pricking of conscience engendered by orthodoxy. In the story that Eliot himself has discussed Gabriel, the husband, feels guilty at the end of the story. The feeling of guilt comes from an appeal to the other side, or in other words, the good side of personality. Lawrence, on the other hand, writes about Mellors, the game-keeper, after his affair with Lady Chatterley :

> He had a sense of foreboding. No sense of wrong or sin; he was troubled by no conscience in that respect. He knew that conscience was chiefly fear of society, or fear of oneself.

And it is the pricking of conscience that makes one feel guilty. Eliot is probably wrong in finding "the absence of any moral or social sense in Lawrence's men and women" : however individualistic and hence heretical Lawrence's morality may be, but it is there. Eliot himself realized it later when he observed that Lawrence, "without being a Christian, was primarily and always religious."[63] Lady Chatterley's desertion of Sir Clifford and the acceptance of the game-keeper is a moral act for her, however immoral it may be for others. If Lawrence's men and women, compared with Joyce's, are one-sided, it is because they stick to their individual morality a little too fast.

The personality that Eliot decries in his later essays is equivalent to individual morality resulting from a heretical view of life. And the impersonality that Eliot idealizes in his later phase is an objective moral standard which is the product of an orthodox view of life.

V

In "Religion and Literature" and an unpublished address called "Types of English Religious Verse" Eliot has described different types of religious poetry. The categorization made in "Religion and Literature" has already been reckoned with. In his address he surveys the history of English poetry from the seventeenth century onwards in the light of Christian orthodoxy. He makes a twofold division of English verse—

one covering the seventeenth century English poetry and the other comprehending the poetry of eighteenth and nineteenth centuries. It is evident from his discussion that he looks upon metaphysical poetry as the best religious poetry written in England. The chief quality of this poetry that he singles out is its impersonality. "It is not only free from autobiography," writes Eliot, "but from the consciousness on the part of the author of being a Christian. The writer vanishes from his own mind in the presence of what he contemplates."[64] This is, indeed, an extreme position, since the metaphysicals, though they accept the objectivity of Christian orthodoxy, are not free from personal elements altogether. "The question of one's own salvation" that Eliot deems a by-product of the romantic movement is very much there in metaphysical poetry. In a highly perceptive account of religious poetry Helen Gardner does not fail to notice the personal side of metaphysical poetry. As against Eliot, she believes that "many of the most beautiful of the religious lyrics of the century are autobiographical, or arise out of particular circumstances, whether actual or imagined."[65] Helen Gardner's threefold division of religious poetry throws tremendous light on the problem of religious verse, including Eliot's. In the first category she places medieval and eighteenth-century religious verse. Of medieval religious poetry she says that in it "the feelings expressed are common, unindividualized." The second cetegory comprises metaphysical poetry of the seventeenth century in which there is "a strongly individual handling of what are common things"; and the third category consists of the romantic poets who individualize religion. "In the nineteenth century," writes Helen Gardner "the poet is expected to create not only his poem but also his subject matter."[66]

The main point that Eliot and Helen Gardner have in common is this : that genuine religious poetry is that which accepts Christian orthodoxy and gives it an individual form. The poetry that lacks personality, like the medieval and eighteenth-century poetry, or, for that matter, the poetry that lacks impersonality such as that of the nineteenth century falls short of this criterion.

Having examined different types of religious poetry, it is worthwhile to turn to Eliot's own poetry and see where it finds its place. Eliot approves of only two types of religious poetry—metaphysical poetry which is the poetry of limited awareness, and the poetry such as that of Dante which is the poetry of general awareness. The latter is superior to the former. Eliot's contention is that in the poetry of general awareness what we find is not only the treatment of religious subject matter but the whole range of subject matter treated in the religious spirit. It is general awareness that Eliot finds in the works of Dante and Joyce, for example. Dante has treated the whole range of human experience from hell to paradise in the Christian religious spirit, and Joyce manifests the Christian spirit in his appeal to the total personality involving Good and Evil.

Eliot's early poetry which culminates in *The Waste Land* is the poetry of general awareness in the sense that it is not limited to a particular area of experience but covers a wide range from life in a modern metropolis to the religious experiences in east and west. But since the spirit informing it is not Christian but anthropological, it is not religious poetry. A comparison between Eliot's early poetry and Dante's *The Divine Comedy* will bring out how Eliot's poetry is not Christian. As has been pointed out, the central theme of Eliot's early poetry including *The Waste Land* is what one finds in the third canto of the *Inferno* dealing with the Vestibule inhabited by the Futile. It will be wrong to identify the whole of the *Inferno* with *The Waste Land*, since it is only a tiny part of the *Inferno* on which the latter rests. When Dante describes those inhabiting the *inferno*, one feels the undercurrent of Christian orthodoxy. People are punished according to the sins committed by them. But the inhabitants of the Waste Land are without sin or virtue. In the preceding section I have quoted Joyce to show how his characters feel a sense of guilt. I do not contend that the feeling of guilt stems only from religious belief but it certainly goes with religious awareness. And when we come to Eliot's characters in his early poetry, we find that for all their degenerate behaviour they do not feel guilty at all. The most emphatic instance in point is the typist girl in *The Waste Land*.

Eliot's poetry after *The Waste Land* is specifically Christian. If the early poetry culminates in *The Waste Land*, the later poetry culminates in the *Four Quartets.* Stephen Spender has said, and rightly, that "without Dante, as the supreme example of an orthodox writer, *After Strange Gods* could hardly have been written."[67] Similarly, without Dante as the supreme example of a Christian poet the *Four Quartets* could hardly have been written. When I make this remark, I do not have in mind only the pastiche of Dante in "Little Gidding," of which Eliot says that this section of the poem—not the "length of one canto of the *Divine Comedy*—"cost me far more time and trouble and vexation than any passage of the same length that I have ever written."[68] What mainly unites the *Four Quartets* with *The Divine Comedy* is the way Christian orthodoxy has been poeticized. In short, the *Four Quartets* as well as *The Divine Comedy* gives us the poetic equivalent of Christian orthodoxy. Of "Ash Wednesday" and the *Four Quartets,* the former resembles a metaphysical poem, while the latter *The Divine Comedy.* In metaphysical poetry we discern an individual handling of the aspects of orthodoxy : the orthodoxy is impersonal, while the handling is personal. It is in the harmony of the two that Helen Gardner finds tradition and the individual talent combined. Even a cursory glance at the Divine poems of Donne, or the poems in Herbert's *The Temple,* will bring out the generality of their themes. But the generality becomes individualized because of the treatment it receives at the hands of the poet. Take, for instance, Donne's "Good Friday, 1613. Riding Westward". The theme the poem deals with is a general one : the theme of Christ's crucifixion. But the poet gives it an individual handling as is evidenced by the following lines :

> Hence is't, that I am carryed towards the West
> This day, when my soules forme bends towards the East,
> There I should see a Sunne, by rising set,
> And by that setting endlesse day beget;
> But that Christ on this Crosse, did rise and fall.
> Sinne had eternally benighted all.

In the lines preceding this extract, Donne has described how a heavenly body loses its own motion by being subjected to foreign motions. And then he goes on to describe in the above lines how he is divided between the East where Christ was crucified and which stands for all that goes with Christ, and the wordly pleasures associated with the West. Thus what is a general theme becomes an individual experience. One discerns a similar individualizing of orthodoxy in Herbert's *The Temple*, in "Denialle," for instance, that deals with spiritual desolation.

The individualizing of orthodoxy that one finds in the metaphysical poets is different from the reinterpretation of orthodoxy in a writer like Blake. The latter is what Eliot would call eccentricity, or heresy. The individuality of a metaphysical poet lies in the treatment : he does not reinterpret orthodoxy but only makes use of it in his own way. But a writer like Blake creates an individual orthodoxy before giving it an individual treatment. This is a romantic approach which expects of a poet to be original both in experience and expression. Helen Gardner rightly says of the romantics as compared with the metaphysicals : "If the seventeenth-century poet is like an architect using materials provided by others and designing his building on an accepted model, the nineteenth-century poet is brick-maker, quarryer, brick-layer and stonemason as well as architect."[69] Thus the work of a romantic is all his own.

We have noticed above that there are two ways of individualizing orthodoxy—one is to give it an individual handling only, and the other to give it an individual treatment after reinterpreting it. Coming to Eliot's poetry we find that it certainly is not of the latter type. Is it of the former type then ? Eliot himself has touched upon the nature of religious poetry in the modern age : "It is to be expected," he says "that the religious poetry of our time will be concerned primarily with giving poetic form to theological thought, and will tend to have more kinship with that of the seventeenth century, than with that of the nineteenth."[70] Is Eliot's own poetry then like that of the metaphysicals in the treatment of orthodoxy ? Helen Gardner has something significant to say on the nature of Eliot's religious poetry.

> Eliot's achievement was to manage to express a rigorous acceptance of the tradition of Western Christianity in a language and through symbols that owe nothing to the traditional language and traditional symbols of the

> Church. The blend of an extreme individuality of language, a highly personal and yet not eccentric idiom; of an imagery that is also highly personal, yet is made of the stuff of ordinary experience, and is in no way exotic; and of a highly original formal inventiveness, with an extreme orthodoxy of belief is Eliot's distinctive achievement.[71]

Helen Gardner's point comes down to this: that Eliot's religious poetry combines the extremes of impersonality and personality, in other words, it is on the one hand, strictly orthodox and, on the other, highly personal. The impersonality lies in the rigorous acceptance of orthodoxy and personality in giving it an individual form. There are two questions that strike one at this stage. First, does what Helen Gardner say of Eliot's poetry hold for metaphysical poetry as well? And, secondly, does Helen Gardner's generalization apply to the whole of Eliot's religious poetry or only to part of it? Helen Gardner has referred to Eliot's "Marina", but I should like to leave out all the shorter poems and concentrate on the two major poems of the later Eliot, namely "Ash Wednesday" and the *Four Quartets*. I believe that Helen Gardner's generalization does not apply to "Ash Wednesday" which is very much like a metaphysical poem. As against Gardner, I maintain that the language used in the poem is not devoid of "the traditional language and traditional symbols of the Church." The language of "Ash Wednesday" is, in fact, highly liturgical.

> Pray for us sinners now and at the hour of our death
> Pray for us now and at the hour of our death
>   Lord, I am not worthy
> Lord, I am not worthy
>   but speak the word only
> O my people, what have I done unto thee.

The first section of "Ash Wednesday" reads like the "Confession" with which the Church service begins. Words like "eagle" and "violet" have theological associations. A noticeable feature of "Ash Wednesday", that distinguishes it from Eliot's early poetry, is the nature of the protagonist. Unlike the protagonists of the early poetry, the speaker of "Ash Wednesday" is a type, the type of penitent, though not without individuality.[72] Being like an individual in the congregation the penitent combines individuality with generality. The shift from the plural to the singular and back to the plural in the following lines, for instance, points to the fusion of the impersonal experience embodied in the "Confession" and the poet's own experience.

And pray to God to have mercy upon us
And I pray that I may forget
These matters that with myself I too much discuss
Too much explain
Because I do not hope to turn again
Let these words answer
For what is done, not to be done again
May the judgement not be too heavy upon us

It is this weaving of a design of personal experiences against an impersonal background that brings "Ash Wednesday" close to Donne's "Good Friday, 1613, Riding Westward".

The problems of impersonality that Eliot confronted in his later poetry differ from those he faced in his early poetry. In the early poetry the experience is personal and the problem is how to depersonalize it, while in the later poetry the experience is general and therefore the problem is how to individualize it. That is to say, the problem that Eliot has to resolve in the later poetry is just the opposite of his problem in the early poetry. Eliot resolves his problem in "Ash Wednesday" by speaking in his own person, and placing the images and symbols which are highly personal side by side with those which are liturgical. The following is an instance in point :

At the first turning of the third stair
Was a slotted window bellied like the fig's fruit
And beyond the hawthorn blossom and a pasture scene
The broad backed figure drest in blue and green
Enchanted the maytime with an antique flute.
Blown hair is sweet, brown hair over the mouth blown,
Lilac and brown hair;
Distraction, music of the flute, stops and steps of the mind
over the third stair,
Fading, fading; strength beyond hope and despair
Climbing the third stair.

Lord, I am not worthy
Lord, I am not worthy
but speak the word only

The image of stair reminds one of the ten steps of the mystic ladder described in St John of the Cross's *The Dark Night of the Soul*, and also the mount Purgatory in Dante's *The Divine Comedy*. The experience formulated is not an individual but a general experience which one feels in the course of establishing communion with God. The last three lines are quoted from Matthew : 8:8. But if there is this impersonal design, on the one hand, there is, on the other, the individuality of the poet expressed in the erotic description of "a slotted window" and "a pasture scene". The "I" of the lines from Matthew takes the place of the protagonist in the context of the poem.

In "Ash Wednesday" and the *Four Quartets* the poet appears in his own person. In the former he typifies the penitent, while in the latter his voice is an individual one. This personal element in the later poetry comes in to balance the impersonality of orthodoxy. The experience formulated in the *Four Quartets* is an impersonal experience and so the poet can safely appear in the poem to feel it. As a result we get such direct utterances of the poet as could not be expected in his early poetry.

So here I am, in the middle way, having had twenty years—
Twenty years largely wasted, the years of *l' entre deux guerres*—
Trying to learn to use words, and every attempt
Is a wholly new start, and a different kind of failure
Because one has only learnt to get the better of words
For the thing one no longer has to say, or the way in which
One is no longer disposed to say it. And so each venture
Is a new beginning . . . .

The poet appears in his own person, but the experience that he expresses is not unrelated to the general idea of the whole poem, particularly the section called "East Coker" in which the above lines appear. The idea is stated right at the outset of "East Coker": "In my beginning is my end." Helen Gardner's generalization about Eliot's religious poetry applies almost fully to the *Four Quartets*. The theme of Christ's Incarnation marking the intersection of time and Eternity has been effectively communicated through images and symbols which are Eliot's own. The poem attains a unique balance of personality and impersonality which is nowhere else to be found in English poetry. On the one hand, orthodoxy has been accepted rigorously and, on the other, the expression given to it is highly personal, and shorn of the liturgical language that informs "Ash Wednesday." Eliot's religious poetry in the *Four Quartets*, of limited awareness though it is, is a unique achievement in the history of English religious poetry.

CHAPTER FIVE

Dissociation of Sensibility (I)

The term "dissociation of sensibility" was first used by Eliot in 1921 in his review of Grierson's edition of *Metaphysical Lyrics and Poems of the Seventeenth Century,* later included as "The Metaphysical Poets" in *Homage to John Dryden.* In the same year appeared his essay on Andrew Marvell on the occasion of the poet's tercentenary. In fact, if one is studying Eliot's writings on metaphysical poetry in chronological order, one should start with his review of Donne's sermons which he wrote in 1919. After the two essays in 1921 he wrote in 1923 two pieces—one each on John Donne and Andrew Marvell—both being reviews of the selections of poems of the two poets. In 1925 Eliot reviewed for the *TLS* Mario Praz's book on Donne and Crashaw. And in 1926 he delivered the "Clark Lectures" on the metaphysical Poets at Trinity College, Cambridge, which are as yet unpublished. In 1927 he reviewed for *Dial* Edmund Blunden's *On the Poems of Henry Vaughan* and in 1928 wrote a piece on Richard Crashaw. In 1929 he gave a talk on the Sermons of Donne. In *The Listener* for 1930, Eliot wrote a series of articles on the poetry of the early seventeenth century in which he discussed the metaphysical poets from Donne to Cowley and Dryden. To the memorial volume on Donne edited by Theodore Spencer in 1931 he contributed a piece on "Donne in Our Time." In 1932 he wrote on George Herbert in the series called "Studies in Sanctity." In 1938 he lectured on George Herbert to Friends of Salisbury Cathedral, and also contributed a note on the two odes of Cowley to the volume on seventeenth-century literature presented to Sir Herbert Grierson. Then there was a long gap in Eliot's writings on the metaphysical poets and the next piece to appear was his pamphlet on George Herbert written for the British Council in 1962.

From the above stocktaking of Eliot on metaphysical poetry it should be obvious that his writings on the school of Donne are spread over a long passage of time. The time factor is of crucial significance in any discussion of Eliot's theory of the dissociation of sensibility. As the first phase of Eliot's criticism ended in 1921, everything published after this date needs to be viewed in the altered context. And this factor gathers further significance in view of Eliot's conversion to Anglo-Catholicism in 1927. It must needs be emphasized here that the conversion to Christianity was most likely to impinge upon Eliot's attitude towards metaphysical poetry, which is for the most part Christian. As we shall notice presently, the critics of Eliot have simply bypassed these significant factors involved in Eliot's discussion of the metaphysical poets.

In the first place, too much attention has been paid to the two essays—"The Metaphysical Poets" and "Andrew Marvell"—in *Homage to John Dryden* to the neglect of Eliot's other publications on the metaphysical poets. As regards the essay on "Donne in Our Time", it is customary with critics to refer to it in order to demonstrate how the later Eliot has detracted from Donne. Most critics have found the clue to the dissociation of sensibility in Eliot's collocation of the metaphysical poets with the French symbolists. And the collocation suits particularly the critics who seek to establish that Eliot is a romanticist despite his avowed classicism. I shall refer here to two critics whose publications—both classics of modern criticism—were divided by nearly three decades. In *Axel's Castle* published as early as 1931, Edmund Wilson discussed modern symbolist writers and grouped Eliot with Yeats, Valéry, Joyce and Gertrude Stein. And in *Romantic Image* (1957) Frank Kermode asserted that Eliot with his emphasis on the poetic image is a romanticist and bracketed him with Yeats, Symons and Hulme. In point of fact, the step from Wilson to Kermode is very easy to take. It is a commonplace of criticism that the French symbolists drew heavily on Poe, and Poe is looked upon by Anglo-Saxon critics as a romanticist who laid the English romantics, particularly Coleridge, under contribution. But Edmund Wilson is not blind to the differences between the romantics and the symbolists. What surprises one is that nowhere in his book does Kermode refer to Wilson, not even when drawing on the analogy of Axel. One suspects that he simply wants to dodge the entire issue regarding the differences between the romantics and the symbolists raised so emphatically by Wilson. Moreover, unlike Kermode, Wilson is alive to the differences among the symbolists themselves and separates symbolists like Corbière and Laforgue with their conversational-ironic technique from those like Mallarmé and Valéry who constitute the serious-aesthetic tradition of symbolism. According to Wilson, Eliot resembles the former rather than the latter. Furthermore, he distinguishes the modern symbolists including Eliot from a symbolist like Rimbaud who went to the extent of giving up literature in order to get "away to a life of pure action and a more primitive civilization." Wilson has not touched on the theory of the dissociation of sensibility but if he had, he would have arrived at more or less the same conclusion as Kermode, except that he would have called it symbolist rather than romantic imagistic doctrine.

Among the other critics who have discussed the dissociation, of sensibility Basil Willey and F.R. Leavis deserve special attention. Both the critics have gone outside literature to account for the dissociation. Willey believes that the realms of prose and poetry were separated by the Cartesian spirit, and it was this separation that precipitated the dissociation of sensibility. And in his discussion of Locke he points out that "the cold philosophy such as that of Locke destroyed the union of thought and feeling." That is to say, the dissociation of sensibility was the separation of the poetic virtue, i.e., feeling from the prosaic virtue, i.e., thought. Leavis does not go outside literature at such length as Willey but, like the latter, he upholds that the change in language that caused the dissociation of sensibility was brought about by the change in civilization that took place in the seventeenth century. "No one, I suppose, will dispute," writes Leavis "that the 17th century witnessed an immense, comprehensive and momentous change in ethos, in civilization, in the English language."[1] Leavis, like Kermode, believes that the theory of the dissociation of sensibility was, in effect, an attempt to re-write the history of English poetry,[2] and that the essence of the unified sensibility that Eliot found in the metaphysical poets lies in "concreteness", a term that he uses several times. In Milton, whom together with Dryden, Eliot saddled with the responsibility of the dissociation of sensibility, Leavis finds "a marked restriction of the part played by evoked sensuous effects and evoked specific varieties of energy—and absence, in sum, of arresting concreteness."[3]

There are critics who have concerned themselves with tracing the source of Eliot's dissociation of sensibility rather than explicating the theory. Bateson and Burne have traced the term to Gourmont who uses the word "sensibility" in connection with the word "dissociate" in his essay on "La Sensibilite de Jules Laforgue."[4] Both believe that Eliot has adapted the term instead of accepting it literally. F.N. Lees demonstrates the similarity between Eliot's dissociation of sensibility and Arthur Hallam's diagnosis of the contemporary poetry.[5] Eric Thompson traces the source of Eliot's theory to the philosophy of F.H. Bradley.[6]

There is one point which all the interpretations of the dissociation of sensibility have in common, i.e., that the theory rests on the "sensuous apprehension of thought." There is difference of opinion as to the nature of thought but none as regards sensuousness. The point which has gone more or less unnoticed is that with the development of Eliot, the theory takes on a new complexion. The critics have not failed to notice the change in Eliot's attitude towards Donne, but they have overlooked the important fact that his withdrawal from Donne coincided with his movement towards George Herbert. Both Donne and Herbert are metaphysical poets, but the later Eliot with his Christian bias has more in common with Herbert than with Donne. And this change in attitude implies a significant mutation in his theory of the dissociation of sensibility.

In dealing with the metaphysical poets, the early Eliot's concern is with the poetic quality embodied in their works and not the theology which goes into their poetic compositions. Even a cursory glance at the two essays on the metaphysicals in *Homage to John Dryden* will reveal to us that Eliot does not restrict the metaphysical quality of "sensuous apprehension of thought" to the so-called metaphysical, or, for that matter, Christian poets only. Besides the Elizabethans like Shakespeare, Marlowe, Webster, Jonson, the classical writers such as Catullus, Propertius, Ovid, and the French writers such as Baudelaire, Gautier and Laforgue manifest the metaphysical quality. Among the metaphysicals themselves, Eliot finds the metaphysical quality in both secular and religious metaphysical poetry. In a most significant statement on the dissociation of sensibility in *The Sacred Wood* Eliot groups the metaphysicals with other writers :

> The quality in question [i.e., the metaphysical quality] is not peculiar to Donne and Chapman. In common with the greatest—Marlowe, Webster, Tourneur, and Shakespeare—they had a *quality of sensuous thought, or of thinking through the senses, or of the senses thinking*, of which the exact formula remains to be defined. If you look for it in Shelley or Beddoes, both of whom in very different ways recaptured something of the Elizabethan inspiration, you will not find it, though you may find other qualities instead. There is a trace of it only in Keats, and, derived from a different source, in Rossetti.[7] (italics mine)

Needless to say, the metaphysical quality is not restricted to the metaphysicals : traces of it are discernible in poets so different from them as Keats and Rossetti. Eliot says in his essay on "Andrew Marvell" that the hold on human values, the grasp of human experiences that we find in the Elizabethan and Jacobean poets "leads towards, and is only completed by the religious comprehension."[8] Eliot's emphasis on "religious comprehension" sounds fortuitous in view of the interpretation of the metaphysical quality advanced by him. The very fact that he finds the metaphysical quality in both religious and secular poetry is evidence enough to refute the contention that religion is essential to it. I believe that this ill-founded assumption derives from the fact that metaphysical poetry is for the most part religious poetry, too.

The later Eliot with his penchant for Christian values plays down the importance of Donne and, looking upon Dante as the greatest metaphysical poet, sets much value on George Herbert. The definition of metaphysical poetry advanced by him in the "Clark Lectures" is a clear pointer to the shift in Eliot's attitude towards the metaphysical poets. Defining metaphysical poetry right at the outset of his first lecture he writes :

> If you identify "metaphysical" with "philosophical" and limit "philosophical" to those poets who have given expression to a system or some view of the universe, and man's place in it, which has some philosophical equivalent . . . then the definition is perfectly clear.[9]

We can notice how the emphasis has shifted from the "sensuous apprehension" to the philosophical thought. In the essays on "The Metaphysical Poets" and "Andrew Marvell", Dante and Lucretius, Donne and the other metaphysicals, the French symbolists were all grouped together, whereas in the "Clark Lectures" Dante providing, as he does, the emotional equivalent to a coherent philosophical system, emerges as the ideal metaphysical poet and the other poets are assessed with respect to him. The metaphysicals and the French symbolists are all inferior to Dante in the metaphysical quality of giving sensuous embodiment to thought. It is the thought, the philosophical thought, that becomes the pivotal point of value judgement.

By the year 1930 when Eliot delivered the broadcast talks on metaphysical poetry, published subsequently in *The Listener*, Eliot's concept of metaphysical poetry had undergone a further change. In the "Clark Lectures", Donne is still a philosophical poet, but in the 1930 broadcast talk on Donne, he is removed from the category of philosophical poetry. Eliot distinguishes sharply between philosophical and metaphysical poetry and places Donne where he belongs, and not with philosophical poets like Dante, Lucretius and Goethe. Drawing on Santayana's *Three Philosophical Poets* he advances the following distinction between philosophical and metaphysical poetry :

> Philosophical poetry is poetry in which the poet has done one of two things. He has either written a poem to express in verse a particular theory of the universe which he has taken over from some philosopher—Lucretius wrote his poem to expound the philosophy of Epicurus and Demo-

> critus in verse and Dante expounded substantially the philosophy of St Thomas Aquinas in verse—or else he makes his own system of philosophy and expresses that in verse; and the latter is more what Geothe did. But in philosophical poetry the poet *believes* in some theory about life and the universe and makes poetry of it. Metaphysical poetry, on the other hand, does not imply belief; it has come to mean the poetry in which the poet *makes use* of metaphysical ideas and theories.[10]

What I am driving at is not merely that Eliot's attitude towards Donne changes, but also his concept of metaphysical poetry as such takes a new turn. Eliot has come to value the importance of belief, and of all the metaphysical poets, Donne seems most incapable of believing anything. Consequently, in the altered context the poets with genuine beliefs, George Herbert for instance, are likely to take precedence over Donne.

II

The element of concreteness that goes with poetic imagery has been brought out by all the critics of Eliot dealing with the theory of the dissociation of sensibility. Some critics have confused image with symbol but the image is invariably at the centre of their discussion. And it is suprising that the critics who set so much weight on image have left out of account the significant movement in the first two decades of the present century called imagism. If for Kermode the modern image is a romantic image, then the question naturally arises as to how imagist poetry, with which modernism began and with which Hulme and Pound were so closely associated, is different from the poetry it sharply reacted against, namely romantic poetry, particularly its decadent phase in the eighteen nineties of which Arthur Symons, on whom Kermode writes a full-length chapter, formed a significant segment.

That Eliot had close links with the imagists cannot be denied, although it is difficult to decide whether or not he started his literary career under their influence. And still more difficult is to decide whether Hulme or Pound or Ford was the real pioneer of imagism. Grover Smith has traced the source of one of Eliot's early poems, "Death of St Narcissus," to Pound's "A Girl" and Hulme's "Conversion", both published in Pound's *Ripostes* (1912). [11] S. K. Coffman and Peter Jones have also demonstrated the imagists' correspondence with and possible influence on Eliot. [12] Anyone examining the literary climate of the first two decades of the present century can easily see Eliot's association with the imagists. Eliot meeting Pound in London in 1914 and the subsequent encouragement he received from the latter are too well-known to need labouring. Among the imagists who remained in the movement until it died out in 1917, Eliot had his closest ties with Richard Aldington. He succeeded Aldington as the editor of the *Egoist* when the latter was called up for military service in the first World War, and appointed him as the assistant editor of his *The Criterion*. On the other hand, Aldington wrote a favourable review of *The Sacred Wood* and a longish piece on Eliot's poetry (1924). All the imagists, except for Amy Lowell, were among the contributors to *The Criterion*. All these links between Eliot and the imagists are easy to see. What is difficult to establish is that Eliot's career was initially shaped, or for that matter, decisively influenced by the imagists.

Eliot's early poems published in the *Harvard Advocate* between 1907 and 1910 were written when Hulme was organizing his Poet's Club in London. Eliot never met Hulme, and it is doubtful if he had heard of him until after "Prufrock" was completed in 1911. As regards knowing Hulme indirectly through the works of Pound who, as an imagist, had certain things in common with the former, Eliot's own confession cannot be ignored : "I was introduced to *Personae* and *Exultations* in 1910, while still an undergraduate at Harvard. The poems did not then excite me, any more than did the poetry of Yeats." [13]

When Eliot started his career as a poet, he was much fascinated by the French symbolists, particularly Laforgue. Having disclaimed the influence of Pound or Yeats on his early career Eliot writes : "I was too much engrossed in working out the implications of Laforgue." [14] And he was initiated into the French symbolists including Laforgue by Symons's book on them. It was sheer coincidence that both Eliot and the imagists turned to the French symbolists around the same time, and the ; ommon area that we discern between the early

Eliot and the imagists can be traced to their common interest in French symbolism. As regards the contributions under which Eliot laid Remy de Gourmont, the French critic of the symbolist movement, Eliot himself admits that his attention was drawn to Gourmont by Ezra Pound.

Despite certain parallels between Eliot and the imagists there are striking differences between them which have not received sufficient notice. In order to get at these differences it is necessary to have in mind the distinction between the imagists and the French Symbolists. In spite of their avowed interest in the French symbolists, the imagists claimed that they detested symbolism. Pound who edited the first anthology of imagist poetry drew a clear line between symbolism and imagism.

> The symbolists dealt in "association", that is, in a sort of allusion almost of allegory. They degraded the symbol to the status of a word, they made it a form of metronomy. One can be grossly "symbolic", for example, by using the word "cross" to mean "trial." The symbolist's *symbols* have a fixed value, like numbers in arithmetic, like 1, 2 and 7. The imagist's images have a variable significance like the signs a, b, and x in algebra . . . . the author must use his *image* because he sees it or feels it, ***not*** because he thinks he can use it to back up some creed ...... or some system of ethics or economics. [15]

What Pound's argument comes down to is that the imagists are not symbolists, an argument not essentially different from that advanced by Amy Lowell in her distinction between *internality* and *externality*. The quality called internality Lowell considers "the most marked quality in the poetry of the nineties," and in contrast finds modern poetry, i.e., poetry written by her and her circle as characterized by *externality*, i.e., "an interest in things for themselves and not because of the effect they have on oneself." The emphasis on externality, is well borne out by her pronouncement that " 'Imagism,' 'Imagist,' refers more to the manner of presentation than to the thing presented. It is a kind of technique rather than a choice of subject." [16]

If we combine Amy Lowell's *internality* and *externality*, we will come close to having a clear idea of Eliot's poetry. As both Jones and Coffman point out, the externality or objectivity in Eliot's poetic theory and practice is not valued for its own sake but as communicating effectively the poet's feeling. The gravamen of the charge brought against the Imagists by their contemporaries was the lack of what we find in Eliot, a definite personality, a point of view, an emotional force. Conrad Aliken who admired Eliot's poetry to the extent of trying to rope in a publisher for its publication, and introducing its author to Ezra Pound, was the most severe critic of the imagists. To him, the main flaw of imagist poetry was the lack of vitality.

> They give us frail pictures—whiffs of windy beaches, marshes, meadows, city streets, dishevelled leaves; pictures pleasant and suggestive enough. But seldom is any of them more than a nice description, coolly sensuous, a rustle to the ear, a ripple to the eye. Of organic movement there is practically none. [17]

It is the "organic movement" in Eliot's poetry that distinguishes him from the imagists. If we judge the imagists on Eliot's criterion, they are impersonal in a pejorative sense, impersonal without personality, with the inevitable result that the linguistic ingenuity takes precedence over the felt experience. This is confirmed by Eliot's own remark that "the aim of 'imagism' . . . . was to induce a peculiar concentration upon something visual, and to set in motion an expanding succession of concentric feelings."[18]

Another point on which Eliot differs with the imagists is the question of the relation between prose and poetry. In "The Borderline of Prose" he countered Richard Aldington's concept of a prose-poem. And in his contribution to the symposium on the prose-poetry controversy he took issue with Richard Aldington, another contributor to the same symposium, on the distinction between prose and poetry. I am not here concerned with the entire prose-poetry controversy but only a particular point in it, namely the element of intensity in a poetic composition. This is a significant point which marks off Eliot from all the imagists including Pound. An imagist poem is intense throughout, which is why it is always short. In her Preface to *Some Imagist Poems* 1915 Amy Lowell stated as the final principle of imagism that "concentration is of the very essence of poetry." What Lowell means by "concentration" is what Eliot means by "intensity", though the latter separates his term from "concentration." [19] Eliot does not admit it in so many words but he will undoubtedly be in agreement with the imagists as far as a short poem or what we call lyric is concerned. The differences between the two arise on the question of the possibility of a long poem. If a poem is expected to be intense throughout, then a long poem is impossible. The question, in fact, goes back to Poe, referred to by Eliot himself, who said, to use Eliot's paraphrase, "that no poem should be more than 100 lines." "Poe demands," writes Eliot "the static poem, that in which there shall be no movement of tension and relaxation, only the capture of a single unit of intense feeling."[20] This is a pronouncement which the imagists would at once assent to. But Eliot does not rule out the possibility of a long poem which will balance tension with relaxation, since "no long work can maintain the same high tension throughout." He finds such a balance not only in epics like *The Divine Comedy*, the *Odyssey* and the *Aeneid* but also in prose works such as Gibbon's History and Newman's Apology.

Thus Eliot's emphasis on concreteness or sensuousness does not imply that he is an imagist. For Eliot an image in verse or prose is the point of intensity, and he would like to reserve the word "poetry" for this intensity whether occurring in a poem or prose. That Eliot values poetic imagery is evident from the following statement :

> The work of poetry is often said to be performed by the use of images, by a cumulative succession of images each fusing with the next; or by the rapid and unexpected combination of images apparently unrelated, which have their relationship enforced upon them by the mind of the author. This appears to be true.[21]

But this does not suggest that the unified sensibility is nothing but concreteness or sensuousness. In fact, the theory of the dissociation of sensibility is much more complex than has been taken to be by the critics of Eliot. What has misled most critics is their inability to see that Eliot has used the same term in different senses. It is this inability that lies behind Bateson's finding paradoxical Eliot's use of the term "sensibility" in two different senses. Bateson accounts for the paradox in terms of Eliot's indebtedness to Remy de Gourmont. But I think that it is in the very nature of Eliot to use terms in different senses.

There are three terms which must be adequately clarified before the dissociation of sensibility can be explained, namely emotion, feeling and thought. In the preceding chapter I have discussed the term "emotion" and pointed out how it has been used in different senses and how in one sense it is synonymous with feeling. But the term "feeling" itself has not been used in one sense only. The critics go wrong in assuming that it has just one implication in Eliot's criticism. They have identified feeling with sensation which is the product of imagery. Bateson, for instance, says that "*feeling* means sensation."[22] And Allen Austin expresses a similar view in his remark that "the term 'felt' . . . has been correctly interpreted by Basil Willey as 'image' (a combination of sensation and, emotion)."[23] But the term "feeling" has been used by Eliot in two different senses; first, as a synonym for emotion, and. secondly, as meaning sensuousness produced by imagery. Feeling is juxtaposed sometimes with "emotion" and sometimes with "thought." When it occurs with emotion, it connotes sensation or sensuousness, but when it occurs with thought it sometimes implies sensuousness and sometimes emotion. To point out the two different senses of the term "feeling" I am giving below two extracts from the same essay each containing the term :

> In Chapman especially there is a direct sensuous apprehension of thought, or a recreation of thought into *feeling*, which is exactly what we find in Donne.[24] (italics mine)

> The poets in question [i.e., the metaphysical poets] have, like other poets, various faults. But they were, at best, engaged in the task of trying to find the verbal equivalent for states of mind and *feeling*.[25] (italics mine)

The term "feeling" in the first extract is equivalent to "sensuous apprehension" while in the second it implies "emotion" and sensuousness is covered by "the verbal equivalent."

As regards the term "thought" as used by Eliot, like "feeling" it has been reduced by most critics to a single implication. But, in fact, the word "thought" has different meanings in different contexts and juxtapositions. Allen Austin says that the complexity of Eliot's dissociation of sensibility lies not in the term "feeling" but in the term "thought," and goes on to point out the two different senses it has been used in. "The term 'thought' in Eliot's definition," writes Austin "refers to abstract ideas in relation to the dissociated sensibility but it refers to wit or play of intellect in relation to the unified sensibility."[26] I find no evidence in Eliot's criticism of the separation between the two senses of the term "thought" as mentioned by Austin, though the term has certainly been used in two different senses. The term "thought" in the two senses occurs in both the unified and dissociated sensibilities. The first of the two senses is exactly that mentioned by Austin, i.e., wit or play of intellect. The second sense I would call "metaphysical idea" rather than "abstract idea."

The two senses of the term "thought" call for further elaboration. We must bear in mind that every metaphor or simile is not a conceit, just as every conceit is not a metaphysical idea. The "play of intellect" above may or may not be expressed through images. (The image itself may be divided into two types, namely literal image and poetic image, the former being an equivalent of sensuousness and the latter having a point of comparison along with sensuousness such as we find in similes, metaphors and symbols. What I mean by an image here is poetic image.) I am quoting below the lines that Eliot himself instances from Andrew Marvell's "To His Coy Mistress" in order to demonstrate how intellect can operate in two different ways :

> Had we but world enough and time,
> This coyness, lady, were no crime,
> . . . I would
> Love you ten years before the Flood,
> And you should, if you please, refuse
> Till the conversion of the *Jews*;
> My vegetable Love should grow
> Vaster than Empires and more slow.

If we leave out the last two lines there is no poetic image but only the play of intellect. It is in the last two lines that the poetic images from vegetation and empire are brought in. But it must not be forgotten that wit or play of intellect in metaphysical poetry usually operates through images.

As regards the two kinds of thought—wit and metaphysical idea—they often combine in metaphysical poetry; that is to say, wit is displayed through the use of metaphysical ideas. But before going on to discuss the combination of the two it is worthwhile to examine how they separate. In a typical metaphysical poem disparate experiences are fused; in other words, images quite remote from one another are brought in conjunction. Metaphysical imagery, drawn as it is from different spheres of knowledge, demands erudition on the part of the poet. We are reminded of Dr Johnson's remark that "the metaphysical poets were men of learning, and to show their learning was their whole endeavour."[27] The following lines from Donne have been cited by both Dr Johnson and Eliot as an example of metaphysical wit :

On a rounded ball
A workman, that hath copies by, can lay
An Europe, Afrique and, an Asia,
And quickly make that, which was nothing, All.
So doth each teare
which thee doth weare,
A globe, yea world by that impression grow,
Till thy tears mixed with mine doe overflow
This world, by waters sent from thee, my heaven dissolved so.

The poet brings in geography to describe love just as in another poem, "A valediction : forbidding mourning" he brings in mathematics, "twin campasses", to describe the peculiar relation that obtains between lovers. The above lines are metaphysical in the sense of the play of intellect through imagery drawn from remote spheres. But they are not metaphysical in the sense of the use of an idea borrowed from a metaphysician. I shall have to go a little beyond the first phase of Eliot's criticism to clarify the difference between wit and metaphysical idea.

In his "Clark Lectures", Eliot advances a definition of metaphysical poetry which has already been discussed.

According to this definition a metaphysical poet is one who gives an emotional equivalent of metaphysical thought. Metaphysics being a branch of philosophy, Eliot has used the two terms interchangeably. Though Eliot does not admit it explicitly, by metaphysical poetry in the strict sense he implies poetry which uses for poetic purposes metaphysical ideas set forth by metaphysicians. In the seventh of his "Clark Lectures" he affirms that of all the metaphysical poets Donne and Crashaw are the only ones who are fully metaphysical. And it is not for nothing that of all the metaphysicals, Eliot relates only Donne and Crashaw to the Spanish mystics and saints—Donne to St Ignatius and Crashaw to St Theresa. In order to be a metaphysical poet in the strict sense of the term one has to have a metaphysical bent of mind which Eliot finds only in Donne and Crashaw who were influenced by the Spanish metaphysicians. As Eliot points out time and again, Donne, a voracious reader as he was, was very well grounded in philosophy and made use of philosophic ideas for poetic purposes. It is where he makes such a use that he is metaphysical in Eliot's restricted sense. One can instance Donne's "The Ecstasy" Where the Neoplatonic idea of "ecstasy" (standing outside one's own body) has been rendered poetically. Of his experience of ecstasy Plotinus writes :

> Many times it has happened : Lifted out of the body into myself ; becoming external to all other things and self-centered ; beholding a marvellous beauty : then, more than ever, assured of community with the loftiest order; enacting the noblest life, acquiring identity with the divine stationing within it by having attained that activity; poised above whatsoever in the intellectual is less than the Supreme; yet, there comes the moment of descent from intellection to reasoning, and after that sojourn in the divine, I ask myself how it happens that I can now be descending, and how did the soul enter into my body, the Soul which even within the body is the high thing it has shown itself to be.[28]

The soul goes out of the body to experience ecstasy but it cannot remain in the ecstatic state forever and has to come back to the body. Explaining the descending of the soul into the body, Plotinus distinguishes between that part of the soul which is spirit and that which is Nature and the world of sense. To him the world of sense is not evil but beautiful. In Donne's poem the soul goes out of the body and returns to it. Like Plotinus, Donne recognizes the beauty of the physical world which is indispensable for spiritual union. Besides platonism, Donne draws on scholastic philosophy to underline the "interdependence of body and soul" and suggest that "the complete unity of two lovers, though their souls already enjoy oneness, is not realized until their bodies also are joined.[29]

Eliot controverts Grierson's argument that "The Ecstasy" formulates Donne's "metaphysic of love", i.e, Donne believes in the metaphysical ideas expressed in the poem and points out that Donne simply uses metaphysical ideas for poetic purposes. But the difference between Grierson and Eliot is an insignificant point in the present context. The significant point is that "The Ecstasy" is a complete metaphysical poem, as it offers the emotional equivalent of metaphysical ideas.

In his discussion of the Elizabethan and Jacobean writers, particularly the metaphysical poets, Eliot emphasizes frequently what he calls the "emotional equivalent of thought." The first formulation of this notion occurs in the essays on "Imperfect Critics" and "Philip Massinger" : in the former he uses the term "sensuous thought" and in the latter he talks of "the intellect . . . at the tips of the senses." In his essay on "The Metaphysical Poets" he uses the phrase "a direct sensuous apprehension of thought."[30] In the "Clark Lectures", the terms conveying the idea of the feeling of thought occur at several places. I am giving below just one extract containing this idea :

> With all the psychological differences that I have tried to indicate, between himself and Dante, Donne was still able to find *the emotional equivalent of highly abstract, or generalized ideas.*[31] (italics mine)

Explaining what he means by the poet who thinks, Eliot writes in "Shakespeare and the Stoicism of Seneca" : "The poet who 'thinks' is merely the poet who can express the emotional equivalent of thought." These quotations from different essays by Eliot bring out the importance that he attaches to the feeling of thought. And Donne's "The Ecstasy" is an apt example of how thought is felt. The term "sensuousness" used by Eliot in this context should not be confused with the visual effect : "the odour of a rose," a phrase used in the complaint against Tennyson and Browning is itself a pointer to the olfactory sensation.

III

The relationship between metaphysical and Eliot's poetry has been explored at great length. As early as 1929, George Williamson produced a full-length study of the parallels between Donne and Eliot. To him Eliot is the twentieth-century counterpart of Donne. The main points of similarity between Donne and Eliot he points out are conceit, incorporation of erudition into poetry, and colloquial diction and phrasing. Writing several years after Williamson, Cleanth Brooks, in a highly perceptive account of the nature and tradition of modern poetry, demonstrates the resemblances between the modern poets with Eliot at the centre and Donne and his circle. He concedes that the modern poets are the counterparts of the metaphysicals in their use of metaphor.[32] There is, however, one important difference between Williamson and Brooks. Williamson tacitly acquiesces in Eliot's oft-quoted pronouncement that the unified sensibility as embodied in metaphysical poetry disappeared sometime in the seventeenth century. Brooks does believe that the nature of metaphor changed in the late seventeenth century but to him the difference between metaphysical poetry and the poetry that followed, i.e., Augustan, romantic and Victorian poetry, is a difference in degree only. What is characteristic of metaphysical poetry is characteristic of "all poetry, poetry being essentially one."

At the other extreme from Williamson and Brooks stands a critic like F.M. Kuna in whose opinion the concept of metaphysical poetry as evolved by Eliot does not apply to metaphysical poetry at all : it applies only to modern poetry such as written by Eliot.[33] Between Williamson and Brooks on the one hand, and Kuna on the other stands Joseph E. Duncan who finds both parallels and differences between the metaphysicals and Eliot.[34]

The weakness of the critics dealing with Eliot on metaphysical poetry is that they tend to take an extreme stance. Of the critics mentioned above it is only Duncan who takes a middle course. There is much truth in what Duncan says : Eliot does resemble as well as differ from the metaphysicals. It must not be forgotten that Eliot was simultaneously interested in the metaphysicals and the French symbolists and the differences between Donne and Eliot that critics have discovered are due possibly to the mingling in the latter's mind of the two movements separated by nearly three centuries. As regards the justification of Eliot's interpretation of metaphysical poetry, nobody can blame him for advancing an interpretation tinged by his own preoccupation. No interpretation is absolutely objective : a certain amount of subjectivity is bound to creep in. Looking upon the metaphysical revival in retrospect, Eliot himself confessed and vindicated the element of subjectivity in it.

> That there was an element of fashion in our enjoyment and exploitation of Donne it would be vain to deny; but there was nothing capricious about the fashion. For at any particular moment it may happen that the poets who are beginning to write find a particular poet, or a particular type or school of poetry, such as Donne and the school of Donne—and for our time Laforgue and some other French poets as well—with whom or which they have close sympathy, and through whom or which they elicit their own talents.[35]

That there are points of affinity between Donne and Eliot is beyond question. For all his attempts Kuna fails to separate Eliot completely from Donne. While discussing Donne's "A bracelet of bright hair about his bone" he can only say that the metaphysical quality discerned by Eliot in the line "does not very often occur in 'metaphysical poetry' "; which is to say that it does occur sometimes. Kuna's argument that in a Donne conceit both the elements are concrete, while in an Eliot conceit one element is concrete while the other abstract does not carry conviction. Donne's poetry is not completely devoid of conceits combining concrete and abstract elements and Eliot's poetry, on the other hand, is full of conceits where both the elements are concrete. I am giving below a few examples from Eliot of the metaphysical conceit in Kuna's sense :

The moon has lost her memory.
A washed-out smallpox cracks her face,
Her hand twists a paper rose.
("Rhapsody on a Windy Night")

"Our sentimental friend the moon !
Or possibly (fantastic, I confess)
It may be Prester John's balloon
Or an old battered lantern hung aloft
To light poor travellers to their distress."
("Conversation Galante")

In his essay on "The Metaphysical Poets" Eliot talks of what he calls "characteristically 'metaphysical' " device : "the elaboration (contrasted with the condensation) of a figure of speech to the furthest stage to which ingenuity can carry it."[36] Eliot refers to Cowley's comparison of the world to a chess-board in "To Destiny" and Donne's of two lovers to a pair of compasses. The most emphatic example of such a comparison in Eliot's poetry, to which critics have already drawn attention, occurs in "Prufrock" in the image of fog as a cat :

The yellow fog that rubs it back upon the window-panes
The yellow smoke that rubs its muzzle on the window-panes
Licked its tongue into the corners of the evening,
Lingered upon the pools that stand in drains,
Let fall upon its back the soot that falls from chimneys,
Slipped by the terrace, made a sudden leap,
And seeing that it was a soft October night,
Curled once about the house, and fell asleep.

This is an example of the metaphysical wit expressed through an image. But the unified sensibility may exist without metaphysical thought in the strict sense or, for that matter, without feeling as poetic imagery. When the play of intellect combines with feeling as emotion, we get such a unified sensibility which occurs more frequently in Eliot than in Donne. There are no poetic images, for example, in the following lines from "Prufrock" but the play of intellect combined with feeling is obvious :

And indeed there will be time
To wonder, "Do I dare?" and, "Do I dare?"

Time to turn back and descend the stair,
With a bald spot in the middle of my hair—
They will say : "How his hair is growing thin! "
My morning coat, my collar mounting firmly to the chin,
My necktie rich and modest but asserted by a simple pin—
They will say : "But how his arms and legs are thin!"
Do I dare
Disturb the universe?
In a minute there is time
For decisions and revisions which a minute will reverse.

The amalgamation of disparate experiences that Eliot finds in a poet like Donne is present throughout his early poetry. Comparing the poet's experience with the ordinary man's, Eliot writes : "The latter [the ordinary man] falls in love, or reads Spinoza, and these two experiences have nothing to do with each other, or with the noise of the typewriter or the smell of cooking; in the mind of the poet these experiences are always forming new wholes.[37] The word "love" in this quotation reminds one of Prufrock's love and the amount of reading that combines with it to form new wholes. One needs to point only to Michelangelo and Shakespeare brought into conjunction with Prufrock's love. The unification of disparate experiences that Eliot and Donne have in common presupposes erudition on the part of the poet. One has only to look at the poems in *Poems*, 1920, let alone *The Waste Land*, to have an idea of Eliot's learning. Even poems which appear simple such as "Mr Eliot's Sunday Morning Service" and "A Cooking Egg" are, in fact, loaded with scholarship. The amount of learning that goes into the making of a short poem like "Mr Eliot's Sunday Morning Service" is simply amazing. Several disciplines like theology, biology, and painting have been laid under contribution. The very first word of the poem, which is Eliot's own coinage, is likely to put one off. But the word is highly significant and charged with different shades of meaning. The poem running from "polyphiloprogenitive" to "polymath" gives us not dry learning but the emotional equivalent of it. According to the *Shorter Oxford Dictionary*, the word "philoprogenitive" means "inclined to the production of offspring, prolific." By adding the prefix "poly" with its implication of "many" to "philoprogenitive" Eliot aptly describes "the sapient sutlers of the Lord," particularly

Origen known to have written as many as 6,000 books. And Origen, who was so prolific as a theological scholar, was just the opposite of one "inclined to production of offspring" as he had castrated himself as a bachelor. The two meanings of "philoprogenitive" with the added force of "poly" contrast with each other and bring forth layers of meaning. The addition of the prefix "poly" to "philoprogenitive" is fully justified in view of the exceptional prolificness of Origen. This is only a random instance of emotional experience emanating from learning. Eliot's poetry abounds in such examples of learning becoming experience.

As said above, a metaphysical poet in the strict sense of the term uses for poetic purposes the ideas derived from metaphysicians. Donne uses the neo-Platonic ideas in "The Ecstasy." Is Eliot a metaphysical poet in the strict sense? First, what is metaphysics? And, secondly, is it necessary for a poet to derive his metaphysical ideas from a metaphysician? Metaphysics is usually defined as dealing with the problem of unity in diversity. According to the *New Catholic Encyclopedia* metaphysics is concerned "to investigate the way in which the many are interrelated to the one in some form of real unity." This is the definition that James Smith accepts in his essay on metaphysical poetry which he defines as the verse "to which the impulse is given by an overwhelming concern with metaphysical problems; with problems either deriving from, or closely resembling, in the nature of their difficulty, the problem of the many and the one."[38] Metaphysics thus becomes almost an all-inclusive term and theology, it has been pointed out, is an integral part of it. According to the *Encyclopaedia Britannica*, "theological philosophy in general, or natural theology, has always constituted a large part of what has been derided and championed as 'metaphysics'."[39] The early Eliot is not a metaphysical poet in the sense in which Donne is one in using for poetic purposes ideas set forth by metaphysicians like St Ignatius. But nevertheless Eliot is a metaphysical poet, if only because he uses theological notions in his poems such as "Gerontion," "Mr Eliot's Sunday Morning Service" and *The Waste Land*. The idea of logos, or of Trinitarianism is very much a metaphysical idea suggesting the relationship between the one and the many. Eliot's repetition of

"In the beginning was the Word" in "Mr Eliot's Sunday Morning Service" is highly significant in this context. Gerontion" and *The Waste Land*—and it is as well to recall here that Eliot wished to use the former as a prelude to the latter—abound in metaphysical fragments.

As regards sensuousness being an integral part of the unified sensibility, Eliot does value imagery but not so much as the imagists. Attention has been drawn to Pound's definition of an image as "an intellectual and emotional complex in an instant of time." The combination of intellect and emotion does suggest the unified sensibility but one must be on guard against reading too much into Pounds's definition. (A more important source of Eliot's theory is F.H. Bradley.)[40] Pound was an imagist but Eliot was not, despite his occasional resemblances with the imagists. Sensuousness engendered by imagery was at the very centre of the imagist credo but Eliot does not go as far as the imagists in placing emphasis on sensuousness. Pound's pruning of *The Waste Land* becomes particularly significant in this context. When the facsimile of the original manuscript of *The Waste Land* with Pound's annotations came out, the opinion generally expressed by the reviewers was the ratification of Eliot's own admission that Pound turned *The Waste Land* "from a jumble of good and bad passages into a poem." Bernard Bergonzi, for instance, said that "most of the material that was cut out, whether by Eliot himself or Pound, deserved to go."[41] But in what way is the published poem different from the manuscript? Writing nearly a decade before the manuscript was discovered, Hugh Kenner wrote that Pound eliminated "everything not of the first intensity." And the view was confirmed by Donald Gallup in his account of the outcome of Pound's pruning in a piece written after the discovery but before the publication of the manuscript. Gallup examines the correspondence between Eliot and Pound relating to *The Waste Land*. He explains the difference between Eliot's and Pound's critical attitudes. Eliot's concept of a long poem—and *The Waste Land* is certainly one—was different from Pound's. Gallup quotes Eliot's pronouncement in "The Music of Poetry" on the balance of greater and lesser intensity in a long poem. "The Music of Poetry" was published in 1942, but the argument advanced by

Eliot in this essay has been expressed by him in several other pieces both before and after the publication of *The Waste Land*.[42] Gallup compares Eliot's view with Pound's expressed in a letter to Harriet Monroe :

> The test of a writer is his ability for . . . concentration AND for his power to stay concentrated till he gets to the end of his poem; whether it is two lines or two hundred.[43]

This is obviously an imagist doctrine that does not allow for any relaxation in the poem. And Pound's pronouncement is almost similar to Poe's which Eliot sums up in his essay on Poe and with which he expresses his disagreement.

> A long poem may gain by the widest possible variations of intensity. But Poe wanted a poem to be of the first intensity throughout : it is questionable whether he could have appreciated the more philosophical passages in Dante's *Purgatorio*.[44]

Eliot wrote *The Waste Land* with his own concept of a long poem at the back of his mind, and Pound pruned it in the light of his own views. Eliot said in his interview for *Paris Review* that "he [Pound] was a marvellous critic because he didn't try to turn you into an imitation of himself. He tried to see what you were trying to do."[45] But, as Gallup has pointed out, Pound's "Caesarean operation" did change the structure of the poem. "At least part of what the central poem gained," writes Gallup "in concentration, intensity, and general effectiveness through Pound's editing was at the sacrifice of some of its experimental character."[46] If we closely examine *The Waste Land* as published in 1922, we shall find that there are two long passages which are not consonant with the general structure of the poem. The passages I have in mind are both narratives, one each dealing with the typist girl-carbuncular young man affair and the cockney women. If those two passages are left out, the poem will read precisely like an imagist poem with the same intensity throughout. What I am suggesting is that sensuousness or what Hulme calls the handing over of sensations bodily[47] is not the sole characteristic of the unified sensibility. The critics who equate the unified sensibility with sensuousness or concreteness are wrong : in theory as well as in practice Eliot does not show any such equation. If the three narratives, one each in "The Burial of the Dead" (dealing with the night life of London). "The Fire Sermon" (describing a fashionable lady in imitation of Pope) and "Death by Water" (dealing with the voyage and shipwreck echoing Dante's and Tennyson's Ulysses) had been retained, they, along with the two passages mentioned above, would have made the less intense part of the poem more conspicuous and set it in opposition to the more intense one. The less intense part of the poem is radically different from imagist poetry. When critics talk of sensuousness as basic to the unified sensibility, they mean primarily visual effect, though they do not admit it openly. The passages of less intensity contradict these critics' arguments. I hasten to add that sensuousness, particularly visual, is a very important aspect of Eliot's poetry but it cannot be identified with the unified sensibility.

CHAPTER SIX

Dissociation of Sensibility (II)

Eliot's conversion to Christianity in 1927 brought about a change in his attitude to literature in general as well as to individual writers. After his conversion he began to look upon the writers of the past as well as his contemporaries as a neo-scholastic. Eliot's firm grounding in the Elizabethan and Jacobean literature is too well-known to call for further emphasis. Eliot exalted this literature, particularly for embodying the unified sensibility which, he said, disappeared sometime in the seventeenth century. An intriguing question that Eliot's conversion raises is whether he can still hold the literature of the English Renaissance in the same estimation in which he held it earlier. The immediate answer will be that it depends on how he looks upon the Renaissance itself. The Renaissance on the continent as well as in England has been interpreted variously. What will concern us here is the interpretation of the Renaissance that Eliot himself accepts or, in other words, the way he interprets it. Douglas Bush has discussed at some length the different approaches to the Renaissance. Of the two main approaches he writes : "One view extends the Renaissance backward to include the Middle Ages, the other extends the Middle Ages forward to include the Renaissance."[1] Bush himself is inclined towards the latter view. Both the views, as Bush points out, have one important point in common, i.e., they do not look upon the Renaissance as marking a complete break with the Middle Ages. The earlier view that there was a complete break between the Middle Ages and the Renaissance has been found untenable. It has been pointed out that the earlier view was founded upon the erroneous notion of the Middle Ages as dark and uncivilized, the notion first expressed by the Renaissance humanists themselves who had pitted themselves against medievalism.

Coming to Eliot we find that in his later phase he has expressed an ambivalent attitude towards the Renaissance. One can well envisage the dilemma in which Eliot finds himself, though at the same time one can see the way out of it which he ignores. The later Eliot acquiesces in the interpretation of the Renaissance as advanced by men like Babbitt and Hulme who reckon the Renaissance the source of modern secularization, in other words, hold that there was complete break between medievalism and the Renaissance. Babbitt divides humanism into two categories, namely utilitarian as represented by Bacon, and emotional as represented by Rousseau, and sets himself in opposition to both. The humanism as it has come down to us from the Renaissance, he wants to be replaced by what he calls critical humanism with its emphasis on the inner check. Hulme launches a severe attack on English humanism stemming from the Renaissance in his essay on "Humanism and the Religious Attitude." He finds an absolute difference between the Middle Ages and the Renaissance and makes a watertight division between the two historical periods, the first from St Augustine to the Renaissance and the second from the Renaissance to his own time. The former, Hulme says, is religious, while the latter is humanistic. And "it is necessary to realize," writes Hulme "that there is an absolute, and not a relative, difference between humanism . . . and the religious spirit."[2] Hulme does not tire of disparaging the Renaissance and all that emanated from it and exalting the Middle Ages.

Although both Babbitt and Hulme decry the Renaissance, they have significant points of difference. In the first place, Babbitt separates the classical literature from that produced by the English humanists, while Hulme lumps them together. Babbitt and Hulme are at one in their attack on the Renaissance, but whereas Babbitt evolves a new humanism out of the assemblage of ideas and literatures, classical and oriental, Hulme dislikes any attempt at a fresh formulation of humanism. Hulme wrote almost at the time when Babbitt was most enthusiastic about his humanism that "all attempts to 'explain' religion on a humanist basis, whether it be Christian or an alien religion like Buddhism, must always be futile."[3] Babbitt was doing precisely what Hulme considered futile. He took a keen interest in Buddhism and rated the Buddha very high as a thinker. He was not opposed to Christianity but could accept it only so far as it could be assimilated to his critical humanism. That he discovered in Buddhism the source of his humanism is evident from his observation that "a man may safely go into himself if what he finds there is not, like Rousseau, his own emotion, but like the Buddha, the law of righteousness."[4] Babbitt in his turn deemed futile what Hulme was doing. His attack on dogma and outer authority on which Hulme set so much value is clear from the following statement :

> A civilization that rests on dogmas and outer authority cannot afford to face the whole truth about the imagination and its role. A civilization in which dogma and outer authority have been undermined by the critical spirit, not only can but must do this very thing if it is to continue at all.[5]

Eliot sides with both Babbitt and Hulme as far as diagnosis is concerned but sides with the latter and denounces the former when it comes to prescription. He quotes Hulme with approval in his second essay on Baudelaire and "Second Thoughts about Humanism" and takes issue with Babbitt in "The Humanism of Irving Babbitt" and "Second Thoughts about Humanism."

Eliot's view of the Renaissance as a revolt against the Middle Ages and starting the process of secularization is evidenced by his attacks on the Renaissance at several places in his writings. His attacks are at times so subtle that they are likely to be overlooked at first glance. I shall dwell upon the explicit attacks before passing on to the implicit ones.

> In the Elizabethans, the Roman Stoicism is visible beneath *the Renaissance anarchism*.[6] (italics mine)

> You can hardly say that Shakespeare believed, or did not believe, *the mixed and muddled skepticism* of the Renaissance.[7] (italics mine)

> Thomas Hobbes was one of those extraordinary little upstarts whom *the chaotic motions of the Renaissance* tossed

> into an eminence which they hardly deserved and have never lost.[8] (italics mine)

The italicized portions leave us in no doubt as to the esteem in which Eliot holds the Renaissance. That he is in line with Hulme and sharply opposed to humanists like Babbitt and Foerster is obvious from his "Second Thoughts about Humanism." Commenting on Hulme versus the humanists he writes :

> I agree with what Hulme says : and I am afraid that many modern Humanists are explicitly or implicitly committed to the view which Hulme denounces; and that they are, in consequence, men of the Renaissance rather than men of our own time. . . . It is to the immense credit of Hulme that he found out for himself that there is an *absolute* to which men can *never* attain.[9]

Eliot buttresses his argument by bringing in a quotation from Hulme's "Humanism and the Religious Attitude" which begins with the remark that "I hold the religious conception of ultimate values to be right, the humanist wrong."[10] Hulme was a neo-scholastic and Eliot, after his conversion to Christianity, could be fully in accord with him.

Eliot's attacks on the Renaissance are at times indirect and as such likely to escape our attention. I shall mention in this connection the attacks on the Renaissance implied in "Shakespeare and the Stoicism of Seneca" and "Machiavelli" (an essay published in *For Lancelot Andrewes* but not reprinted in *Selected Essays*). Eliot holds that both Seneca and Machiavelli were distorted by the Elizabethans so much so indeed that they resembled the image of Nietzsche. Of the Shakespearean tragedies he says :

> There is, in some of the great tragedies of Shakespeare, a new attitude. It is not the attitude of Seneca, but is derived from Seneca; it is slightly different from anything that can be found in French tragedy, in Corneille or in Racine; it is modern, and it culminates, if there is ever any culmination, in the attitude of Neitzsche.[11]

And in his essay on Machiavelli he writes :

> There is a form of self-satisfaction and self-deception, which merely propogates the Jew of Malta—Neitzsche

> myth of Machiavelli. In Elizabethan England the reputation of Machiavelli was merely manipulated unconsciously to feed the perpetually recurring tendency to Manichaean heresy; the desire for a devil to worship.[12]

I am not concerned here with what in actual fact were the attitudes of Seneca and Machiavelli, and whether or not Eliot got them right. My sole concern here is with what Eliot thinks of the Elizabethans. For Eliot the Elizabethan attitude is the Neitzschean attitude. And of Neitzsche Bertrand Russell writes that to him "Christianity is the most fatal and seductive lie that ever existed."[13] That is to say, the Elizabethan attitude is the opposite of the Christian attitude, which is further ratified by Eliot's remark in "Seneca in Elizabethan Translation" that "Christian piety and pity . . . disappears with Elizabethan verse."[14]

Eliot's attacks on the Renaissance and the literature that it produced put him in a dilemma. The early Eliot had set much value on the Elizabethan literature, the decline of which resulted in the dissociation of sensibility. If Eliot had looked upon the Renaissance, like Douglas Bush, as primarily an extension of the Middle Ages, he would have placed himself safely outside the dilemma. It is generally agreed that a radical change in attitude, literary as well as philosophical, took place in the seventeenth century after the decline of the Elizabethan literature, which includes in it metaphysical poetry.[15] And this was precisely the view that the early Eliot expressed when he wrote: "In the seventeenth century a dissociation of sensibility set in, from which we have never recovered."[16] The dilemma of Eliot is due to his looking upon the Renaissance with Babbitt and Hulme.

The ambivalence in Eliot's attitude towards the Renaissance becomes apparent, when he comes to discuss the metaphysical poets. The early Eliot had grouped the metaphysical poets of the Jacobean period with the Elizabethans. The later Eliot could possibly detract from the Elizabethans but could not retract his evaluation of metaphysical poetry, which was for the most part Christian. Consequently, in his discussion of the metaphysical poets the later Eliot takes a stance different from the one he takes while discussing the

Elizabethans. Summing up the "Clark Lectures" (1926) devoted to the metaphysical poets Eliot writes :

> What I have tried to do is to maintain literary values in the centre of the picture, to consider different periods of poetry by poetic values, and merely to indicate the extra-literary causes of the differences in literary value. In doing so, I have indicated a theory of what I call the "disintegration of the intellect." So far as I am concerned, this disintegration means merely a progressive deterioration of poetry, in one respect or another, since the XIIIth century.[17]

Of the prerequisites of metaphysical poetry he says :

> Metaphysical poetry involves the existence of a background of thought, of a definite system or fragments of definite systems. Behind Dante there was Aquinas, behind Donne the fragments of every philosophical system and every theological system up to his own time; and although the whole was chaos, the fragments were still sharp and identifiable.[18]

It is obvious from these extracts that the "disintegration of the intellect," i.e., the disassociation of sensibility set in just after the monumental achievements of the thirteenth century. And as the "disintegration of the intellect" tantamounts to the degeneration of poetry, the metaphysical poetry of the seventeenth century is inferior to that of Dante, for example. Nevertheless, the theological background which is a prerequisite of metaphysical poetry was there, though not so coherent as in the thirteenth century, for the metaphysical poets to make use of. This is the point that Eliot repeats in his talk on metaphysical poetry in 1930. Of the religious sensibility of the seventeenth century he says :

> In its religious sensibility the seventeenth century seems to me the third most interesting period in the history of Christianity; the others being the early period which saw the development of dogma in the Greek and Latin churches and the thirteenth century.[19]

If we accept Eliot's interpretation, then it is difficult to account for his attitude towards the Elizabethans. As the Elizabethans preceded the metaphysicals, judged by Eliot's continual "disintegration of the intellect" they were furnished with a better theological background than the latter. If Eliot had looked upon the metaphysicals as revolting against the Elizabethans, a view not unusual now,[20] he would have found a way out of his dilemma, though not without contradicting his earlier stance.

Frank Kermode who has examined Eliot's dilemma, though without going into its full complexity, expresses his belief in the untenability of the recurrence of the dissociated sensibility.[21] But in the passage quoted above Eliot himself points out the recurrence in three different periods of the religious sensibility which goes into the making of metaphysical poetry. In his "Clarks Lectures" he discusses at length the appearance of metaphysical poetry in the thirteenth (Dante, Guido Cavalcanti, etc.), seventeenth (the metaphysicals) and nineteenth (the French symbolists) centuries. As we have noticed, Eliot's dilemma is not due to the difficulty of the recurrence of the dissociated or unified sensibility but to his earlier stance.

If Eliot's conversion to Anglo-Catholicism caused an ambivalence in his attitude towards the writers of the English Renaissance, it was also responsible for his progressive devaluation of Donne and exaltation of Herbert. The early Eliot admired Donne and the poet who came next to Donne in the assessment was Andrew Marvell. It is surprising that in the two essays in *Selected Essays* by which Eliot on metaphysical poetry is best known—"The Metaphysical Poets" and "Andrew Marvell"—there is not a single quotation from Herbert and in the essay on Marvell, Herbert is not even mentioned. The first relatively detailed account of Herbert came as late as 1930. If Eliot's first writing on metaphysical poetry was on Donne, the last was on George Herbert.

If we compare Eliot's writings on Donne with those on Herbert, we shall find that his depreciation of the former goes side by side with his exaltation of the latter. The first piece on Donne by the later Eliot plays down the importance of Donne though in a subtle way. He makes a point which he repeats much more forcefully in "Donne in Our Time." He says that "those who take Donne as a contemporary will be taking him as a fashion only."[22] Eliot dismisses this view of Donne and points to the metaphysical quality of his poetry which places him above the nineteenth century poets. But does not Eliot himself look upon Donne as a contemporary? The view he dismisses here he himself has half a mind to accept in "Donne in Our Time" where he writes : "That there was an element of fashion in our enjoyment and exploitation of Donne it would be vain to deny it ; but there was nothing capricious about the fashion."[23] When I say "half a mind" I mean that Eliot does not reckon the Donne revival in the present century a matter of fashion *only*, though he does find an element of fashion in the revival. In "Donne in Our Time" Eliot almost veers to the other extreme in his assessment of Donne when he observes that "in Donne, there is a manifest fissure between thought and sensibility;" that is to say, Donne suffers from the dissociation of sensibility.

If Donne comes down in Eliot's assessment Herbert goes up. Comparing Herbert and Donne as religious poets he said in his lecture at Salisbury Cathedral (1938) that "religious poetry was more incidental for Donne, and more essential for Herbert" and that "with Donne I feel that there is always something of the particular and private sinner which remains, as a kind of sediment, even in his most religious verse." The later Eliot is aware of the difference between Donne and other metaphysical poets, and hence his attempt to separate them.

> We must . . . dissociate Donne from the "school of Donne"; so far as these followers enjoy any particular vogue in our time, it is a popularity reflected from that of Donne or partly one arising from a new interest in devotional verse.[24]

This dissociation of Donne from other metaphysical poets, particularly George Herbert, has far-reaching implications. Eliot does not seem to be sure of Donnc's religious piety, though he tries to give the contrary impression. In his BBC talk on Donne he said : "I believe that his [Donne's] religion was quite sincere"[25] and in "Donne in Our Time" he wrote : "it was . . . possible for Donne to be, and I am sure that he was, genuinely *devout*."[26] But Eliot does not mean what he says and suspects, though tacitly, that Donne's religion is the religion of a man who only wants to feel what religion is like. In the same essay in which he considers Donne "genuinely devout" he intimates that "the kind of religious faith expressed in Donne's religious writings is wholly consistent with the employment in his poetry of many scraps of various philosophies that appear there."[27] Eliot says time and again that Donne, unlike Dante or any other medieval poet, was interested in what it feels like to cherish philosophic ideas rather than their truth or falsity. Similarly, Donne is interested more in the idea of religion than in religion as such. That this is Eliot's view is testified by his comment on the development of Donne. He does not agree with those who divide Donne's life into two periods, "one dissolute and irreligious, the other a revulsion to intense and austere piety" and holds that "it is one and the same man in both early and later life."[28] Eliot takes issue with those who exaggerate the erotic, or, for that matter, mystical element in Donne's poetry. It is this exaggeration which is responsible for the view that there was a complete division in Donne's life. What Eliot is driving at is that the erotic element in the early Donne is not of necessity his personal experience, just as his later penitence is not always genuinely felt. He admits that he cannot "take very seriously Donne's later remorse or repentance."

The devaluation of Donne and his separation from poets like Herbert became necessary for the later Eliot just as the exaltation of Donne and his association with other metaphysical poets was necessary for the early Eliot. The early Eliot's association of Donne with the other metaphysicals emphasised the metaphysical technique which he valued so much, while the later Eliot's dissociation of Donne from the other metaphysicals stressed his Christian point of view. Not being sure of Donne's religious piety he thought he had better separate him from other metaphysicals whose religion could not be called in question. Eliot speaks of the "school of Herbert" including in it Vaughan and Crashaw. Differentiating Donne from Herbert he writes :

> The difference that I wish to emphasize is not that between the violence of Donne and the gentle imagery of Herbert, but rather a difference between the dominance of intellect over sensibility and the dominance of sensibility over intellect. Both men were highly intellectual, both men had very keen sensibility ; but in Donne thought

seems in control of feeling, and in Herbert feeling seems in control of thought.[29]

Donne's poetry betrays the dominance of intellect, while Herbert's shows the dominance of feeling, though both are intellectual poets as against the reflective poets such as Tennyson and Browning. But the later Eliot is the more sympathetic towards poetry with the dominance of feeling over intellect. Herbert's feeling is genuinely felt and as such has greater appeal than Donne's to the religious poets including Eliot.

II

The later Eliot emphasizes the metaphysical thought which for him is the Christian thought rather than the metaphysical conceit. At several places in his later criticism he distinguishes between a conceit such as found in metaphysical poetry and a metaphor or simile employed by poets like Dante and Shakespeare. In his early writings he finds "a direct sensuous apprehension of thought" in the metaphysicals as well as in Dante and Shakespeare. "The poets of the seventeenth century," he wrote in his celebrated piece on "The Metaphysical Poets," "the successors of the dramatists of the sixteenth, possessed a mechanism of sensibility which could devour any kind of experience. They are simple, artificial, difficult, or fantastic, as their predecessors were; no less nor more than Dante, Guido Cavalcanti, Guinicelli, or Cino."[30] Thus the four qualities enumerated—simplicity, artificiality, difficulty, and fantasticality—the metaphysicals have in common with poets like Dante and Cavalcanti. But only two years later, reviewing Marvell's *Miscellaneous Poems*, he distinguished sharply between conceits of a poet like Marvell and the imagery of Dante and Shakespeare. After his remark that Marvell is highly conceited he advances his definition of a conceit. "In a conceit," he says "two things very different are brought together, and the spark of ecstasy generated in us is a perception of power in bringing them together."[31] And he illustrates this definition from Marvell's "Might a Soul bath there and be clean/Or slake its Drought ?" Eliot points to "the suddenness of the transference from material to spiritual water" in Marvell's lines. He contrasts Marvell's conceit with the imagery employed in Shakespeare's "She looks like sleep/ As she would catch another Antony/ In her strong toil of grace." In Shakespeare's lines, he says, there is a fusion instead of a contrast : "a restoration of language to contact with things."[32] Eliot leaves us in no doubt as to which of the two he prefers. He discerns in Dante precisely what he finds in Shakespeare. After adducing lines from Dante he comments : "these are not conceits. They have a rational necessity as well as suggestiveness ; they are, like the words of Shakespeare above, an *explication* of the meaning."[33]

In his "Clark Lectures" (1926) Eliot discusses at length the distinction between the imagery of poets like Dante and Cavalcanti and the conceits in the metaphysicals. He makes it abundantly clear that in Dante the interest of the reader centers on what is being communicated, and the images are employed only as a means of communication. In the metaphysical poets, on the other hand, the interest lies in the ingenuity displayed in the employment of conceits. Of the difference between an image and a conceit he writes "A conceit is the extreme limit of the simile and metaphor which is used for its own sake, and not to make clear an idea or more definite an emotion."[34] In his talk on the poets of the seventeenth century he again touches on the difference between the two types of of images. Of the conceit he says that it "is used for its own sake and for the intellectual pleasure of far-fetched comparisons."[35]

The point to note in the above shift from the metaphysical conceit used for its own sake to the imagery employed for the sake of meaning is not so much the shift of emphasis from one technique to another as the general drift towards what is communicated. The imagery employed by Dante and Shakespeare is only a means subjugated to what they want to formulate. Thus the "what" takes precedence over the "how."

The emphasis laid upon what is communicated is in conformity with the nature of Eliot's later poetry. It is the experience to be bodied forth which is of prime significance for the later Eliot. And the experience is invariably Christian. In "Shakespeare and the Stoicism of Seneca" he writes : "The poet who 'thinks' is merely the poet who can express the emotional equivalent of thought. But he is not necessarily interested in the thought itself."[36] The thought that the later Eliot idealizes is the Christian thought, and hence his regret over "the divorce of philosophy from theology."[37] Though he says that the poet's interest in thought is not necessary, what he really implies is that the greatness of a poet depends on how far he is able to identify his personal experience with the thought. It is this that explains the superiority for Eliot of Dante over Shakespeare and Donne. What places Dante at such a high pedestal in Eliot's assessment is the exquisite craftsmanship combined with almost one-to-one correspondence between Dante's own experience and St. Thomas's philosophy.

When one examines Eliot's poetry in the light of what he says about Dante, one naturally looks for a philosophical system to which it corresponds. What was the philosophic thought to which the later Eliot was giving poetic expression ? Eliot has emphasized the philosophic thought, particularly in his discussion of metaphysical poetry including in it both Dante and Donne. Eliot has distinguished at several places in his later criticism between the thought in Dante's poetry and that in Donne's. I am speaking here not of the way thought is treated but the quality of thought. Eliot refutes the argument that Donne's was a medieval mind. In his BBC talk on Donne, Eliot said : "Nor is there any evidence for saying that Donne had a 'medieval mind' ; or that his merit is to have expressed a dualism of medieval and modern in his work."[38] In "Donne in Our Time" he takes exception to Miss Ramsay's thesis that Donne's mind was medieval, and goes on to say that "his mind was decidedly the mind of a man of his own time : but it was legal and controversial rather than philosophical and theological."[39]

There are two main points that distinguish the medieval mind from the mind of Donne ; first, the belief in the philosophical ideas poeticized and, secondly, the dualism of body and soul. The medieval mind *believes* in the truth of philosophy pressed into the service of poetry, while Donne simply plays with philosophic ideas for their own sake. The latter's "delight in ideas as ideas, in theories as theories is anything but medieval."[40] And, again, "to be interested in philosophies for their own sake, apart from their degree of truth, is not a medieval attitude."[41]

The separation of body and soul, like the use of philosophic ideas for their own sake, is a modern and not a medieval concept. The only difference in the medieval period is "between higher and lower, more and less worthy loves. . . . There is no imagined struggle of soul and body, only one struggle toward perfection."[42] In Donne, on the other hand, the dichotomy of body and soul exists ; and in a crude form at that.

In his discussions Eliot gives the impression that he is for the medieval concept in which there is no separation of body and soul. His exaltation of the medieval concept over the seventeenth-century one is a pointer to it. But when we approach Eliot's poetry without any preconceived notions, we discern that it resembles metaphysical poetry rather than *The Divine Comedy*. Among the metaphysicals, the poet to whom the later Eliot comes closest is Herbert, not Donne.

It is significant to note here that in his later essays Eliot repeatedly compares Herbert's religious piety with that of St John of the Cross upon whom he looks almost as an ideal by which to judge the religious experience of others. Comparing Dante with St John of the Cross he said in his review of Edmund Blunden's essay on Vaughan : "A genuine mystical *statement* is to be found in the last canto of the *Paradiso* ; this is primarily great poetry. An equally genuine mysticism is expressed in the verses of St John of the Cross : this is not a statement, but a riddling expression ; it belongs to great mysticism, but not to great poetry."[43] (We shall revert to the difference between the two later.) In his BBC talk on the seventeenth-century poetry he discusses at some length the Spanish mystics and saints. "The greatest", writes Eliot "were St Theresa and St John of the Cross, both Carmelites. I think that St John was the greater, or rather that his writings are very much more important than St Theresa's ; but probably Theresa had the greater influence."[44] In another BBC talk he deemed "St John of the Cross perhaps the greatest of all European mystics."[45] In an article published in 1932 Eliot bracketed Herbert with St John of the Cross. Lecturing to Friends of Salisbury Cathedral he again compared Herbert with St John of the Cross. "Indeed the only poetry that I can think of," said he "which belongs to quite the same class as Herbert—as expression of purity and intensity of religious feeling, and, as I am told by those who can appreciate Spanish literature more accurately than I, for literary excellence—is St John of the Cross."[46] There is, however, a difference between the two comparisons between Herbert and St John of the Cross. In the first he restricts his comparison to religious piety, while in the second he includes in it the "literary excellence" as well.

I have said that Eliot's later poetry is nearer to Herbert than to Donne. But where does Dante stand then? In a quotation above, Dante is recognized as a mystic, and the difference between him and St John of the Cross has been pointed out. The comparison between Dante and St John of the Cross is of the same nature as that between the latter and Pascal; in other words, there is no wholesale indentification between the two as between Herbert and St John of the Cross. There are points of similarity as well as dissimilarity. Of Pascal he writes:

> His [Pascal's] despair, his disillusion, are, however, no illustration of personal weakness; they are perfectly objective, because they are essential moments in the progress of the intellectual soul, and for the type of Pascal they are the analogue of the drought, *the dark night*, which is an essential stage in the progress of the Christian mystic.[47] (italics mine)

"The dark night" is evidently a reference to St John of the Cross. But at another place Eliot differentiates Pascal from St John of the Cross, saying that the latter is "primarily for readers with a special determination of purpose", while the former can be recommended "to those who doubt."[48]

The essay on Pascal provides me with the cue to the distinction between Dante and St John of the Cross. Of the three orders analysed by Pascal—of nature, of mind, and of charity—Eliot says that they are *discontinuous* in the sense that "the higher is not implicit in the lower as in an evolutionary doctrine it would be."[49] And the footnote to this remark refers us to T.E. Hulme's *Speculations* "for an important modern theory of discontinuity, suggested partly by Pascal."[50] That is to say, Pascal and Hulme can be grouped together. And Dante derived from St Thomas Aquinas precisely what Eliot finds the absence of in Pascal. St Thomas is known for combining the contraries and there is no conflict as such between the "natural" and the "supernatural" As the *Encylopaedia Britannica* says, "he is a man for the 'both' not the 'either or,' who sees a continuity between life and thought, mind and sense, faith and reason, law and freedom." The continuity between the natural and the supernatural orders in Aquinas is given a poetic form by Dante in *The Divine Comedy.* Dante enters the supernatural world without shedding off his worldly existence, and the Beatrice he meets in paradise is the same Beatrice as he met on earth. Eliot finds mysticism, and rightly, in the last canto of *Paradiso* but the process which leads Dante to the beatific vision goes back to his earthly existence. Mysticism at the end of the *Comedy* should not delude one into thinking that it is central to the massive structure of the poem. What Russell says of Aquinas holds as well for Dante. "There are three ways of knowing God," writes Russell "by reason, by revelation, and by intuition of things previously known only by revelation. Of the third way, however, he says almost nothing. A writer inclined to mysticism would have said more of it than of either of the others, but Aquinas's temperament is ratiocinative rather than mystical."[51] And so is Dante's temperament.

Dante and St John of the Cross have basic differences despite the similarity brought out by Eliot. The earthly existence which Dante and Beatrice retain even in paradise, the mystic is stripped of at the very first stage of his journey to the communion with God. In *The Ascent of Mount Carmel* St John of the Cross intimates that "there are three reasons for which this journey made by the soul to communion with God is called night. The first has to do with the point from which the soul goes forth, for *it has gradually to deprive itself of desire for all the worldly things which it possessed, by denying them to itself*; the which denial and deprivation are, as it were, night to all the senses of man."[52] (italics mine) And at the very outset of *The Dark Night of the Soul* which deals with the Passive Night as *The Ascent* deals with the Active Night, St John of the Cross points out how the soul enters the dark night of sense by dying to all worldly things. Eliot often refers to the verses of St John of the Cross, particularly when comparing him with a creative writer. The following lines from St John of the Cross depict the state in which the mystic's soul awaits the communion with God :

> I live without inhabiting
> Myself—in such a wise that I
> Am dying that I do not die.

The "death" is the state of negation—sensual as well as spiritual. The quotation from St John of the Cross in the epigraph to *Sweeney Agonistes* gives us the very essence of St John of the Cross. "Hence the soul cannot be possessed of the divine union, until it has divested itself of the love of created beings." The dichotomy of "the love of created beings" and the divine love is well brought out by this quotation. And it is this dichotomy that separates St John of the Cross from Dante.[53]

The dichotomy of body and soul that one finds in the metaphysicals and St John of the Cross is at the very centre of Eliot's poetry. We can make a twofold division of Eliot's later poetry, one comprising such poems as "Journey of the Magi," "Animula" and "Ash Wednesday," and the other consisting of the *Four Quartets*. While the former shows the conflict between body and soul and the attempt at shedding off bodily associations, the latter depicts the soul's communion with God. The conflict between two lives, one worldly and the other Divine, that informs the poems of the first division puts Eliot in line with the metaphysicals, particularly Herbert. Donne's religious piety is suspect, and the dichotomy of the two worlds in a poem like "Good Friday, 1613 ; Riding Westward" is a statement of dichotomy going well with Donne's dialectical reasoning rather than the actual conflict experienced by the poet. Herbert's conflict, on the other hand, between the attraction of the material world and that of the Divine life is genuinely felt by him. One has only to look at poems like "Affliction" and "The Collar" to realize the genuineness of his religious experience and the conflict engendered by it. There are striking parallels between these poems and Eliot's "Ash Wednesday." The dichotomy of the two worlds that Eliot discovers in the seventeenth century is expressed in the following lines of Herbert :

Whereas my birth and spirit rather took
The way that takes the town;
Thou didst betray me to a lingring book,
And wrap me in a gown.
I was entangled in the world of strife,
Before I had the power to change my life.
("Affliction")

"The world of strife" is the strife between two worlds—one the material world in town and the other the world of God. Eliot's Ariel poems such as "Journey of the Magi" and "Animula" also describe a similar conflict. The three wise men from the East coming to glimpse the infant Christ—a step towards the Divine life—regret at times "The Summer palaces on slopes, the terraces, and the silken girls, bringing sherbet." The Magi are simply caught up between two worlds and cannot decide whether they were led all the way for Birth or Death. They know it to be sure that there was a Birth, the birth of Christ, but the "bitter agony" that it caused them makes them feel that it was also Death, their death. Being unable to stand the agony of Death they return to their kingdoms, though on return they feel that they are not at ease here either. They fail to realize that Death which was so painful to them is the prerequisite of birth, the spiritual rebirth. Animula, like the Magi, is described between two worlds, one from which she has come and the other into which she is born. Animula who "issues from the hand of God, the simple soul" later "issues from the hand of time the simple soul." She, like the Magi, is "unable to fare forward or retreat."

"Ash Wednesday" the first major poem of the later Eliot, is informed throughout by the dichotomy of body and soul. The very opening section of the poem points in two opposite directions, one from which the protagonist has departed and the other for which he is making. The world to which he does not hope to turn again is the material world, of "this man's gift and that man's scope ;" the world "where trees flower and springs flow."

Before elaborating on the dichotomy of body and soul in "Ash Wednesday" I should like to forestall a possible objection. It has been pointed out that the Lady described in the second section of the poem is the equivalent of Dante's Beatrice.[54] And if we stretch the analogy to its logical conclusion, the Lady, like Dante's Beatrice, reconciles the earthly existence with the divine vision. There is no doubt that the Lady in the poem is meant to be Beatrice and the critics have not failed to notice the analogy. But before one accepts the analogy, one must question whether Eliot's Lady plays the same role as Dante's Beatrice. Beatrice moves from her earthly existence as a Florentine girl to the Virgin type in heaven. Anybody reading Dante's *Purgatorio*, particularly canto XXX, is deeply impressed by the height of imagination and the exquisite craftsmanship that go into the description of Beatrice combining in her heaven and earth. Dante sees Beatrice in a white veil and instantly begins to feel "The old, old love in all its mastering might." He turns to Virgil to say,

> There is scarce a dream
> That does not hammer and throb in all my blood,
> I know the embers of the ancient flame.

But Virgil had already left. "The old love" and "the ancient flame" communicate effectively the love that Dante felt for the Florentine girl, the love that he describes in *La Vita Nuova*. And it is this Beatrice that rises up to the Virgin figure. Eliot's attempt to portray the counterpart of Beatrice is a failure for the simple reason that he places his emphasis, wittingly or unwittingly, almost exclusively on the Divine side of Beatrice with the result that it is difficult to distinguish this Lady from the Virgin Mary whom she "honours in meditation." The supplication to the Lady in the paradoxical language applies to her only so far as she is the type of the Virgin. Nevertheless Eliot intends to suggest the worldly side of the Lady as is obvious from the fourth section of the poem.

> Going in white and blue, in Mary's colour,
> Talking of trivial things
> In ignorance and in knowledge of eternal dolour.

On the one hand, the Lady is going in Mary's colour while, on the other, she is "talking of trivial things." As a human being she is ignorant of the "eternal dolour", whereas, as the Virgin she is congnizant of it. But the worldly side of the Lady is very indistinct and insignificant in the poem. For all her resemblances with the Virgin, Dante's Beatrice cannot be replaced by the latter. But the same is not true of Eliot's Lady. At times one wonders why Eliot has separated the Lady from the Virgin. And the only explanation one can find is in his trying to imitate Dante. (That in his later poetry Eliot makes conscious efforts at imitating Dante is witnessed by the "compound ghost" in "Little Gidding.") If the purpose of the separation is to point to the two worlds—one earthly and the other Divine, one that the protagonist discards and the other that he accepts—then the purpose is defeated, since Dante's Beatrice cannot be employed for this purpose.

The predominant note of "Ash Wednesday" reflects St John of the Cross rather than Dante. The very title of the poem is a pointer to St John of the Cross. Ash Wednesday is the first day of Lent when Christians repent for their past sins and seek God's assistance to turn away from the world and towards Him. This is the significance of the word "turn" in the very first stanza of the poem. Critics have found paradoxical the word "turn", saying that it implies at once "the hopelessness of the return to joys of sense and the hopelessness of the return to God."[55] This explanation is due to critics' presupposition that in this poem Eliot, like Dante in *The Divine Comedy*, is attempting to combine the two worlds. It is surprising that even Leonard Unger, who centres his exegesis of "Ash Wednesday" on its relation to St John of the Cross's mystical works, particularly *The Dark Night of the Soul*, overlooks the significance of the word "again" in the very first line of the poem. From the use of Guido Cavalcanti's "In Exile at Sarzana" in the poem he elicits the conclusion that "the ideas of devotion to a woman and the religious experience of approaching union with God are held by Eliot in a single conceptual pattern."[56] But, in fact, there is no woman whom the protagonist of "Ash Wednesday" inclines to associate himself with. The word "again" suggests that the world to which he does not hope to turn is the one he has been to before, the world which is suggested by the reference to Guido Cavalcanti's lady. For all the devotion on the part of the protagonist to the lady described in Guido's poem the lady remains the lady of the world and does not rise to the type of the heavenly Beatrice. It is this world represented by Guido Cavalcanti's lady to which the protagonist of "Ash Wednesday" does not hope to turn again. In point of fact, it is this world that holds the protagonist back on his journey to the union with God, as one finds in the third section of the poem. The different stairs that the protagonist climbs are the different stages of his journey. At the first turning of the second stair the protagonist looks back only to see his earlier shape "struggling with the devil." And at the first turning of the third stair he views through the "slotted window" "the hawthorn blossom and a pasture scene." These sensuous descriptions point to the distractions and struggles felt by the protagonist. The "slotted window" and "antique flute" have obvious sexual overtones. The physical associations constitute only a distraction for the protagonist. Even in the last section of the poem the protagonist feels divided between two worlds. Although he does not hope to turn again yet,

> the *lost* heart stiffens and rejoices
> In the *lost* lilac and the *lost* sea voices
> And the *weak* spirit quickens to *rebel*
> For the bent golden-rod and the lost sea smell
> Quickens to *recover*
> The cry of quail and the whirling plover
> And the blind eye creates
> The empty forms between the ivory gates
> And smell *renews* the salt savour of the sandy earth
> (Leonard Unger's italics)

As Unger has pointed out,[57] the italicized words suggest how, in spite of himself, the protagonist is feeling nostalgia for the delightful manifestations of the worldly life which he had stripped himself of at one stage.

The conflict between body and soul that permeates poems like "Journey of the Magi," "Animula," and "Ash Wednesday" is absent from the *Four Quartets*. This is the reason why I am placing the *Four Quartets* under a separate category. Here I must point out the difference between dichotomy and conflict. The dichotomy of body and soul marks the *Four Quartets* as much as "Ash Wednesday". The difference between the two poems lies in conflict. Of the two major works of

St John of the Cross, one (*The Ascent of Mount Carmel*) deals with the Active Dark Night, while the other (*The Dark Night of the Soul*) deals with the Passive Dark Night. In the two works which are, in effect, only one work with two parts, St John describes the long process through which the mystic has to pass in order to arrive at the stage where he establishes communion with God. The conflicts and distractions that the mystic feels in the process are described by Eliot in "Ash Wednesday." In the *Four Quartets* Eliot does point to the process resting on the dichotomy of the two worlds but leaves out the conflict in the process. How far Eliot goes in imbibing the influence of St John of the Cross is evident from the lines in "East Coker" which are almost a literal transcription of the lines in the first book of *The Ascent of Mount Carmel.* Towards the close of the book St John of the Cross describes in verse "the two roads which are on either side of the path of perfection."[58]

> In order to arrive at having pleasure in everything
> Desire to have pleasure in nothing.
> In order to arrive at possessing everything,
> Desire to possess nothing.
> In order to arrive at knowing everything
> Desire to know nothing.
> In order to arrive at that wherein
> thou hast no pleasure
> Thou must go by a way wherein thou
> hast no pleasure.
> In order to arrive at that which thou knowest not
> Thou must go by a way that thou knowest not.
> In order to arrive at that which thou possessest not,
> Thou must go by a way that thou possessest not.
> In order to arrive at that which thou art not,
> Thou must go through that which thou art not.

The lines which Eliot writes in imitation of these lines run as follows :

> In order to arrive there,
> To arrive where you are, to get from where you are not,
> You must go by a way wherein there is no ecstasy.
> In order to arrive at what you do not know
> You must go by a way which is the way of ignorance.
> In order to possess what you do not possess

You must go by the way of dispossession.
In order to arrive at what you are not
You must go through the way in which you are not
And what you do not know is the only thing you know
And what you own is what you do not own.
And where you are is where you are not.
(East Coker, III)

The striking parallel between the two quotations is indicative of the deep impact that St John of the Cross exercised on Eliot. The two worlds, one to be dispossessed and the other to be possessed—are clearly separate. The critics of Eliot have paid almost excessive attention to his imitation of Dante in the description of the "compound ghost" in "Little Gidding", but have not paid sufficient attention to his imitation of St John of the Cross. Even Helen Gardner, who does not fail to notice the similarity between the two quotations above, touches on Eliot –St John relationship only in passing.[59] What is striking about the above quotations is not merely the parallel between St John of the Cross and Eliot but the difference between the latter and Dante that they point to by implication.

It is hardly possible to exaggerate the influence of St John of the Cross on the later Eliot. The *Four Quartets*, particularly the first half, is throughout charged with the vocabulary of the Spanish mystic. Terms like "old man," "darkness," "wait," "empty" which occur frequently in the *Four Quartets* remind one at once of St John. Eliot goes to the extent of referring in "Burnt Norton" to the mystic ladder with ten steps described in *The Dark Night of the Soul*. One can easily give numerous instances from the *Four Quartets* which have parallels in St John of the Cross. The two most striking instances are one each in "Burnt Norton" (the second passage of the first movement) and "East Coker" (the first passage of the third movement). In the former Eliot describes the Active Dark Night of sense and spirit which is the subject of *The Ascent of Mount Carmel* and in the latter the Passive Dark Night of the Soul which is dealt with in *The Dark Night of the Soul*. The evacuation of the world of "sense," "faith" and "spirit" described in the former is the Active Dark Night of sense and spirit, while the "darkness of God" in the latter is the Passive Dark Night.

The above parallel between St John of the Cross and Eliot goes to show that the later Eliot acquieces in the division of the world into body and soul that he discerns in the seventeenth century. George Herbert has been compared by Eliot to St John of the Cross. That is to say, Herbert rises in Eliot's scale in direct proportion to the weight that the latter sets on St John of the Cross. It is not for nothing that the last of the *Quartets* derives its title from "Little Gidding" which was frequented by George Herbert and to Nicholas Farrar of which he submitted the manuscript of *The Temple* for appraisal.

Among the metaphysicals it is Herbert and among the mystics it is St John of the Cross whom the later Eliot resembles most. But we have noticed above that a metaphysical poet who embodies the unified sensibility gives a poetic form to philosophic thought. What philosophic system is rendered poetically in the *Four Quartets*?

III

The two main philosophers that critics have pointed to as having provided Eliot with the philosophical background are Bradley and Bergson.[60] Eliot argues at several places that a poet should not seek to fabricate a philosophy of his own but instead use the philosophy set forth by others. As we have already noticed, he criticizes Blake for creating a philosophy of his own and admires Dante for making use of the philosophy of St Thomas Aquinas. Like Dante, he says, Lucretius lends a poetic form to philosophic thought. In his essay on "Shakespeare and the Stoicism of Seneca" Eliot writes that "Dante had behind him the system of St Thomas, to which his poem corresponds point to point."[61] Is there any philosopher who can be an Aquinas to Eliot?

When we think of Eliot as a "philosophical poet" in the sense in which he himself has defined the term, we think primarily of the *Four Quartets*. As the *Quartets* deals with the Christian dogma of the Incarnation, the only philosophy that can be embodied in the *Four Quartets* is the philosophy that is rooted in Christianity. In order to be an Aquinas to Eliot a philosopher must have not merely a philosophical system but a philosophical system resting on Christian dogmas. Dante, whom Eliot always looks upon as an ideal, draws on the philosophy of St Thomas Aquinas which is, without doubt, a Christian philosophy. It is worthwhile to consider the nature of philosophy in the *Four Quartets* before touching on the Christian aspect of it.

It is somewhat surprising that Eliot uses fragments from a pre-Christian philosopher of 500 B.C. as the epigraph to a poem which is patently Christian. The three extracts from Heraclitus forming the epigraph to "Burnt Norton" (though, in effect, applicable to all the *Quartets*) read as follows :

> Though the law of things is universal in scope, the average man makes up the rules for himself.
>
> The way up and the way down are one and the same.
>
> Though the Word governs everything, most men live in centres of their own.[62]

Although there are certain Heraclitean ideas in the *Four Quartets* such as the death of the four elements of air, earth, water and fire in the second movement of "Little Gidding," the dominance of the element of fire in the whole of "Little Gidding," and the reconciliation of opposites pervading the whole poem (it is significant to note that the second of the three fragments above is reproduced with some modification in the third movement of "The Dry Salvages" as "The way up is the way down, the way forward is the way back.") yet the Heraclitean philosophy is certainly not the most dominant philosophy in the poem. In the first place, there are present in the *Four Quartets* the philosophic ideas which are not Heraclitean and, secondly, there are other philosophers who lay a better claim than Heraclitus to be an Aquinas to Eliot. The predominant philosophic notion in the *Four Quartets* is the intersection of time and Eternity. The Heraclitean flux does not admit of a "still point" where there is "neither arrest nor movement." I must add that the Heraclitean flux as far as it goes is very much present in the *Four Quartets*. "You cannot step twice into the same river," writes Heraclitus "for fresh waters are ever flowing in upon you." And again, "the sun is new every day." This idea of a constant change informs not merely the *Four Quartets* but Eliot's plays, particularly *The Cocktail Party.*[63] It is the "still point" in flux that differentiates Eliot's philosophy from that of Heraclitus. Another vital point of difference between Heraclitus and Eliot is that though Heraclitus believes in God and places Him above other things, yet his God is certainly not the Christian God, while Eliot is an orthodox Christian in the *Four Quartets*.

It is difficult to say where precisely Eliot derives the concept of time from. As said above, the critics of Eliot have pointed to Bradley or/and Bergson as the source of Eliot's philosophy. Surprisingly enough, a Christian philospher of A.D. 400, St Augustine, has only been referred to by the critics of Eliot, particularly when examining the opening lines of the *Four Quartets* but never accorded the same place as Bradley or Bergson.[64] It is clear from the discussions of the *Four Quartets* that it is either Bradley or Bergson who is an Aquinas to Eliot. Thus St Augustine's role in the philosophy of time in the poem is reckoned no more than casual. But, in fact, St Augustine is the only philosopher who has all the points that Eliot makes in the *Four Quartets*. St Augustine has always loomed large on Eliot's mental horizon. "Mixing memory and desire" in the opening lines of *The Waste Land* is Augustinian[65] and St Augustine has been juxtaposed with the Buddha in "The Fire Sermon." It is the same *Confessions* from the fifth book of which Eliot quotes in "The Fire Sermon" that sets forth in the eleventh book the philosophy of time embodied in the *Four Quartets*.

The time as described in the *Four Quartets* operates on three levels and all the three levels one finds in St Augustine. On the first level is the mechanical concept of time with its threefold division into past, present and future. This concept has been refuted by both St Augustine and Eliot. St Augustine demonstrates the untenability of the threefold division of time, saying that both past and future are rooted in the present. The only way, he argues, we can distinguish between past, present, and future is to say that there is "a present of things past, a present of things present, and a present of things future."[66] It is this Augustinian view that Eliot expresses in the opening lines of the *Four Quartets*.

Time present and time past
Are both perhaps present in time future
And time future contained in time past
If all time is eternally present
All time is unredeemable.

The word "unredeemable" has been interpreted variously. Kristian Smidt, for instance, writes : " 'Redeemable' in this context I take to apply both to the past, which one would wish to buy back and change, and to time as such, which needs to be redeemed from being merely a quasi-spatial, deterministic succession of moments."[67] And commenting upon the last two lines above, Graham Hough says that "to redeem the time means to make the most of the time, to embrace every opportunity, for right action; and it also surely includes the intention of atoning for the past and making resolutions for the future. If all time is simultaneously spread out like a map these intentions and resolves are illusory."[68] There is all the difference between Smidt and Hough and it is Smidt who has got the point right. The main difference between Smidt and Hough is that for Smidt, Eliot formulates in the opening lines of "Burnt Norton" a concept of time that he does not accept, whereas for Hough he accepts it. It is surprising that Graham Hough who attempts a detailed analysis of the concept of time in the *Four Quartets* misses Eliot's point made at the very opening of the poem. Of "all time is eternally present" he remarks that "it is not quite clear what meaning we are to attach to this." The word "unredeemable" in the above quotation is charged with meaning and one who misses the meaning of this word will miss the basic point about the concept of time in the *Four Quartets*.

The concept of time as the eternal present including both past and future is both Augustinian and Bergsonian. (Graham Hough points to only the Augustinian aspect and Smidt only to the Bergsonian, though the latter also points to the solution that Eliot finds in St Augustine.) And also Bradleyan. In fact, there are striking similarities between the Augustinian, the Bergsonian and the Bradleyan concepts of time. The Augustinian eternal presence has already been discussed. The Bergsonian real time and the Bradleyan immediate experience both centre on the idea of the eternal present, a stream of time with no before or after. T.E. Hulme, who might be credited with exercising the Bergsonian influence on Eliot,[69] writes in his account of the Bergsonian philsophy of the intensive manifold : "In the mechanical world . . . time might flow with infinite rapidity and the entire past, present and future be spread out all at once. But inside us it is very different."[70] The time with past, present and future clearly spread out is the concept of time that St Augustine also demolishes. And the time inside us is the time as eternal present with no past or future. In the mechanical time future is predictable, but in the real time future is unpredictable and "the whole of your past life is in the present." The similarity to the Bergsonian time of the Bradleyan immediate experience or the finite centre can be demonstrated by reproducing two extracts adduced by Eliot from Bradley's *Essays on Truth and Reality* in his "Leibniz's monads and Bradley's finite centres." In both the extracts Bradley speaks of the finite centre or immediate experience.

> It comes to itself as all the world and not as one world among others. And it has properly no duration through which it lasts. It can contain a lapse and a before and after, but these are subordinate.[71]

> It has, or it contains, a character and on that character its own past and future depend.[72]

The immediate experience with no duration in the proper sense and containing its own past and future is both Augustinian and Bergsonian. The immediate experience is as unpredictable as the Bergsonian *duree* and like the Augustinian present it has no proper duration. As the future is constantly passing through the present into the past St Augustine wonders what could be the duration of the present and arrives at the conclusion that "if an instant of time be conceived, which cannot be divided into the smallest particles of moments, that alone is it, which may be called present."[73] I must point out, parenthetically, that Bradley differs from both St Augustine and Bergson on one point, i.e., in admitting a lapse and before and after of the immediate experience. Nevertheless so long as it lasts it is similar to Bergson's real time and St Augustine's eternal present.

Having discussed the parallels between St Augustine, Bradley and Bergson, it is worthwhile to turn to one vital difference between St Augustine on the one hand, and Bradley and Bergson on the other. It is this difference that is hinted at in the opening lines of "Burnt Norton," particularly in the word "unredeemable." Here comes in the third level of time in the *Four Quartets*, a level absent from both Bradley and Bergson but present in St Augustine. This time is a fixed point in the eternal flux which St Augustine identifies with the Christian God. It has been pointed out that both Bergson and Bradley go a long way towards accepting the Christian God but they do not go far enough to accept Him.[74] And it must be stressed that any account of the philosophical system in the later Eliot must place Christianity at the very centre. If one is pushing Christianity into the background while discussing Eliot's use of philosophy, one is likely to go wrong. In her discussion of "The Philosophy of F.H. Bradley and the Mind and Art of T.S. Eliot" Anne C. Bolgan shunts off to a footnote the point which ought to have been the very focus of her attention, I mean the point about Christianity.[75] She admits that Bradley does not give credence to the Christian God and yet asserts that Eliot's "life and mind and art . . . must be seen as gathered around the spinal cord of Bradley's philosophy."[76] In fact, if we compare Bradley and Bergson in the light of Christian orthodoxy, Bergson certainly comes closer to it than Bradley. To be sufficiently convinced of this one has only to look at the relevant portions of Bradley's *Appearance and Reality* and Bergson's *Two Sources of Morality and Religion*. Bradley's monism precludes the possibility of the Christian God. "If you identify the Absolute with God," writes Bradley "that is not the God of religion. If again you separate them God becomes a finite factor in the Whole."[77] Sympathetic towards religion though he is, ("there is nothing more real than what comes in religion") his definition of religion flies in the face of Christianity.[78] Bergson, on the other hand, accepts the dynamic religion which manifests itself in mysticism, although he discards the static or natural religion. That he is sympathetic towards Christianity is evident from his remark that "complete mysticism is that of the great Christian mystics."[79] As a matter of fact, if he had taken the step which he wanted to towards the end of his life, he would have been the counterpart of Eliot in the *Four Quartets*.[80] But as far as Bergson's philosophy goes, it does not admit of the point of fixity in the flux of real time which one finds in Eliot. Hence it is not fanciful to suppose that Eliot got the third level of his concept of time neither in Bradley nor in Bergson but in St Augustine, who writes answering those who question, "What was God doing before He made heaven and Earth ?"

> Who speak thus, do not yet understand Thee, O Wisdom of God, light of souls, understand not yet how the things be made, which by Thee, and in Thee are made; yet they strive to comprehend things eternal, whilst their heart fluttereth between the motions of things past and to come, and is still unstable. Who shall hold it, and fix it, that it be settled awhile, and awhile catch the glory of that ever-fixed Eternity, and compare it with the times which are never fixed, and see that it cannot be compared; and that a long time cannot become long, but out of many motions passing by, which cannot be prolonged altogether ; but that in the Eternal nothing passeth, but the whole is present; whereas no time is all at once present : and that all time past, is driven on by time to come, and all to come followeth upon the past, and all past and to come is created, and flows out of that which is ever present ? Who shall hold the heart of man, that it may stand still, and see how eternity ever stillstanding, neither past nor to come, uttereth the times past and to come ?[81]

It is this glimpse of "ever still standing" Eternity at the still point of the flux of time that is central to the problem of time in the *Four Quartets*. And it is this Eternity that redeems the time by making it stand still for a moment and thereby free from movement. Thus "all time" is not unredeemable for Eliot as well as for St Augustine, since it can be redeemed by Eternity.[82] It is significant to note St Augustine's distinction between the momentary standing still of the flux of time and the ever standing still of Eternity. Eternity has no past or future and hence can stand still for ever, but the flux of time can stand still only for a moment gathering in itself both past and future. It is this still point in the everflowing passage of time that Eliot describes in the following lines :

> At the still point of the turning world. Neither flesh nor fleshless ;
> Neither from nor towards ; at the still point there the dance is,
> But neither arrest nor movement. And do not call it fixity,
> Where past and future are gathered. Neither movement from nor towards,
> Neither ascent nor decline. Except for the point, the still point,
> There would be no dance, and there is only the dance.
>
> ("Burnt Norton," II)

The "still point" is both the point of the Incarnation of Christ and the point at which the Incarnation is glimpsed. At the "still point" opposites reconcile : Eternity takes on the human form and the human beings get the "hints and guesses" of Eternity.

Eliot's case is more complicated than Dante's. One knows for certain the source of Dante's philosophy, but in the case of Eliot it is very difficult to put one's finger on one philosopher. At any rate, if we have got to think in terms of just one philosopher, then St Augustine takes precedence over others including Heraclitus. The complication in Eliot's case is obvious from the fact that one's choice falls upon St Augustine, while Eliot derives from Heraclitus the epigraph to "Burnt Norton" which, as has been said, is applicable to all the Quartets. The reason why St. Augustine gets preference over other philosophers is that his writings cover all the points which Eliot makes. I am far from suggesting that other philosophers did not at all impinge on Eliot. Bradley and Bergson, besides Heraclitus, exercised their imfluence on him, but to be an Aquinas to Eliot one has to have all the aspects of the philosophy of time given poetic form in the *Four Quartets*.

The *Four Quartets* is a philosophical poem dealing with the problem of time. The problem relates to the intersection of the Eternal moment and the flux of time. But, as Eliot has pointed out, the poet is concerned not with the philosophy as such but with the poetic rendering of philosophy. Of the relation between poetry and philosophy he writes :

> The poet can deal with philosophic ideas, not as matter for argument, but as matter for inspection. The original form of a philosophy cannot be poetic. But poetry can be penetrated by a philosophic idea, it can deal with this idea when it has reached the point of immediate acceptance, when it has become almost a physical modification.[83]

Thus in poetry a philosophic idea becomes a "physical modification." But what is it that turns the former into the latter ? Eliot has made the above pronouncement in his discussion of Dante who is a great philosophical poet. In Dante's *The Divine Comedy* the philosophy of St Thomas Aquinas is, to use Eliot's own term, "realized." Of all the devices that a poet employs to transform a philosophic idea into poetry, imagery plays the dominant role. And of all the images, the visual images are most effective. I have already discussed sensousness as an important ingredient of the unified sensibility in the early Eliot. The sensuousness of Eliot's later poetry is somewhat different from that of his early poetry. And this is because of the change in the nature of imagery employed. As Maxwell has pointed out, the imagery in the early poetry is predominantly urban, whereas that in the later poetry is predominantly natural. Eliot's own predilection for nature imagery is evidenced by his admission that

> In New England I missed the long dark river, the ailanthus trees, the flaming cardinal birds, the high limestone bluffs where we searched for fossil shell-fish ; in Missouri I missed the fir trees, the bay and golden rod, the song of sparrows, the red granite and the blue sea of Massachusetts. [84]

Maxwell quotes the following passage to point out the personal element in the imagery in Eliot's later poetry, but a more remarkable point about the passage is the nature of images that the later Eliot recapitulates :

> The song of the bird, the leap of one fish, at a particular place and time, the scent of one flower, an old woman on a German mountain path, six ruffians playing cards at nightfall at a small French railway junction where there

> was a watermill : such memories have a symbolic value, but of what we cannot tell for they come to represent the depths of feeling in which we cannot peer.[85]

The bird, the fish, the flower, the mountain path, the nightfall, the watermill are all nature images. This goes to show how Eliot has gone adrift from urban imagery which he admired in Baudelaire. I do not imply any watertight division between Eliot's early and later poetry as regards the nature of imagery. There are nature images in his early poetry (in the opening lines of *The Waste Land*, for instance) just as there are urban images in his later poetry (the London tube image in "East Coker" and the train image in "The Dry Salvages," for example).

Nature imagery in Eliot's later poetry formulates the philosophy of time discussed above. The point of intersection of the timeless with time is delineated through various images. In the first movement of each of the quartets, Eliot describes through nature imagery how the passive soul destitute of worldly associations is acted upon by Eternity. In "Burnt Norton" the dry pool is acted upon by the sunlight ; in "East Coker" "the light falls across the open field," in "The Dry Salvages" "the river is within us, the sea is all about us" (this image is slightly different from the other images in that it describes the union of the human soul with Eternity rather than the former being acted upon by the latter) and, finally, in "Little Gidding" "The brief sun flames the ice, on pond and ditches." The sunlight in the three images is symbolic of the beatific vision. The sea with its very vastness and stability suggests Eternity. In the employment of nature imagery for the communication of mystical experience, Eliot differs from the Spanish mystics including St John of the Cross. Examining the poetry of the early seventeenth century Eliot says that "in the Spanish mystics there is a strong vein of what would now be called eroticism" which "does render them liable to the indignities of Freudian analysis."[86] In his poetry St John of the Cross often compares himself to a bride and God or Christ to a bridegroom. His poetry is informed by a strong erotic element. Eliot, on the contrary, uses nature imagery and as such falls in line with Dante rather than the

Spanish mystics or the metaphysical poets. The metaphysical conceit which is so important an element of Eliot's early poetry almost disappears from his later poetry : it has been replaced by symbols and imagery drawn from nature.

As against Graham Hough, I believe that Eliot's nature imagery is not pantheistic. One can easily discern the difference between nature in the *Four Quartets* and in Wordsworth's poetry. Eliot's nature, unlike Wordsworth's, is not in itself an object of worship, but is employed as a symbol to body forth the intersection of time and Enternity.

Sensuousness is an important element in the early as well as the later poetry of Eliot. Sensuousness in the early poetry is engendered by urban imagery, while that in the later poetry is produced by nature imagery. As has been said, sensuousness cannot be identified with the unified sensibility, though it certainly is an important element of the latter. Philosophical thought may be given poetic form by devices other than imagery. Stephen Spender rightly points out that "with all their excellent qualities, when we compare "East Coker" and "Little Gidding" with Eliot's earlier poetry there seems a loss of sensuousness, together with a gain in seriousness."[87] But in the first place, the loss of sensuousness does not diminish poetic excellence. And, secondly, the balancing of sensuous and abstract images constitutes the very pattern of the *Four Quartets*, the pattern which is essentially the same as the one *The Waste Land* originally had. The fusion of thought and feeling which is the unified sensibility characterizes the abstract passages as much as the sensuous ones.

CHAPTER SEVEN

Eliot's Critical Achievement

In my study of Eliot I have tried to be as fair to him as one possibly can be. I have sought to explain his critical concepts objectively and not infrequently taken his critics to task for taking him out of context and not making sufficient critical discrimination. This is particularly evident from my discussion of Eliot's theories of impersonality and the dissociation of sensibility. I have pointed out how critics have not sufficiently realized that the terms "personality" and "impersonality" as well as "thought", "emotion" and "feeling" have been used by Eliot in different senses. This emphasis on critical discrimination stems from my deep-rooted conviction that a writer must be viewed in the proper context. The examples of writers being denounced for what they never intended are legion. Coleridge's criticism of Wordsworth comes to mind. Coleridge does not realize the experimental nature of Wordsworth's theory of poetry as set forth in his Preface to the *Lyrical Ballads* with the result that he frequently attacks Wordsworth on the wrong counts. Every critical pronouncement by a critic ought to be construed in context.

The present study investigates the development of Eliot's theory of poetry. As Eliot himself admits, his critics have overlooked the fact that, like his poetry, his criticism develops with the result that they have found out contradictions between his statements made at two different stages of his development. To take a random instance, Eliot has discovered both the unified and dissociated sensibilities in Donne but there is no contradiction here. At one stage (1921, "The Metaphysical Poets") Eliot feels that Donne's poetry embodies the unified sensibility, while at a later stage (1931, "Donne in Our Time") he arrives at the conclusion that in Donne there is "a manifest fissure between thought and sensibility." The two statements coming at two different stages point to the development of Eliot's critical career rather than his inconsistency.

The foregoing discussion should not lead one to think that I have unqualified praise for Eliot or, for that matter, am blind to his weak points. The main weakness of Eliot seems to me his inability to strike a proper balance between art and morality, the kind of balance that has been attained by critics like Mathew Arnold and F.R. Leavis. In his early phase he is preoccupied with technique, and his critical concepts are essentially achievements on the technical level, while in the later phase he concerns himself primarily with Christian orthodoxy. Thus, the balance between art and morality is disrupted at one stage by the technical preoccupation and at the other by the religious preoccupation. I am not suggesting that a work of art should be didactic in nature but at the same time there is no denying that some kind of moral vision artistically rendered is an essential feature of great literature. This moral vision may or may not have behind it Christian sanctions. Even the concept of morality will vary from writer to writer but so long as the moral values are mature and given proper artistic form, we shall accept them despite personal differences. These values constitute the strength of a work of art, while didacticism by which I mean moral values directly stated is a blemish. Eliot's religious criterion in *After Strange Gods* is puerile if only because he isolates it completely from the technical excellence. What one expects a mature critic like Eliot to do is to apply a critical standard which rests on a proper balance of experience and expression. The separation of the two in case of Eliot is most conspicuous in his discussion of Ezra Pound who is Eliot's ideal by the early aesthetic standards, and the object of severe attack by the later Christian standards.

II

The critical attitude of Eliot has been a matter of controversy among the critics. M.C. Bradbrook believes that in the early criticism Eliot displays "nervous stiffness and defensive irony while the later criticism exhibits rather a haughty humility."[1] C.L. Barber, in his chapter on "The Power of Development" contributed to Matthiessen's book, points out a difference between Eliot's early and later criticism, saying that the former is what Eliot himself calls "a by—product of my private poetry workshop", while the latter "has rarely been of this kind." In his criticism since the later thirties, says Barber, Eliot "returns in several of his pieces to figures who have *not* been sympathetic to him, such as Byron, Milton, Kipling, doing justice, discovering qualities he had missed, with wonderful perceptivity but without the excitement of adding to a whole developing view of poetry."[2] What Barber finds in Eliot's later criticism, Bradbrook discovers in the whole of Eliot. She maintains that Eliot is capable of getting over his personal [taste in order to appreciate the writers, except for a few, who are very different from himself, and that this capability is not marred by the progress of his poetry and criticism. This capacity, says Bradbrook, "to appreciate the virtues of writers who are personally uncongenial guarantees his integrity." In point of fact, Barber is nearer the truth than Bradbrook, though it is difficult to agree entirely with either. Eliot continues in his later criticism to look upon poetry and criticism in the light of his own poetry, i.e., the later poetry, though at the same time he can also demonstrate virtues in writers who are very much unlike himself. Thus it is a mixed attitude that we discern in the later criticism. In *After Strange Gods* Eliot applies religious standards which are a by-product of the markedly religious poetry begun with "The Hollow Men" and fails to appreciate a writer like D.H. Lawrence who is different from himself and holds in high esteem James Joyce with whom he is strikingly identical. One can see how Eliot's own religious point of view, the by-product of his religious poetry, is operating in his evaluation of Lawrence and Joyce.

Eliot's later criticism has vital links with his later poetry, since in both there is a marked religious note. Nevertheless, in his later phase, Eliot often tries to be sympathetic towards writers with whom he has differences, and gives an objective assessment of them by placing himself at their point of view. This is particularly true of the essays in *On Poetry and Poets*,

The essay on "Johnson as Critic and Poet" is typical of Eliot's attitude in this book. In his discussion and assessment of Johnson's criticism and poetry he evolves a historical attitude and seeks to explicate Johnson by putting him in the eighteenth century setting. One of the two values of studying the *Lives of the Poets*, says Eliot is that "by studying them, and in so doing attempting to put ourselves at their author's point of view, we may recover some of the criteria of judgement which have been disappearing from the criticism of poetry."[3] Recounting his approach to Johnson in "To Criticize the Critic" Eliot writes : "In a lecture on Johnson's *Lives of the Poets*, published in one of my collections of essays and addresses [*On Poetry and Poets*], I made the point that in appraising the judgements of any critic of the past age, one needed to see him in the context of that age, to *try to place himself at the writer's point of view*."[4] (italics mine) And Eliot's attempt to place himself at the writer's point of view to do justice to his work is characteristic of *On Poetry and Poets*, There are writers such as Byron, Kipling and Goethe with whom he has, as he himself confesses, not much in common. In his essay on Byron he says : "It is sometimes desirable to approach the work of a poet completely out of favour, by an unfamiliar avenue."[5] And of his study of Rudyard Kipling he writes : "I confess . . . that introspection into my own processes affords no assistance—part of the fascination of the subject is in the exploration of a mind so different from one's own."[6] Goethe, again, Eliot finds different from himself. "For anyone like myself" says he "who combines a Catholic cast of mind, a Calvinistic heritage, and a puritanical temperament Goethe does indeed present some obstacles to be surmounted."[7] Thus Eliot is very well aware of the fact that writers like Byron, Kipling and Goethe are unlike himself and so he must get over his personal predilections in order to appreciate their virtues. He appreciates Byron's skill as the writer of narrative verse, Kipling for his unique position as the writer of verse, and Goethe who was previously criticized for "dabbling in both philosophy and poetry and making no great success of either" is now regarded as one of those few poets who have achieved a rare combination of spiritual wisdom and poetic excellence. This attempt on the part of Eliot to place himself at the writer's point of view indicates his critical maturity. The business of a critic is to see what the writer is about in a particular work, and, how far he has succeeded in achieving the aim he has set himself. He should not, as the early Eliot frequently does, impose his preconceived notions on the writers under examination.

III

Of the three critical concepts that have been discussed the theory of the 'dissociation of sensibility' has the soundest footing and will interest students of literature longer than the other two concepts. After all the theories of tradition and impersonality are not very original contributions. If we take it that the two theories are interlinked, Babbitt and Pound must get due credit for pioneering them. Moreover, tradition and impersonality cannot be laid down as essential qualities of great poetry. Shakespeare violates the theory of tradition and Yeats that of impersonality in the sense in which Eliot has used them. But can one say that they are not great writers ? A writer can achieve greatness while discarding these theories. But the same cannot be said about the theory of the dissociation of sensibility. One can safely assert that whenever poetry is great, it embodies the unified sensibility. The only lacuna of the theory is its historicity which will continue to be a matter of controversy among critics. As a matter of fact, it is difficult to accept Eliot's belief that there was no great poet in England between the metaphysicals and the moderns. Leavis has demonstrated convincingly that Pope is in line with the metaphysicals. And someone may establish that Keats falls in line with them. Every such argument hits at the historical basis of the theory of the dissociation of sensibility. But if we set aside the question of historicity, we shall find that the theory is basically sound as great poetry never exists without the fusion of thought and emotion. Though we can trace the theory back to Coleridge's theory of the imagination (Eliot himself is the first important modern critic to draw attention to the celebrated passage in the *Biographia Literaria* where Coleridge talks about the reconciliation of opposites), it is Eliot of all the critics who best demostrates how the two components unify. It can be said that Eliot's most significant achievement as a critic is his theory of the dissociation of sensibility.

Notes and References

CHAPTER ONE

1. "To Criticize the Critic," *To Criticize the Critic* (London : Faber and Faber, 1965), p. 14.
2. Ibid.
3. *The Achievement of T.S. Eliot*, Third edition with a chapter by C.L. Barber, (London : Oxford University Press, 1969), p. VIII.
4. Introduction, *The Literary Essays of Ezra Pound* (London : Faber and Faber, 1968, first published in 1954), p. XI.
5. Introduction, Paul Valéry, *The Art of Poetry*, translated by Denise Folliott (New York : Pantheon Books, 1958), p. IX.
6. Wilson, *Six Essays on the Development of T.S. Eliot* (London : The Fortune Press, 1948); Maxwell, *The Poetry of T.S. Eliot* (London : Routledge and Kegan Paul, 1969, first published in 1952).
7. "Author and Critic". The John Hayward bequest, King's College, Cambridge, pp. 8-9.
8. *Between Fixity and Flux* (Washington : The Catholic University of America Press, 1966), p. 2.
9. *Poetry and Morality* (London : Chatto and Windus, 1968), p. 92.
10. "The Metaphysical Poets," *Selected Essays* (London : Faber and Faber, 1966), p. 287.
11. "In Memoriam," ibid., p. 337.
12. Ibid., p. 328.
13. Ibid.
14. Op. cit., p. 153
15. Ibid., p. 59.
16. Ibid., pp. 49-59.
17. "The Frontiers of Criticism," *On Poetry and Poets* (London : Faber and Faber, 1969), p. 106.
18. Foreword, J.M. Murry, *Catherine Mansfield and Other Literary Studies* (London : Constable, 1959) p. VII.
19. *The Waste Land : A Facsimile and Transcript*, ed. Valerie Eliot (London : Faber and Faber, (1971), p. XXV.
20. "The Function of Criticism," *Selected Essays*, p. 27.
21. *The Sacred Wood* (London : Methuen, 1964), p. 16.
22. *Chapbook*, II (March 1920), p. 3.
23. "The Function of Criticism", p. 33.
24. *The Sacred Wood*, p. VIII.

25. "Religion and Literature," *Selected Essays*, p. 388.
26. "Dante," ibid., p. 258.
27. Ibid.
28. Op. cit., p. 252.
29. "The Music of Poetry," *On Poetry and Poets*, p. 32.
30. "Donne in our Time," *A Garland for John Donne*, ed., Theodore Spencer (Cambridge, Mass : Harvard University Press, 1931), p. 11.
31. Ibid., p. 8.
32. "Baudelaire" *Selected Essays*, p. 420.
33. Ibid., p. 428.
34. Op. cit., p. 90.
35. *To Criticize the Critic*, p. 130.
36. Ibid.
37. "The Metaphysical Poets," *Selected Essays*, p. 286.

CHAPTER TWO

1. "Ezra Pound : His Metric and Poetry," *To Criticize the Critic*, p. 177.
2. *On Poetry and Poets*, p. 50.
3. Quoted by Buckley, *Poetry and Morality*, p. 92.
4. Ibid.
5. Ibid.
6. Ibid., p. 126.
7. See "To Criticize the Critic," *To Criticize the Critic*, p. 17.
8. Op. cit., p. 90.
9. Quoted by Margolis, *T.S. Eliot's Intellectual Development* (Chicago : The University of Chicago Press, 1972), pp. 11-12. A copy of the twelve-page descriptive syllabus is in the library of King's College, Cambridge. The extract quoted by Margolis occurs in the second lecture called "The Reaction Against Romanticism." The syllabus, except for page 6, is without pagination.
10. Op. cit., p. 22.
11. Quoted by Margolis, p. 22.
12. Op. cit., p. 36.
13. Bergonzi, "There is no hint in *The Sacred Wood* which contains 'Tradition and the Individual Talent' that the author is a poet with propogandist aims." *T.S. Eliot* (New York : Macmillan, 1972), p. 57; Margolis, see above, p. 34; Stanley K. Coffman, *Imagism* (New York: Octagon Books, 1972), p. 220.
14. "T.S. Eliot in Prose," *Poetry*, XXXXII (April, 1933), p. 48.
15. *The Art of T.S. Eliot* (London : The Cresset Press, 1949), p. 99.
16. *Poetry and the Sacred* (London : Chatto and Windus, 1968), pp. 211-12.
17. Ibid., p. 212.
18. *T.S. Eliot : The Man and His Work*, ed. Allen Tate (Harmondsworth : Penguin Books, 1971), pp. 43-44. Richards' view was first expressed in "A Background for Contemporary Poetry," *The Criterion*, III (July 1925), p. 520. Eliot refuted Richards' view in "A Note on Poetry and Belief." *The Enemy*, I (January 1927), pp. 16-17.

Richards added a note on Eliot's comment in *Poetries and Sciences*, [a reissue of *Science and Poetry* (1926)] (London : Routledge and Kegan Paul, 1970), p. 64.

19. *The Destructive Element* (London : Jonathan Cape, 1938), pp. 145-46.
20. *The Poetry of T.S. Eliot*, pp. 149-50.
21. "Ulysses, Order, and Myth, *Dial* LXXV (November 1923), p. 483.
22. Op. cit., p. 94.
23. I am emphasizing only the way Joyce and Eliot have used their sources and not identifying the *Odyssey* with anthropology. For the difference between the *Odyssey* and the Grail legend as retold by Miss Jessie Weston see A. Walton Litz, "The Waste Land Fifty Years After," *Eliot in His Time*, ed, A. Walton Litz (London : Oxford University Press, 1973), p. 6
24. *A Glossary of Literary Terms* (New York : Holt, Rinehart and Winston, 1971) p. 102.
25. Ibid.
26. *From Ritual to Romance* (New York : Doubleday, 1957, first published in 1920), p. 149.
27. *The Golden Bough* (London : Macmillan, 1919, first published in 1906), part 2, vol. 1, p. 309.
28. Ibid., p. 311.
29. Ibid., p. 312.
30. Ibid., p. 301.
31. *Aspects of Modern Unitarianism*, ed. Alfred Hall (London : The Lindsey Press, 1922). p. 64.
32. For the controversy over humanism see Herbert Read "Humanism and the Absolute," *The Criterion*, VIII (December 1928), pp. 270-76 : G.K. Chesterton, "Is Humanism a Religion?," ibid. (April 1929), pp. 382-93; Allen Tate, "The Fallacy of Humanism," ibid. (July 1929), pp. 661-81; Norman Foester, "Humanism and Religion," ibid., IX (October 1929), pp. 23-32; Ramon Fernandez, "A Humanist Theory of Value," ibid. (January 1930), pp. 228-45; J Middleton Murry, "The Detachment of Naturalism," ibid. (July 1930), pp. 642-60. Eliot's own contributions on humanism were not published in *The Criterion* though he made as many as three on the subject, namely "The Humanism of Irving Babbitt," *Selected Essays*, pp. 471-80; "Second Thoughts About Humanism," ibid., pp. 481-91; "Religion Without Humanism," *Humanism and America*, ed. Norman Foester (New York : Farrar and Rinehart, 1930), pp. 105-112.
33. *Rousseau and Romanticism* (Cleveland : The World Publishing Company, 1968), p. 287; see also "Humanism : An Essay at Definition," *Humanism and America*, ed. Norman Foester, pp. 43-44.
34. W. Whitaker, *Aspects of Modern Unitarianism*, ed. Alfred Hall, p. 86.
35. Alfred Hall, ibid., p. 121.
36. Babbitt does not say in so many words that Confucious and the Buddha are superior to Christ, but that this is his stand is evident from his speculations. See "Humanism : An Essay at Definition," pp. 30-31, 37.

37. Unfortunately, critics like Helen Gardner and Vincent Buckley who find continuity in Eliot's poetry do not discuss "Gerontion." But if they did their conclusion would be very similar to Grover Smith's. Smith takes the references to Christ in the poem in the Christian spirit and believes that the poem contrasts Europe's secular history with "the unregarded promise of salvation through Christ." *T.S. Eliot's Poetry and Plays*, (Chicago : The University of Chicago Press, 1967), p. 60.
38. *T.S. Eliot : A Critical Essay* (Grand Rapids, Michigan : William B. Eerdmans Publishing Company, 1967), p. 15.
39. Wold Mankowitz "Notes on 'Gerontion'," *T.S. Eliot*, ed. B. Rajan, p. 129.
40. *Modern Poetry and the Tradition* (Chapel Hill : The University of North Carolina Press, 1939), p. 171.
41. *Thought in Twentieth Century English Poetry* (London : Routledge and Kegan Paul, 1972), p 135.
42. *Widening Horizons in English Verse* (London : Routledge and Kegan Paul, 1966), p. 83.
43. "T.S. Eliot and Buddhism," *Philosophy East and West* II, (1952-53), (Hawaii : The University of Hawaii Press), p. 39.
44. " 'The Waste Land' as a Buddist Poem," *The Times Literary Supplement*, 4 May 1973, p. 503.
45. There is some truth in David Ward's remark that "in whatever ways Eliot is opposed to Babbitt's humanism, there is a real continuity between his later Christianity and his earlier humanism." *T.S. Eliot : Between Two Worlds* (London : Routledge and Kegan Paul, 1973), p. 9. It is true that there is no opposition between humanism and Christianity : in fact, they have many points in common. But it must be stressed that humanism and Christianity cannot be identified and that what we discern in the early Eliot is humanism and not Christianity.
46. Op. cit., p. 164.
47. See Northop Frye, *T.S. Eliot* (Edinburgh : Oliver and Boyd, 1968), pp. 56-57; Helen Gardner, p, 105.
48. *Six Essays on the Development of T.S. Eliot*, p. 33.
49. Op. cit., p. 132.
50. Ibid., p. 133.
51. For a detailed discussion of the mystical element in the *Four Quartets*, see below, pp. 207-9, 214-16.
52. Lord Krishna replied : "In this world as I have said, there is a path, O Sinless One : There is the Path of Wisdom for those who meditate, and the Path of Action for those who work." *The Geeta*, translated by Purohit Swami (London : Faber and Faber, 1935), p. 32. (In all probability it was this translation that Eliot used for "The Dry Salvages".)
53. Introduction, *The Bhagawadgita*, translated by S. Radhakrishnan, (London : George Allen and Unwin, 1971), p. 66.

54. *Buddhism in Translations,* edited by Henry Clark Warren (New York : Athenaeum, 1972), p. 109.
55. Philippians : 2 : 12.
56. Op. cit., p. 280.
57. Quoted by J.N.D. Anderson, *Christianity and Comparative Religion* (London : Tyndale Press, 1972), p. 26.
58. Preface, *Thoughts for Meditation,* ed. N. Gangulee (London : Faber and Faber, 1951), p. 13.

CHAPTER THREE

1. Hugh Kenner expresses an extreme view in his comment on "Tradition and the Individual Talent" that it "has been investigated with too much solemnity, as though it were Eliot's 'theory of poetry'. It is not that; it is a meditation on how the old is related to the new, the extensive summation of many *obiter dicta.*" *The Invisible Poet : T.S. Eliot* (London : Methuen, 1969), p. 99. The truth of the matter is that "Tradition and the Individual Talent" is both a theory of poetry and a metaphor demonstrating the relationship between the old and the new.
2. *English Literature in our Time and the University,* p. 68.
3. *Poetry and Morality,* p. 97.
4. *The Critic,* XVIII (April/May 1960), p. 80.
5. "The Aims of Education : The Issue of Religion" *To Criticize the Critic,* p. 119.
6. *The Use of Poetry,* pp. 108-9.
7. "The Aims of Education : The Issue of Religion" *To Criticize the Critic,* p. 119.
8. *Notes Towards the Definition of Culture* (London : Faber and Faber, 1962, first published in 1948), p. 27.
9. *Philosophical Lectures* (London : The Pilot Press, 1949), p. 192.
10. *The Mirror and the Lamp* (New York : W.W. Norton and Company, 1958) p. 171.
11. Cf. ". . .while the whole owes its being to the co-existence of the parts, the existence of that whole is a necessary condition to the survival of the parts; if, for example, a leaf is removed from the parent-plant, the leaf dies." Ibid., p. 174.
12. *Shakespearean Criticism,* ed. T.M. Raysor (London : Constable, 1930), I, p 223.
13. "Tradition and the Individual Talent" *The Sacred Wood,* p. 50.
14. Other writers mentioned are George Saintsbury, by Seán Lucy, *T.S. Eliot and the Idea of Tradition,* p. 32-33, Rilke, by Frank Wood in "Rilke and Eliot : Tradition and Poetry" *The Germanic Review,* XXVII (December 1952), pp. 246-59, and Charles Maurras, by Ants Oras, in *The Critical Ideas of T.S. Eliot,* pp. 95-103.
15. *Poetry and Morality,* p. 88.
16. "The Perfect Critic," The Sacred Wood, p. 1.
17. "To Criticize the Critic", *To Criticize the Critic,* p. 17.

18. "The Literary Influence of Academies," *Essays in Criticism*, ed. G.K. Chesterton (London : J.M. Dent and Sons, 1966), p. 47.
19. "The Three Provincialities (1922), *With a Postscript* (1950)," *Essays in Criticism*, I (January 1951), p. 41.
20. "On the Modern Element in Literature", *Matthew Arnold* : *Selected Prose*, ed. P.J. Keating (Harmondsworth : Penguin Books, 1970), p. 59.
21. "Tradition and the Individual Talent," *The Sacred Wood*, p. 49.
22. See below, p. 61.
23. "On the Modern Element in Literature," p. 59.
24. *Rousseau and Romanticism*, p. 52.
25. See *The New Laokoon* (Boston and New York : Houghton Mifflin Company, 1926, first published in 1910), p. 13.
26. *Literature and the American College* (Boston and New York : Houghton Mifflin Company, 1908), p. 135.
27. Ibid., p. 166.
28. *The Masters of Modern French Criticism* (London : Constable, 1913), p. 362.
29. *Literature and the American College*, p. 230.
30. "Tradition and the Individual Talent," *The Sacred Wood*, p. 48.
31. *Democracy and Leadership* (Boston and New York : Houghton Mifflin Company, 1962, first published in 1924), p. 6.
32. *Literary Essays of Ezra Pound*, p. 280.
33. Ibid., p. 362.
34. "Euripides and Professor Murray," *The Sacred Wood*, p. 77.
35. *Literary Essays of Ezra Pound*, p. 75.
36. Pound formulated this theory only in 1934 but, as K.L. Goodwin has pointed out, "long before 1934 he had been striving to achieve this kind of criticism in his Provencál, his Chinese and his Japanese poems and above all in *Homage to Sextus Propertius*." *The Influence of Ezra Pound* (London : Oxford University Press, 1966), p. 138.
37. See *The Poetry of Ezra Pound* (Berkley and Los Angeles : The University of California Press, 1969), p. 4.
38. This is true of Pound's poetry as well. Discussing Pound's poetry Alice S. Amdur has rightly said that "his mind is not big enough to include anything but technique." *The Poetry of Ezra* Pound (New York : Russell and Russell, 1966), p. 71.
39. "Isolated Superiority," p. 6.
40. "Ben Jonson" *The Sacred Wood*, p. 121.
41. Eliot has defined the historical sense and the historical method, the two terms used interchangeably, at several places. In "The English Tradition," for instance, he writes : "A complete historical method must proceed to interpret the past by the present, as well as the present by the past." *Christendom* X (June 1940), p. 101.
42. "Euripides and Professor Murray," *The Sacred Wood*, p. 77.
43. Ibid.

44. Introduction, *Ezra Pound : Selected Poems*, ed. T.S. Eliot (London : Faber and Faber, 1971, first published in 1928), p. 15.
45. "Tradition and the Individual Talent," *The Sacred Wood*, p. 49.
46. Ibid., p. 52.
47. "Tradition and the Individual Talent," *The Sacred Wood*, p. 49.
48. "A Note on Ezra Pound," *Today*, IV (September 1918), p. 5.
49. Introduction, *Ezra Pound : Selected Poem*, p. 10.
50. Ibid., p. 11.
51. Ibid., p. 15.
52. As critics have pointed out, there are striking parallels between Eliot and Pope. See Maxwell, chapter II, "The New Classicism," pp. 36-47; Helen Gardner, *T.S. Eliot and the English Poetic Tradition* (Nottingham : The University of Nottingham, 1965), pp. 11-12; C.A. Bodelsen, *T.S. Eliot's Four Quartets* (Copenhagen University Publications, Rosenkilde and Bagger, 1958), p. 10.
53. "What is a Classic?" *On Poetry and Poets*, p. 60.
54. "Philip Massinger," *The Sacred Wood*, p. 125.
55. "Imperfect Critics," *The Sacred Wood*, p. 23.
56. "Tradition and the Individual Talent," *The Sacred Wood*, p. 50.
57. "Philip Massinger," ibid., p. 125.
58. "Tradition and the Individual Talent," *The Sacred Wood*, p. 51.
59. Op. cit., p. 204.
60. Thomson goes wrong in making a wholesale identification between allusiveness and the idea of Tradition. See *Poetric Tradition and Eliot's Talent* (New Delhi : Orient Longman 1975).
61. *Tradition and Romanticism* (Hamden, Connecticut : Archon Books, 1964), p. 185.
62. Ibid., p. 200.
63. *Speculations*, ed. Herbert Read (London : Routledge and Kegan Paul, 1960), p. 47.
64. Ibid., p. 104.
65. "Tradition and the Individual Talent," *The Sacred Wood*, p. 48.
66. Op. cit., p. 10.
67. *After Strange Gods*, p. 15.
68. *After Strange Gods*, p. 29.
69. Ibid., p. 59.
70. Ibid., p. 43.
71. Ibid.
72. All the quotations from *The Divine Comedy* refer to Dorothy L. Sayer's translation published in Harmondsworth by Penguin Books, 1971.
73. "The Waste Land : An Analysis," *T.S. Eliot*, ed. B. Rajan, p. 12.
74. Ibid., p. 13.
75. *The Achievement of T.S. Eliot*, p. 22.
76. *Selected Essays*, p. 429.
77. Ibid., pp. 428-29.
78. *The Divine Comedy*, I, p. 89.

79. *The Divine Comedy*, translated and commented by John D. Sinclair, (London : Oxford University Press, 1971), I, p. 54.
80. Matthew : 12:30.
81. Revelation : 10:15-16.
82. "Revelation" *Revelation*, ed. John Baillie and Hugh Martin (London : Faber and Faber, 1937), pp. 1-2.

CHAPTER FOUR

1. "A Romantic Patrician" *The Athenaeum* May 2, 1919, p. 266.
2. *Selected Essays*, p. 26.
3. "Ulysses, Order and Myth," p. 481.
4. See Maxwell, *The Poetry of T.S. Eliot*. p. 36 ; Wheelwright, "A Contemporary Classicist", *The Virginia Quarterly Review* IX (January, 1933), pp. 155-56 ; René Taupin, "The Classicism of T.S. Eliot," *Symposium*, III (January 1932), p. 64 ; Nicoll, "Mr Eliot and the Revival of Classicism", *The English Journal*, XXIII (April 1934), p. 269 ; Read, *Form in Modern Poetry* (London : Vision Press, 1957) pp. 45-46. and *The True Voice of Feeling* (London : Faber and Faber, 1968), p. 140 ; Stead *The New Poetie*, pp. 132-135 ; Kermode, *Romantic Age* (London : Collins, Fontana Books, 1971), pp. 9, 153 ; Bayley, *The Romantic Survival* (London : Chatto and Windus, 1969), p. 79 ; Stanford, "Classicism and the Modern Poet", *The Southern Review*, V (April 1969), pp. 484-85.
5. "The Idea of a Literary Review," *The New Criterion*, IV (January 1926), p. 5.
6. See "A Commentary" *The Monthly Criterion*, V (June 1927), p. 284.
7. "Experiment in Criticism," *The Bookman*, LXX (November 1929), pp. 230-31.
8. *The Use of Poetry*, p. 129.
9. "Shakespearian Criticism I : From Dryden to Coleridge," *A Companion to Shakespeare Studies* ed. H. Granville-Barker and G.B. Harrison (Cambridge : At the University Press, 1949 first published in 1934), p. 294.
10. "To Criticize the Critic." *To Criticize the Critic*, p. 15.
11. *The True Voice of Feeling*, p. 146.
12. Op. cit., pp. 125-176.
13. Speaking of the modern mind in *The Use of Poetry* Eliot concedes that "there is a relation (not necessarily poetic, perhaps merely psychological) between mysticism and some kinds of poetry or some of the kinds of state in which poetry is produced." p. 139. And this statement is bound up with another remark of his that "by the time it [experience] has settled down into a poem it may be so different from the original experience as to be hardly recognisable." Ibid., p. 138. The link between the two pronouncements is not at all difficult to see. If the original experience turns out to be hardly recognizable, it is because the creative process through which it passes operates upon it in a mysterious way.

14. The John Hayward Bequest, King's College, Cambridge, p. 3.
15. Op. cit., p. 146.
16. Op. cit., p. 129.
17. Op. cit., pp. 16-17.
18. Op. cit., p. 273.
19. "To Criticize the Critic," *To Criticize the Critic*, p. 18.
20. Op. cit., p. 273.
21. "Eliot's Classical Standing," *Lectures in America* (London : Chatto and Windus, 1969), p. 33.
22. *The Language of Criticism* (London : Methuen, 1966), p. 94.
23. "T.S. Eliot's Theory of Personal Expression" PMLA, LXXXI (June 1969), p. 305·
24. "Kipling Redivivus," *The Athenaeum*, May 9, 1919, p. 298.
25. "Humanist, Artist and Scientist," *The Athenaeum*, October 10, 1919, p. 1015.
26. "Philip Massinger," *The Sacred Wood*, p. 139.
27. "John Ford," *Selected Essays*, p. 203.
28. "W.B. Yeats," *On Poetry and Poets*, p. 255. It is surprising that Smidt considers Eliot's stance on Yeats as marking a change in Eliot's critical position. See Smidt, p. 43.
29. "W.B. Yeats," *On Poetry and Poets*, p. 255.
30. "What is Minor Poetry ?" *On Poetry and Poets*, pp. 46-47.
31. *Selected Essays*, p. 68.
32. Ibid.
33. "Philip Massinger," *The Sacred Wood*, p. 128.
34. Ibid., p. 128.
35. "A Brief Introduction to the Method of Paul Valéry," *Le Serpent Par Paul Valéry*, translated by Mark Wardle (London : Gobden—Sanderson, 1924), p. 14.
36. "Hamlet and His Problems," *The Sacred Wood*, p. 100.
37. "Tradition and the Individual Talent," *The Sacred Wood*, p. 57.
38. Ibid.
39. *The Sacred Wood*, p. 56.
40. *Selected Essays*, p. 114.
41. *The Sacred Wood*, p. 53.
42. "The Three Voices of Poetry," *On Poetry and Poets* p. 95.
43. *The Poet in the Poem* (Berkeley and Los Angeles : The University of California Press, 1960), p. 57.
44. "The Objective Correlative of T.S. Eliot," *Critiques and Essays in Criticism*, ed. R.W. Stallman (New York : The Ronald Press, 1949), p. 396.
45. "T.S. Eliot's Objective Correlative," p. 136.
46. *New Bearings in English Poetry* (London : Chatto and Windus, 1967), pp. 90-91.
47. "*Four Quartets* : A commentary," *T.S. Eliot*, ed. B. Rajan, p. 60.
48. *Selected Essays*, p. 368.

49. Mrs Eliot reproduces an extract quoted by the late Professor TheodoreSpencer during a lecture at Harvard University, and recorded by the late Henry Ware Eliot, Jr., Eliot's brother, which runs as follows : "Various critics have done me the honour" says Eliot "to interpret the poem in terms of the criticism of the contemporary world, have considered it, indeed, as an important bit of social criticism. To me it was only the relief of a personal and wholly insignificant grouse against life ; it is just a piece of rhythmical grumbling. *The Waste Land* : *a facsimile and transcript*, p. 1. That Eliot in *The Waste Land* was concerned to express his personal emotion is confirmed by Eliot's own admission that "I wrote 'The Waste Land' simply to relieve my own feelings." *On Poetry* (Richmond, Virginia : Whittet and Shipperson, 1947), p. 10.
50. John Peter's article was first published in 1952, but all the copies of the issue of *Essays in Criticism* in which it appeared were destroyed at Eliot's instruction. The article with a postscript reappeared in *Essays in Criticism*, XIX (April 1969), pp. 140-75. On p. 143 he compares *The Waste Land* to *In Memoriam.*
51. *Selected Essays*, p. 334.
52. *From Ritual to Romance*, pp. 63-64.
53. Op. cit., p. 26.
54. "Religion and Literature," *Selected Essays*, p. 399.
55. Ibid.
56. René' Wellek "The Criticism of T.S. Eliot," *The Sewanee Review* Vol.. LXIV (July 1956), pp. 414-15.
57. "Types of English Religious Verse," (1939) The John Haywrd Bequest, Kings' College, Cambridge, p. 21.
58. Ibid., p. 12.
59. Ibid., p. 14.
60. *After Strange Gods*, p. 54.
61. *Selected Essays*, p. 393.
62. Explaining how Lawrence invests Christianity Graham Hough writes: "For Christianity the life of the flesh receives its sanction and purpose from a life of the spirit which is eternal and transcedent. For Lawrence the life of the spirit has its justification in enriching and glorifying the life of the flesh of which it is in any case an epiphenomenon." *The Dark Sun* (London : Gerald Duckworth, 1970), p. 253.
63. Foreword. Father William Tiverton, *D.H. Lawrence and Human Existence* (London : Rockliff, 1951), p. VIII.
64. "Types of English Religious Verse," p. 14.
65. *Religion and Literature* (London : Faber and Faber, 1971), pp. 189-90.
66. Ibid.
67. *The Destructive Element*, p. 154.
68. "What Dante Means to me ?" *To Criticize the Critic*, p. 129.
69. *Religion and Literature*, pp. 162-63.

70. "Types of English Religious Verse," p. 21.
71. *Religion and Literature*, p. 170.
72. Carl Wootan finds the Objective Correlative of "Ash Wednesday" in the Catholic Mass and demonstrates the parallel between the penitent in "Ash Wednesday" and the Mass celebrant. See "The Mass: "Ash Wednesday's" Objective Correlative," *Arizona Quarterly* XVII (Spring 1961), pp. 31-42.

CHAPTER FIVE

1. *The Seventeenth Century Background* (London : Chatto and Windus, 1967), p. 294.
2. *English Literature in Our Time and the University*, p. 73.
3. Ibid , p. 98.
4. See F.W. Bateson "Dissociation of Sensibility, "*Essays in Criticism* I (July 1951), pp. 305-8 ; Glenn S. Burne, *Remy de Gourmont : His Ideas and Influence in England and America* (Carbondale : Southern Illinois University Press, 1963), pp. 135-37.
5. Dissociation of Sensibility ; Arthur Hallam and T.S. Eliot," *Notes and Queries*, CCXII, New Series XIV (August 1967), pp. 308-9.
6. "Dissociation of Sensibility," *Essays in Criticism*, II (April 1952), p. 208.
7. "Imperfect Critics," *The Sacred Wood*, p. 23.
8. *Selected Essays*, p. 297.
9. Op. cit., p. 8.
10. "Rhyme and Reason : The Poetry of John Donne," p. 502.
11. *T.S. Eliot's Poetry and Plays*, p. 34.
12. See S.K. Coffman *Imagism* (New York : Octagon Books, 1972), pp. 216-20, and Peter Jones, Introduction, *Imagist Poetry*, ed. Peter Jones (Harmondsworth : Penguin Books, 1972), pp. 26-27, 38.
13. "On a Recent Piece of Criticism," pp. 91-92.
14. Ibid., p. 92,
15. Quoted by Peter Jones, p. 21.
16. *Tendencies in Modern American Poetry* (New York : Macmillan, 1919), p. 244.
17. Quoted by Glenn Hugh, *Imagism and the Imagists* (California : Stanford University Press, 1931), p. 51.
18. Introduction, *Marianne Moore : Selected Poems* (London : Faber and Faber, 1935), p. 9.
19. "It [intensity] must not be confused with concentration which is stating or implying much in proportion to the space occupied, or with length, which is a different matter from either." "Prose and Verse," *Chapbook*, XXII (April 1921), p. 4.
20. Ibid.
21. "Prose and Verse," p. 7.
22. "Dissociation of Sensibility,", p. 305.
23. "T.S. Eliot's Theory of Dissociation," *College English*, XXIII (January 1962), p. 310.

24. "The Metaphysical Poets," *Selected Essays*, p. 286.
25. Ibid., p. 289.
26. "T.S. Eliot's Theory of Dissociation," p. 310.
27. *Lives of the English Poets*, ed. L. Archer Hind (London : J.M. Dent, 1961), I, p. 11.
28. Quoted by Betrand Russell, *History of Western Philosophy* (London : Allen and Unwin, 1971), pp. 294-95.
29. C.M. Coffin, *John Donne and the New Philosophy* (London's Routledge & Kegan Paul, 1958), p. 20.
30. *Selected Essays*, p. 286.
31. Op. cit., p. 143.
32. "The significant relationship is indicated by the fact that the metaphysical poets and the modernists stand opposed to both the neoclassic and romantic poets on the issue of metaphor." *Modern Poetry and the Tradition*, p. 11.
33. "I shall try to demonstrate that all the well-known statements in Eliot's essay can be applied only to modern poetry and that their application to seventeenth-centuty poetry is only a symptom of the peculiar *parti pris* of our time for the metaphysical poetry." "T.S. Eliot's Dissociation of Sensibility and the Critics of Metaphysical Poetry," *Essays on Criticism* XXIII (July 1963), p. 243.
34. See *The Revival of Metaphysical Poetry* (Minneapolis: The University of Minnesota Press, 1959), pp. 151-53, 155.
35. "Donne in Our Time," pp. 5-6.
36. *Selected Essays*, p. 282.
37. "The Metaphysical Poets," *Selected Essays*, p. 287.
38. "On Metaphysical Poetry," *Scrutiny*, II (December 1933), p. 228.
39. *Encyclopaedia Britannica*, XV (1970), p. 260.
40. Cf. "There is no greater mistake than to think that feeling and thought are exclusive—that those beings which think most and best are not also those capable of the most feeling." *Knowledge and Experience in the Philosophy of F.H. Bradley*, p. 18.
41. "Maps of the Waste Land," *Encounter*, XXXVIII (April 1972), p. 81.
42. See, for example, "Prose and Verse" (1921), p. 5 ; "From Poe to Valéry," (1948) *To Criticize the Critic*, p. 34.
43. Peter Jones, p. 141.
44. "From Poe to Valéry," *To Criticize the Critic*, p. 34.
45. "The Art of Poetry," *Paris Review*, XXI (Spring 1959), pp. 52-53.
46. "T.S. Eliot and Ezra Pound : Collaborators in Letters, "*Atlantic Monthly*, CCXXV (January 1970), p. 54.
47. *Speculations*, p. 134.

CHAPTER SIX

1. *The Renaissance and English Humanism* (Toronto : The University of Toronto Press, 1968), p. 29.
2. *Speculations*, p. 8.
3. Ibid., p. 49.

4. *Rousseau and Romanticism*, p. 28.
5. Ibid., p. 279.
6. "Shakespeare and the Stoicism of Seneca," *Selected Essays*, p. 134.
7. Ibid., p. 137.
8. "John Bramhall, *Selected Essays*, p. 355.
9. "Second thoughts About Humanism," *Selected Essays*, p. 490.
10. Quoted by Eliot, ibid.
11. "Shakespeare and the Stoicism of Seneca," *Selected Essays*, p. 129.
12. "Niccolo Machiavelli," *For Lancelot Andrewes*, pp. 50-51.
13. *History of Western Philosophy* (London : George Allen and Unwin, 1971), p. 733.
14. *Selected Essays*, p. 104.
15. See Basil Willey, *The Seventeenth Century Background*, p. 89., Bertrand Russell, Op. cit, p. 512. The view that the seventeenth century witnessed a radical change in attitude has been refuted at length by Kathleen Nott in *The Emperor's Clothes* (London : William Heinmann, 1954). See particularly chapter V, "Mr. Willey's Lunar Sports," pp. 140-58. There are critics who do not subscribe to Eliot's view that the metaphysical quality of "sensuous apprehension of thought" disappeared after the metaphysical poets. See F.R. Leavis, Revaluation (London : Chatto and Windus, 1962), p. 29. Cleanth Brooks, *Modern Poetry and the Tradition*, p. 39.
16. "The Metaphysical Poets," *Selected Essays*, p. 288.
17. "Clark Lectures," p. 183.
18. Ibid., pp. 159-60,
19. "Thinking in Verse," p. 442.
20. R.H. Fogle, for instance, writes : "Metaphysical poetry reacts against the expansive affirmations, the optimistic humanism and the conventionality of the Elizabethan, much as modern poetry has reacted against the 19th—ciromantics." *Encyclopedia of Poetry and Poetics* (Princeton, New Jersey : Princeton University Press, 1965), p. 230. See also *New Catholic Encyclopedia*, IX (1967), p. 726.
21. "A once-for-all event," writes Frank Kermode "cannot happen every few years; there cannot be, if the term is to retain the significance it has acquired, dissociation between the archaic Greeks and Phidias, between Catallus and Virgil, between Guido and Petrarch, between Donne and Milton." *Romantic Image*, p. 161.
22. "John Donne," p. 332.
23. Op. cit., pp. 5-6.
24. "Donne in Our Time," p. 15.
25. "Rhyme and Reason : The Poetry of John Donne," p. 503.
26. Op. cit., p. 9.
27. "Donne in Our Time," p. 11.
28. "Donne in Our Time," p. 9.
29. Ibid., p. 19.
30. Op. cit., p. 288.
31. "Andrew Marvell," *The Nation and the Athenaeum*, p. 809.

32. Ibid.
33. Ibid.
34. "Clark Lectures," p. 95.
35. "The Devotional Poets of the Seventeenth Century : Donne, Herbert, Crashaw," p. 553.
36. Op. cit., 135.
37. Introduction, Josef Pieper, *Leisure the Basis of Culture* (London : Faber and Faber, 1952), p. 15.
38. "Rhyme and Reason : The Poetry of John Donne," p. 503.
39. Op. cit., p. 8.
40. "Rhyme and Reason : The Poetry of John Donne," p. 503.
41. "Donne in our Time," p. 11.
42. "Clark Lectures," p. 70.
43. "The Silurist," pp. 260-1. By 1961 Eliot had taken a long stride forward in his appreciation of St John of the Cross and had no doubt about the fineness of his poetry. "I can't think of any mystic," he said "who was also a fine poet, except Saint John of the Cross." *The Yorkshire Post*, 29 August 1961, p. 3.
44. "Thinking in Verse : A Survey of Early Seventeenth-Century Poetry," p. 443.
45. "Mystic and Politician as Poet : Vaughan, Traherne, Marvell, Milton," p. 590.
46. "George Herbert," *Salisbury and Winchester Journal*, p. 12.
47. "The 'Pensees' of Pascal," *Selected Essays*, p. 412.
48. Ibid., p. 416.
49. Ibid., p. 416.
50. Ibid.,
51. *History of Western Philosophy*, p. 451.
52. *The Complete Works of St John of the Cross*, ed. E. Allison Peers (London : Burns Oats and Washbourne, 1934), p. 19.
53. While examining St John of the Cross one needs to think in terms of his primary emphasis. It has been pointed out that St John does not believe in the discontinuity between body and soul or, for that matter, between the material and the Divine worlds. See E.W. Trueman Dicken *The Crucible of Love* (London : Longman and Todd, 1963, pp. 328-29, and Gorald Brenan, *St. John of the Cross : His life and Poetry* (Cambridge : At the University Press, 1973), pp. 130-32. In point of fact, St John of the Cross's emphasis falls primarily upon meditation and the final communion with the Divine. And the Saint makes no secret of the fact that bodily attractions as well as those of nature can be only a hindrance in the process.
54. See Grover Smith, *T.S. Eliot's Poetry and Plays*, p. 143; Leonard Unger, *T S. Eliot : Moments and Patterns*, p. 50; E.E. Duncan Jones, "Ash Wednesday," *T.S. Eliot*, ed. B. Rajan, p. 39.
55. Grover Smith, p. 139 See also E.E. Duncan Jones, *T.S. Eliot*, ed. B. Rajan, p. 39.

56. Op. cit., p. 44.
57. Op. cit., pp. 65-66.
58. *The Complete Works of St John of the Cross*, pp. 62-63.
59. See "Four Quartets : A Commentary," *T.S. Eliot*, ed. B. Rajan, p. 66.
60. See E.P. Bollier, "T.S. Eliot and F.H. Bradley : A Question of Influence, *Tulane Studies in English*, XII (1962), pp. 87-111; Peter G. Ellis, "T.S. Eliot, F.H. Bradley and 'Four Quartets'," *Research Studies of Washington State University*, XXXVII (June 1969), pp. 93-111; Anne C. Bolgan, "The Philosophy of F.H. Bradley and the Mind and Art of T.S. Eliot : An Introduction," *English Literature and British Philosophy*, ed. S.P. Rosenbaum (Chicago : The University of Chicago Press, 1971), pp. 251-277; Kristian Smidt, pp. 158-63, 165-81; Philip L. Brun, "T.S. Eliot and Henry Bergson," *The Review of English Studies*, New Series, XVIII (May and August 1967), pp. 146-61 and 274-86.
61. Op. cit., p. 135.
62. The quotations are as paraphrased in Grover Smith, pp. 255-56.
63. . . . we die to each other daily.
    What we know of other people
    Is only our memory of the moments
    During which we know them. And they have changed since then.
    To pretend that they and we are the same
    Is a useful and convenient social convention
    Which must sometimes be broken. We must also remember
    That at every meeting we are meeting a stranger.
    The Cocktail Party, Act I, Scene 3.
64. See, for instance, Grover Smith, p. 257; Graham Hough "Vision and Doctrine in *Four Quartets*," *Critical Quarterly*, XV (Summer, 1973), p. 117. Louis L. Martz brings in St Augustine in more detail than Graham Hough or Grover Smith but even his discussion of St Augustine in the *Four Quartets* is not comprehensive enough. Moreover, Martz does not explain why St Augustine should be reckoned more important than other philosophers in the *Four Quartets*. See *T.S. Eliot : A Selected Critique*, ed. Leonard Unger (New York : Russell and Russell, 1966), pp. 451-52.
65. Cf. ". . . present of things past, memory; present of things present, sight; present of things future, expectation." *The Confessions of St Augustine*, ed. Francis R. Gemme (New York : Airmont Publishing Company, 1969), p. 221.
66. Op. cit., p. 221.
67. Op. cit., p. 171.
68. Op. cit., p. 118.
69. Hulme sought to lend the Christian complexion to the Bergsonian philosophy. His interest in Bergson and his neo-scholasticism are well known. Eliot's interest in T.E. Hulme is borne out by his commentary in *The Criterion* on the occasion of the publication of

Speculations edited by Herbert Read. In this commentary he writes: "In this volume he [Hulme] appears as the forerunner of a new attitude of mind, which should be twentieth century mind, if the twentieth century is to have a mind of its own." *The Criterion* (April 1924), p. 231.

70. Op. cit., p. 195.
71. Quoted in *Knowledge and Experience in the Philosophy of F.H. Bradley*, p. 205.
72. Ibid.
73. Op. cit., p. 219.
74. See Richard Wollheim, *F.H. Bradley* (Harmondsworth; Penguin Books, 1969), Chapter VI, "Morality and God," pp. 229-71. On page 268 Wollheim writes; "God, Bradley tells us, is not ultimately real: but, all the same, he possesses reality to a higher degree than anything else with which we are acquainted." See also Jacques Maritain, *Bergsonian Philosophy and Thomism* (New York: Philosophical Library, 1955) Chapter IX "God," pp. 180-203, and Chapter XVII "The Bergsonian Philosophy of Morality and Religion," pp. 325-45. On pp. 336-37 Maritain writes: "There is nothing more moving, nothing which in a sense better bears witness to the transcendence of the spirit, than to see an untiringly courageous thought, in spite of its philosophical equipment and by virtue of fidelity to the light within, follow a pure spiritual trajectory and thus come to *the very doors* at whose threshhold all philosophy stops short (but which Bergson himself was to pass through some years later.)" (italics mine) What Maritain implies is that Bergson stops at the threshhold of Christianity.
75. Op. cit., footnote no. 23, p. 273.
76. Ibid , p. 256.
77. op. cit , p. 447.
78. See ibid., pp. 438-40.
79. Op. cit., p. 194.
80. Bergson wrote in his will dated Feb. 8. 1937: "May reflections have led me closer and closer to Catholicism, in which I see the complete fulfilment of Judaism. I would have become a convert had I not seen in preparation for years the formidable wave of anti-semitism which is to break upon the world. I wanted to remain among those who tomorrow will be persecuted. But I hope that a Catholic priest will consent, if the Carndinal Archbishop of Paris authorizes it, to come to say prayers at my funeral." Quoted by Maritain, p. 337.
81. Op. cit., p. 216.
82. Cf. "The World is trying the experiment of attempting to form a civilized but non-Christian mentality. The experiment will fail; but we must be very patient in awaiting its collapse, meanwhile redeeming the time: so that the Faith may be preserved alive through the dark ages before us; to renew and rebuild civilization, and save the World from suicide." "Thoughts After Lambeth," *Selected Essays*,

p. 367. If all time were unredeemable Eliot would not write in "Ash Wednesday,"

Redeem
The time. Redeem the unread vision in the higher dream
While jewelled unicorns draw by the gilded hearse.

83. "Dante," *The Sacred Wood*, pp. 162-63.
84. Preface, A.E. Mowner *The American World* (London : Faber and Gwyer, 1928), p. XIV.
85. Quoted by Maxwell, p. 150.
86. "Thinking in Verse," p. 443.
87. "Sensuousness in Modern Poetry," *Penguin New Writing*, XVI (March 1943), pp. 123-24.

CHAPTER SEVEN

1. "Eliot's Critical Method," *T.S. Eliot*, ed. B. Rajan (New York : Russell and Russell 1966), p. 125.
2. F.O. Matthiessen, *The Achievement of T.S. Eliot*, Third edition with a chapter by C.L. Barber (London : Oxford University Press, 1969), p. 199.
3. "Johnson as Critic and Poet," *On Poetry and Poets* (London : Faber and Faber, 1969), p. 192.
4. "To Criticize the Critic," *To Criticize to Critic* (London : Faber and Faber, 1965), p. 16.
5. "Byron," *On Poetry and Poets*, p. 194.
6. "Rudyard Kipling," ibid., p. 237.
7. "Goethe as the Sage," ibid., p. 209.

Bibliography

For items not listed here readers are referred to Donald Gallup's *T.S. Eliot : A Bibliography* (London ; Faber and Faber, 1969) for primary sources, and to Mildred Martin's *A Half-Century of Eliot Criticism* (London : Kaye and Ward, 1972) for secondary sources.

PRIMARY SOURCES

Unpublished Works

All the unpublished works consulted are in the John Hayward bequest, King's College, Cambridge.

Eliot, T.S. "Clark Lectures on the Metaphysical Poetry of the Seventeenth Century." (1926).

——"Poetical and Prosaic Use of Words." [sometime in the 1930s]

——"The last Twenty-five Years of English Poetry." (1939)

——"Types of English Religious Verse." (1939)

——"The Development of Shakespeare's Verse." (1949)

——"The Idea of a European Society." (1949)

——"Author and Critic." (1955)

Published Works

I Books, articles, reviews, and introductions

Eliot, T.S. "Syllabus for Oxford University Extension Lectures" Oxford University Press, 1916.

——"A Note on Ezra Pound." *Today*, IV (September 1918), pp. 39-9.

——"The Post-Georgians." *The Athenaeum*, 11 April 1919, pp. 171-72.

——"A Romantic Patrician." *The Athenaeum*, 2 May 1919, pp. 265-67.

Eliot, T.S. "Kipling Redivivus." *The Athenaeum*, 9 may 1919, pp. 297-98.

——"A Sceptical Patrician." *The Athenaeum*, 23 May 1919, pp. 361-62.

——"The Method of Mr Pound." *The Athenaeum*, 24 October 1919, pp. 1065-66.

——"Humanist, Artist and Scientist." *The Athenaeum*, 10 October 1919, pp. 1014-15.

——"The Preacher as Artist." *The Athenaeum*, 28 November 1919, pp. 1252-53.

——"The Local Flavour." *The Athenaeum*, 12 December 1919, pp. 1332-33.

——*The Sacred Wood*. London : Methuen, 1964, first published in 1920.

——"A Brief Treatise on the Criticism of Poetry." *Chapbook*, II (March 1920), pp. 1-10.

——"Prose and Verse." *Chapbook*, XXII (April 1921), pp. 3-10.

——"London Letter." *Dial*, LXX (April 1921), pp. 448-53.

——"London Letter." *Dial* LXXI (August 1921), pp. 213-17.

——"London Letter." *Dial* LXXXII (May 1922), pp. 511-13.

——"The Three Provincialities (1922), With a postscript (1950)," *Essays in Criticism*, I (January 1951), pp. 38-41.

——"John Donne.." *The Nation and the Athenaeum*, XXXIII 9 June 1923, pp.331-2.

——"Andrew Marvell." *The Nation and the Athenaeum*, XXXIII 29 June 1923, p. 809.

——"Ulysses, Order, and Myth." *Dial*, LXXV (November 1923), pp. 780-83.

——*Homage to John Dryden*. London : The Hogarth Press, 1924.

——"A Brief Introduction to the Method of Paul Valéry," Paul Valéry, *Le Serpent Par Paul Valéry*, translated by Mark Wardle. London : Cobden-Sanderson, 1924, pp. 7-15.

——"A Commentary." *The Criterion*, II (April 1924), pp. 231-35.

——"A Commentary." *The Criterion*, II (July 1924), pp. 371-75

——"An Italian Critic on Donne and Crashaw." *The Times Literary Supplement*, 17 December 1925, p. 878.

Eliot, T.S. "The Idea of a Literary Review." *The New Criterion*, IV (January 1926), pp. 1-6.

——"Creative Criticism." *The Times Literary Supplement*, 12 August 1926, p. 535.

——"Literature, Science, and Dogma." *Dial*, LXXXII (March 1927), pp. 239-43.

——"A Commentary." *The Monthly Criterion*, V (June 1927), pp. 283-86.

——"The Silurist." *Dial*, LXXXIII (September 1927), pp. 259-63.

——"A Commentary." *The Monthly Criterion*, VI (September 1927) pp. 193-96.

——*For Lancelot Andrewes*. London : Faber and Faber, 1970, first published in 1928.

——"Isolated Superiority." *Dial*, LXXXIV (January 1928), pp. 4-7.

——"The Poems English, Latin, and Greek of Richard Crawshaw." *Dial*, LXXXIV (March 1928), pp. 246-50.

——"The Prose of the Preacher. The Sermons of Donne." *The Listener*, 3 July 1929, pp. 22-23.

——"Experiment in Criticism." *The Bookman*, LXX (November 1929), pp. 225-33.

——Introduction, Samuel Johnson, *London* : *A Poem* and *The Vanity of Human Wishes*. London : Frederick Etchells and Hugh Macdonald, 1930. Reprinted as "Poetry in the Eighteenth Century," in *From Dryden to Johnson*: *The Pelican Guide to English Literature*, ed Boris Ford. Harmondsworth : Penguin Books, 1957, pp. 271-77.

——"The Devotional Poets of the Seventeenth Century : Donne, Herbert, Crashaw." *The Listener*, III 26 March 1930, pp. 552-53.

——"Mystic and Politician as Poet : Vaughan, Traherne, Marvell, Milton." *The Listener*, 2 April 1930, pp. 590-91.

——"The Minor Metaphysicals : From Cowley to Dryden." *The Listener*, 9 April 1930, pp. 641-42.

——"John Dryden." *The Listener*, 16 April 1930, pp. 688-89.

——"Religion Without Humanism." *Humanism and America*, ed. Norman Foester. New York : Farrar and Rinehart, 1930, pp. 105-12.

Eliot, T..S "Poetry and Propaganda." *The Bookman*, LXX (February 1930), pp. 595-602.

——"Thinking In Verse : A Survey of Early Seventeenth Century Poetry." *The Listener*, 12 March 1930, pp. 441-43.

——"Rhyme and Reason : The Poetry of John Donne." *The Listener*, 19 March, 1930, pp. 502-53.

——"The Devotional Poets of the Seventeenth Century : Donne, Herbert, Crashaw.'. *The Listener*, 26 March 1930, pp. 552-53.

——Preface, St-John Perse, *Anabasis*, translated by T.S. Eliot. London : Faber and Faber, 1931, pp. 9-12.

——"Donne in Our Time." *A Garland for John Donne*, ed. Theodore Spencer. Cambridge, Mass. : Harvard University Press, 1931, pp. 1-19.

——"A Commentary." *The Criterion*, X (April 1931), pp. 481-90.

——"John Dryden—I. The Poet Who Gave the English Speech." *The Listener*, 15 April, 1931, pp. 621-22.

——"John Dryden—II. Dryden the Dramatist." *The Listener*, V 22 April 1931, pp. 681-82.

——"John Dryden—III. Dryden the Critic, Defender of Sanity." *The Listener*, 29 April 1931, pp. 724-25.

——"George Herbert." *Spectator*, 12 March 1932, pp. 360-61.

——*The Use of Poetry and the Use of Criticism*. London: Faber and Faber, 1964, first published in 1933.

——"A Commentary." *The Criterion*, XII (January 1933), pp. 244-49.

——*After Strange Gods*. London: Faber and Faber, 1934.

——Introduction, Marianne Moore: *Selected Poems*. London: Faber and Faber, 1935, pp. 5-12.

——*Essays Ancient and Modern*. London: Faber and Faber, 1936.

——"Revelation," *Revelation*, ed. John Baillie and Hugh Martin. London: Faber, and Faber, 1937, pp. 1-39.

——"A Note on Two Odes of Cowley," *Seventeenth Century Studies*, ed. John Purves. Oxford: At the Clarendon Press. 1938, pp. 235-42.

——"On a Recent Piece of Criticism." *Purpose*, X (April 1938), pp. 90-94.

Eliot, T.S. "George Herbert." *Salisbury and Winchester Journal* 27 May 1938, p. 12.

——Preface, Charles-Louis Philippe, *Bubu of Montparnasse*. New York: Avalon Press, 1945, pp. 9-14.

——"T.S. Eliot Lacon de Valéry" *Paul Valery Vivant*. Marseille: Cashiers Du Sud, 1946.

——*On Poetry*. Richmond, Virginia : Whittet and Shepperson, 1947.

——*Notes Towards the Definition of Culture*. London : Faber and Faber, 1962, first published in 1948.

——*Christianity and Culture*. New York: Harcourt, Brace and Company, 1949.

——"Shakespeare Criticism: From Dryden to Coleridge." *A Companion to Shakespeare Studies*, ed. H. Granville-Barker and G.B. Harrison (Cambridge: At the University Press, 1949), pp. 287-99.

——Foreword, Father William Tiverton, *D.H. Lawrence and Human Existence*. London: Rockliff, 1951.

——*Selected Essays*. London: Faber and Faber, 1966, this edition first published in 1951.

——Preface, N. Gangulee (ed.) *Thoughts for Meditation*. London; Faber and Faber, 1951 pp. 11-14.

——Introduction, Josef Pieper, *Leisure the Basis of Culture*. London: Faber and Faber, 1952, pp. 11-17.

——Introduction, *Literary Essays of Ezra Pound*, ed. T.S. Eliot. London: Faber and Faber, 1968, pp. IX-XV, first published in 1954.

——*On Poetry and Poets*. London: Faber and Faber, 1969, first published in 1957.

——Introduction, Paul Valéry, *The Art of Poetry*, translated by Denise Folliott. New York : Pantheon Books, 1958, pp. VII-XXIV.

——Introduction, G. Wilson Knight, *The Wheel of Fire*. London : Methuen, 1959, pp. XIII-XX.

——"On Teaching the Appreciation of Poetry." *The Critic*, XVIII (April/May 1960), pp. 13-14, 78-80.

——*George Herbert*. Harlow, Essex : Longman Green, 1968, first published in 1962.

———"Ezra Pound." *Poetry : A Magazine of Verse,* LXVIII (September 1946), pp. 326-38. Reprinted in *Ezra Pound,* ed. Walter Sutton. N.J. : Prentice Hall, 1963, pp. 17-25.

———*Knowledge and Experience in the Philosophy of F.H. Bradley*. London : Faber and Faber, 1964.

———*To Criticize the Critic.* London : Faber and Faber, 1965.

———*The Complete Poems and Plays of T.S. Eliot*. London : Faber and Faber, 1970, first published in 1969.

———*The Waste Land : A Facsimile and Transcript* of the Original Drafts including the Annotations of Ezra Pound, ed. Valerie Eliot. London : Faber and Faber, 1971.

II INTERVIEWS

Hodin, J.P. "T.S. Eliot on the Condition of Man Today." *Horizon,* XII (August 1945), pp. 83-89.

Pellegrini, Allessandro. "A London Conversation with T.S. Eliot." *The Sewanee Review,* LVII (Spring 1949), pp. 287-92.

Hall, Donald. "The Art of Poetry, I : T.S. Eliot." *Paris Review,* XXI (Spring 1959), pp. 47-70.

SECONDARY SOURCES

Books, parts of books, articles, and reviews.

Allan, Mowbray. *T. S. Eliot's Impersonal Theory of Poetry.* Lewisburg : Bucknell University Press, 1974.

Austin, Allen. "T.S. Eliot's Objective Correlative." *The University of Kansas City Review,* XXVI (Winter 1959), pp. 133-40.

———"T.S. Eliot's Theory of Dissociation." *College English,* XXIII (January 1962), pp. 309-12.

———"T.S. Eliot's Theory of Personal Expression." *PMLA,* LXXXI (June 1966), pp. 303-7.

Bateson, F.W. "Dissociation of Sensibility." *Essays in Criticism,* I (July 1951) pp. 302-12.

Bergonzi, Bernard. *T.S. Eliot.* New York : Macmillan, 1972.

———"Maps of the Waste Land." *Encounter,* XXXVIII (April 1972), pp. 80-83.

Bolgan, Anne C. "The Philosophy of F.H. Bradley and the Mind and Art of T.S. Eliot : An Introduction." *English Literature and British Philosophy,* ed. S.P. Rosenbaum

(Chicago : The University of Chicago Press, 1971), pp. 251-77.

Bollier, E.P. "T.S. Eliot and F.H. Bradley : A Question of Influence." *Tulane Studies in English*, XII (1962), pp. 87-111.

Braybrooke, Neville (ed.). *T.S. Eliot : A Symposium for His Seventieth Birthday*. London : Hart-Davis, 1958.

——*T.S. Eliot : A Critical Essay*. Grand Rapids, Michigan : William B. Eerdmans Publishing Company, 1967.

Brombert, Victor. *The Criticism of T.S. Eliot : Problems of an "Impersonal Theory" of Poetry*. New Haven, Yale University Press, 1949.

Brun, Philip Le. "T.S. Eliot and Henry Bergson." *The Review of English Studies*, New Series, XVIII (1967), pp. 149-61, 274-86.

Buckley, Vincent. *Poetry and Morality*. London : Chatto and Windus, 1968.

Burne, Glenn S. *Remy de Gourmont : His Ideas and Influence in England and America*. Carbondale : Southern Illinois University Press, 1963.

Drew, Elizabeth. *T.S. Eliot : The Design of His Poetry*. London : Eyre and Spottiswoode, 1954.

Eliot, Valerie. Introduction, *The Waste Land : A Facsimile and Transcript* of the Original Drafts including the Annotations of Ezra Pound, ed. Valerie Eliot. London. Faber and Faber, 1971.

Ellis, P.G. "F.H. Bradley and 'Four Quartets'." *Research Studies of Washington State University*, XXXVII (June 1969), pp. 93-111.

Evans, B. Ifor. *Tradition and Romanticism*. Hamden, Connecticut : Archon Books, 1964.

Fergusson, Francis. "T.S. Eliot and His Impersonal Theory of Art," *The American Caravan*, ed. Van Wyck Brooks *et al.* New York : Macaulay, 1927, pp. 446-53.

Frye, Northop. *T.S. Eliot*. Edinburgh : Oliver and Boyd, 1968.

Gallup, Donald. "The 'Lost' Manuscripts of T.S. Eliot." *The Times Literary Supplement*, 7 November 1968, pp. 1238-40.

——"T.S. Eliot and Ezra Pound : Collaborators in Letters." *Atlantic Monthly*, CCXXV (January 1970), pp. 49-62.

Gardner, Helen. *The Art of T.S. Eliot*. London : The Cresset Press, 1949.

——*T.S. Eliot and the English Poetic Tradition*. Nottingham : The University of Nottingham, 1965.

Gordon, Lyndall, *Eliot's Early Years*. New York : Oxford University Press, 1977.

Holloway, John. *Widening Horizons in English Verse*. London : Routledge and Kegan Paul, 1966.

Hough, Graham. "Vision and Doctrine in 'Four Quartets.' " *Critical Quarterly*, XV (Summer 1973), pp. 107-27.

Howarth, Herbert. *Notes on Some Figures Behind T.S. Eliot*. London : Chatto and Windus, 1955.

Kenner, Hugh. *The Invisible Poet : T.S. Eliot*. London : Methuen, 1969.

Kermode, Frank. *Romantic Image*. London : Collins, Fontana Books, 1971.

Krieger, Murray. "The Critical Legacy of Matthew Arnold." *The Southern Review*, V (April 1969), pp. 457-74.

Kuna, F.M. "T.S. Eliot's Dissociation of Sensibility and the Critics of Metaphysical Poetry." *Essays in Criticism*, XXIII (July 1963), pp. 241-52.

Leavis, F.R. *New Bearings in English Poetry*. London : Chatto and Windus, 1961.

——*Revaluation*. London : Chatto and Windus, 1962.

——"T.S. Eliot's later Poetry," *T.S. Eliot*, ed. Hugh Kenner. Englewood Cliffs, N.J. : Prentice Hall, 1962, pp. 110-24.

——*Anna Karenina and Other Essays*. London : Chatto and Windus, 1967.

——*English Literature in Our Time and the University*. London : Chatto and Windus, 1969.

——*Lectures in America*. London : Chatto and Windus, 1969.

Lees, F.N. "Dissociation of Sensibility : Arthur Hallam and T.S. Eliot." *Notes and Queries*, LCXII, New Series XIV (August 1967), pp. 308-9.

Litz, A. Walton. *Eliot in His Time*. London : Oxford University Press, 1973.

Lucy, Seán. *T.S. Eliot and the Idea of Tradition*. London : Cohen and West, 1967.

March, Richard and Tambimutu. (eds.) *T.S. Eliot : A Symposium*. London : Editions Poetry, 1948.

Margolis, John D. *T.S. Eliot's Intellectual Development*. Chicago : The University of Chicago Press, 1972.

Martin, Graham. (ed.) *Eliot in Prespective*. London : Macmillan, 1970.

Matthiessen, F.O. *The Achievement of T.S. Eliot*. London : Oxford University Press, 1969.

Maxwell, D.E.S. *The Poetry of T.S. Eliot*. London : Routledge and Kegan Paul, 1969.

McCarthy, Harold E. "T.S. Eliot and Buddhism." *Philosophy East and West*, II (1952-53). Hawaii : The University of Hawaii Press, pp. 31-55.

Nicoll, Allardyce. "Mr T.S. Eliot and the Revival of Classicism." *The English Journal*, XXIII (April 1934), pp. 267-78.

Nott, Kathleen. *The Emperor's Clothes*. London : William Heinemann, 1953.

Oras, Ants. *The Critical Ideas of T.S. Eliot*. Tartu : [K. Mattisen], 1932.

Peter, John. "A New Interpretation of 'The Waste Land' (1952), With Postscript (1969)," *Essays in Criticism*, XIX (April 1969), pp. 140-75.

Pound, Ezra. "Drunken Helots and Mr. Eliot." *Egoist*, IV (June 1917), pp. 72-74.

——"Mr Eliot's Mare's Nest." *The New English Weekly*, 8 March 1934, p. 500

Raine, Craige. " ' The Waste Land' as a Buddhist Poem." *The Times Literary Supplement*, 4 May 1973, pp. 503-5.

Rajan, B. (ed.) *T.S. Eliot . A Study of His Writings by Various Hands*. New York : Russell and Russell, 1966.

Ransom, J. C. *The New Criticism*. Norfolk, Connecticut : New Directions, 1941.

Smidt, Kristian. *Poetry and Belief in the Work of T. S. Eliot*. London : Routledge and Kegan Paul, 1967.

Smith, Grover. *T. S. Eliot's Poetry and Plays*. Chicago : The University of Chicago Press, 1967.

Spender, Stephen. *The Destructive Element*. London : Jonathan Cape, 1938.

——*The Struggle of the Modern*. London : Methuen, 1965.

Stead, C. K. *The New Poetic*. Harmondsworth : Penguin Books, 1967.

Tate, Allen. (ed.) *T. S. Eliot : The Man and His Work*. Harmondsworth : Penguin Books, 1971.

Thompson, Eric. "Dissociation of Sensibility." *Essays in Criticism*, II (April 1952), pp. 207-13.

Tschumi, Raymond. *Thought in Twentieth Century English Poetry*. London : Routledge and Kegan Paul, 1972.

Unger, Leonard. *T. S. Eliot : Moments and Patterns*. Mineapolis : The University of Minnesota Press, 1966.

——(ed.) *T. S. Eliot : A Selected Critique*. New York : Russell and Russell, 1966.

Vivas, Eliseo. "The Objective Correlative of T. S. Eliot," *Critiques and Essays in Criticism*, ed. R. W. Stallman. New York : The Ronald Press, 1949, pp. 389-400.

Ward, David. *T. S. Eliot : Between Two Worlds*. London : Routledge and Kegan Paul, 1973.

Wellek, René. "Criticism of T. S. Eliot." *The Sewanee Review*, LXIV (Summer 1956), pp. 398-443.

Williamson, George. *The Talent of T. S. Eliot*. Seattle : The University of Washington Bookstore, 1929.

Wilson, Edmund. *The Axel's Castle*. London : Collins, Fontana, 1971.

Wilson, Frank. *Six Essays on the Development of T. S. Eliot*. London : The Fortune Press, 1948.

Wootan, Carl. "The Mass : 'Ash Wednesday's' Objective Correlative." *Arizona Quarterly*, XVII (Spring 1961), pp. 31-42.

Wright, George T. *The Poet in the Poem*. Berkeley and Los Angeles : The University of California Press, 1960.

GENERAL

Anderson, J. N. D. *Christianity and Comparative Religion*. London : Tyndale Press, 1972.

Arnold, Matthew. *Essays in Criticism*, ed. G. K. Chesterton. London : J. M. Dent and Sons, 1966.

Arnold, Matthew. *Selected Prose*, ed. P. J. Keating. Harmondsworth : Penguin Books, 1970.

Augustine St. *The Confessions of St Augustine*, ed. Francis R. Gemme. New York : Airmont Publishing Company, 1969.

Babbitt, Irving. *Literature and the American College*. Boston and New York : Houghton and Mifflin Company, 1908.

———*The Masters of Modern French Criticism*. London : Constable, 1913.

———*The New Laokon*. Boston and New York ; Houghton Mifflin Company, 1926.

———"Humanism : An Essay at Definition," *Humanism and America*, ed. Norman Foester. New York : Farrar and Rinehart, 1930, pp. 25-51.

———*Democracy and Leadership*. Boston and New York : Houghton Mifflin Company, 1962.

———*Rousseau and Romanticism*. Cleveland : The World Publishing Company, 1968.

———*On Being Creative*. New York : Biblo and Tannen, 1968.

Bergson, Henry. *Two Sources of Morality and Religion*. London : Macmillan, 1935.

Bradley, F. H. *Appearance and Reality*. London : Swan Sonnenschein, 1902.

Bush, Douglas. *The Renaissance and English Humanism*. Toronto : The University of Toronto Press, 1968.

Coffman, Stanley K. *Imagism*. New York : Octagon Books, 1972.

Coleridge, S. T. *Biographia Literaria*, ed. J. Shawcross, Oxford : At the Clarendon Press, 1907, 2 vols.

———*Shakespearean Criticism*, ed. T. M. Raysor. London : Constable, 1930.

Dante, *The Divine Comedy*. Harmondsworth : Penguin Books, 1971. 3 vols. *Inferno* and *Purgatorio*, translated by Dorothy L. Sayers; *Paradiso*, translated by Dorothy L. Sayers and Barbara Reynolds.

Frazer, J. G. *The Golden Bough*. Part II, *Adonis, Attis, and Osiris*. London : Macmillan, 1919, 2 vols.

Hulme, T. E. *Speculations*, ed. Herbert Read. London : Routledge and Kegan Paul, 1960.

John, of the Cross. St. *The Complete Works of St John of the Cross*, ed. E. Allison Peers. London : Burns Oates and Washbourne, 1934, 3 vols.

———*Poems of St John of the Cross*, translated by Roy Campbell. London : Harvill Press, 1956.

Johnson, Samuel. *Lives of the English Poets,* ed. L. Archer Hind, London : J. M. Dent, 1961. 2 vols.

Maritain, Jacques. *Bergsonian Philosophy and Thomism.* New York : Philosophical Library, 1955.

Pound, Ezra. *The Spirit of Romance.* London : Peter Owen, 1952.

——Radhakrishnan, S. (tr.). Introduction, *The Bhagawadgita,* London : George Allen and Unwin, 1971.

Russell, Bertrand. *History of Western Philosophy.* London : George Allen and Unwin, 1971.

Swami, Purohit. (tr.) *The Geeta.* London : Faber and Faber, 1935.

Warren, Henry Clark. (ed.) *Buddhism in Translations.* New York : Athenaeum, 1972.

Weston, Jessie L. *From Ritual to Romance.* New York : Doubleday, 1957.

Willey, Basil. *The Seventeenth-Century Background.* London : Chatto and Windus, 1967.

Index